the
depression
and
bipolar
workbook

30 ways to lift your mood & strengthen the brain

Chris Aiken, MD

Copyright © 2020 by Chris Aiken

Published by
PESI Publishing & Media
PESI, Inc
3839 White Ave
Eau Claire, WI 54703

Cover: Amy Rubenzer
Editing: Jenessa Jackson, PhD
Layout: Amy Rubenzer & Bookmasters
Illustrations: Eleanor Aiken

ISBN: 9781683732358

Printed in the United States of America.

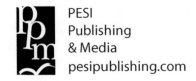

PESI
Publishing
& Media
pesipublishing.com

Dedication

To Jim Phelps, a good friend and gifted mentor, and
Kathrine Ross, who got me started on this path

About the Author

 **Chris Aiken, MD**, is a psychiatrist and psychotherapist whose work focuses on natural and lifestyle approaches to mood disorders. He is the director of the Mood Treatment Center, Editor-in-Chief of *The Carlat Psychiatry Report,* the Bipolar Section Editor for *Psychiatric Times,* and an instructor at the Wake Forest University School of Medicine. He co-hosts the weekly *Carlat Psychiatry Podcast* with Kellie Newsome, PMH-NP.

Dr. Aiken's interest in mood disorders came from experience with close friends who suffered from depression. He began his career as a research assistant at the National Institute of Mental Health and went on to complete medical school at Yale and residency at Cornell and Duke Medical Centers. He remains active in research, and his work has appeared in peer-reviewed journals and books. He lives in North Carolina with his wife Lisa and twin children, David and Eleanor.

Table of Contents

Introduction

Therapy with a Biological Basis

"How is talk therapy going to help when what I have is a chemical imbalance?" Stacey asked when I recommended that she start psychotherapy. I had been treating her depression with medication, but like two thirds of the people who start an antidepressant, she had not recovered. Now I was concerned that the medicine may have contributed to a tenacious side effect: the idea that she didn't have an active role to play in her recovery.

Depression is a passive state. When you ask someone with depression what they did last week, they are likely to tell you what *happened* to them, but not what they did. "When I'm depressed, it's like there's a movie playing in my head of all the things I should be doing, and I can't do them, and the movie just furthers my guilt."

The idea that depression is due to an imbalance of brain chemistry doesn't really help this cause. It also isn't true. Sometimes called the *monoamine hypothesis,* the chemical imbalance theory started out as a way to explain how antidepressants worked. Antidepressants raise levels of serotonin and norepinephrine, so it was a reasonable guess that those chemicals were off-balance in the depressed brain. There's a catch, however. Antidepressants raise those chemicals right away, but they take weeks to work. What's going on in the meantime?

The answer has more to do with brain structure than brain chemistry. In the weeks after starting an antidepressant, the brain undergoes gradual changes in structure, and it's these changes that are responsible for recovery. Namely, there is growth in the *amygdala* (the mood center) and in the nerves that connect that center to the *prefrontal cortex* (where judgment and action take place). Similar changes are seen after successful psychotherapy or healthy lifestyle changes, and this book details specific ways to guide clients in those healing directions.

Recovery from mood disorders also brings changes throughout the body, such as reduced inflammation, stabilization of stress hormones, and a restoration to the daily rhythms of the biological clock. Importantly, some of these pathways respond better to therapy than medication, and I have outlined those therapies throughout this book.

For example, the stress hormone cortisol follows a daily rhythm. It peaks in the morning and falls throughout the day. In bipolar disorder, that hormone stays at peak levels throughout the day, as if on red alert. Social rhythm therapy treats bipolar disorder and restores the ebb and flow of cortisol (Delle Chiaie et al., 2013). Another approach, cognitive behavioral therapy for insomnia, recalibrates the biological gears that drive sleep and, in doing so, also reduces inflammation and treats depression (Irwin et al., 2015). Similarly, behavioral activation turns down the brain's *default mood network,* which is responsible for the ruminative style of thinking so often seen in depression (Yokoyama, 2017).

The Mood Terrain

Clients with mood disorders often seek therapy because they are caught in vicious cycles that they can't break out of. Throughout this book I'll describe the forces that drive those cycles, as well as the suffering they bring. Clients with depression are often trapped in cycles of anxiety and avoidance, while those with mania are fueled by overstimulation and lack of sleep.

In this way, mood disorders operate a bit like addictions. Both entangle clients in habits that are hard to break. Both are common, serious illnesses that affect the body, mind, and every aspect of psychosocial life. A good addiction therapist understands this vast terrain. For example, he or she knows that precautions are in order when a recovered alcoholic sets out to attend a wedding.

Mood disorders have their minefields as well, though they aren't always as intuitive. Changes in sleep, sunlight, diet, travel, screen-time, daily routines, and physical activity can set off new episodes. There are ways to address each of those risks, but it's not as simple as telling clients with depression to get out of bed and get active.

As with addiction, this work is best taken on in the spirit of motivational interviewing. That approach is woven into this text, along with its cousin, harm reduction. For example, clients may not be able to give up electronics at night, but they can at least reduce the harm by using their devices with blue-light filtering lenses.

How to Use this Book

The first step is to understand what mood disorders look like. In part one, I'll show you how they are laid out in the DSM-5 along a spectrum from unipolar depression to bipolar disorder. I'll highlight symptoms that aid the diagnosis of these disorders and provide rating scales to accurately assess them. You'll also learn about their lesser-known symptoms, like rumination and cognitive deficits.

Next, we'll look at what causes these disorders, with worksheets that point the way toward treatment and help engage clients in that direction. The rest of the book details the high-yield interventions for mood disorders. They are laid out from morning to night and connected along a common theme. That is: Clients get better when they have structure to their day, with regular routines and stable rhythms of day and night.

The best interventions are those that clients are motivated to take on. One way to use this book is to present clients with a menu of options so they can choose the steps they want to start with. Understanding their diagnosis, and the causes behind their mood episode, will help you put such a menu together. Try leaving copies of a few of the treatment options in your waiting room. Some clients are more receptive to change when they've discovered it on their own, stashed between the magazines on a coffee table.

The last step is to track the outcome as clients weave these interventions into their lives. Making these changes is not easy, particularly for people with depression, and the benefits have a slow build. After all, if they worked right away, clients probably wouldn't need therapy to stick with them. A weekly mood chart can help clients appreciate their progress.

Mood disorders are fully treatable, and therapy can address their biological origins just as medication can. I hope this work helps your clients understand that they have an active role to play in that recovery and that it moves them closer to it.

30 Ways to Lift Mood, Enhance Therapy, and Strengthen the Brain

1. Diagnosis
Many clients don't fit neatly into the categories of bipolar and depression, and the *DSM-5* has created new categories to recognize those whose mood problems are somewhere in the middle of those extremes. An accurate diagnosis can pave the way to better treatment and, when conveyed with empathy, lighten the burdens of stigma and self-blame (Chapter 1).

2. Temperament
Mood disorders are associated with unique temperaments. Understanding them can help clients accept who they are and live a little more wisely with that knowledge (Chapter 2).

3. Strengths
Mood disorders often come with hidden strengths that clients can capitalize on in their recovery (Chapter 2).

4. Mood charting
Lifestyle changes can take weeks or months to work, so how do you know what's working for your client? Mood charts reveal patterns that can clarify those effects (Chapter 1).

5. Rumination-focused cognitive behavioral therapy (RF-CBT)
This adaptation of CBT uses habit training to reduce rumination, a repetitive style of negative thinking that causes high rates of relapse in depression (Chapter 2).

6. Cognitive rehabilitation
Problems with memory, concentration, and organization are common in mood disorders. Behavioral strategies can help clients overcome these difficulties and regain lost roles in work and relationships (Chapter 2).

7. Expressed emotions in the family
Specific family interactions can influence recovery. Even if your client is in individual therapy, it helps to bring the family in for this education (Chapter 2).

8. Causes and prevention
Depression and bipolar disorder are caused by different types of stresses, and clarifying those helps in treatment and prevention (Chapter 3).

9. Brisk awakening
Rising out of bed is one of the hardest things for people with mood disorders to do, but it's also one of the most effective interventions for depression (Chapter 4).

10. Dawn simulator
Dawn simulators improve energy in the morning by creating a virtual sunrise that gently lifts the brain from deep sleep to full wakefulness (Chapter 4).

11. Careful caffeination
Tea has brain-protecting ingredients that reduce depression and anxiety. Coffee, on the other hand, does some good and some harm (Chapter 4).

12. Music therapy

Music creates positive emotions and alters neurotransmitters in the brain. Some beats get people moving in the morning, while others help bring on sleep (Chapters 4 and 6).

13. Aromatherapy

It's all about the right scent at the right time. Aromatherapy causes complex changes in the brain that can enhance energy, sharpen focus, or induce sleep (Chapters 4 and 6).

14. Air ionization

Ionized air is concentrated in waterfalls, ocean breezes, and rain forests. Air conditioners pull these ions out of the air, but devices that ionize the air are effective antidepressants (Chapter 4).

15. Behavioral activation

Rather than building busy schedules, this therapy helps clients build meaningful lives by choosing actions that are in line with their values (Chapter 5).

16. Opposite action

From impulsive spending to social withdrawal, every symptoms of a mood disorder can also be part of normal life. So, when does a symptom become a disorder? Understanding vicious cycles helps answer that question, and also points the way out. By recognizing early symptoms and acting opposite to them, clients can keep problems from spiraling out of control (Chapter 5).

17. Approach-avoidance

Mood disorders are full of bad feelings. Avoidance moves people away from life in an effort to control those feelings. Approach is the opposite of avoidance. It moves clients toward their goals in spite of their feelings (Chapter 5).

18. Absorbing activity

People with depression are trapped inside their heads, and the scenery in there is usually rather bleak. Absorbing activities help them get out of that space. It's like instant mindfulness: a way of engaging in the present moment for those whose minds are yoked to a rougher train of thought (Chapter 5).

19. Mindful media

Screen time is the default mode for many people, particularly those with depression. While it's hard to argue that there's a benefit to this escape, there are ways to engage electronic media that are less damaging than others (Chapter 5).

20. Brisk walking

This mild form of exercise protects the brain, improves memory, and treats depression about as well as an antidepressant (Chapter 5).

21. Forest therapy

If brisk walking is too strenuous, a stroll in the forest works almost as well. There's something unique about this natural environment that improves mood and health even more than walks in other settings (Chapter 5).

22. Social rhythm therapy

The biological clock is slightly broken in people with mood disorders, and this therapy helps clients develop daily routines to keep it running on time (Chapter 5).

23. Evening wind-down

The hour before sleep is a critical time for brain activity, and a wind-down routine in that time can ease sleep and stabilize mood (Chapter 6).

24. Blue light blockers

The eyes have special receptors that only respond to the blue wavelength of light. Evening blue light dampens the hormones involved in sleep, and it's been linked to insomnia, depression, and a host of health risks. Technology is the source of this light, but it can also be used to filter it out (Chapter 6).

25. Dark therapy

This simple behavioral therapy is very effective against mania, mixed states, and rapid cycles of mood (Chapter 6).

26. Hot bath

In the natural world, temperature drops at night, triggering sleep. A carefully timed hot bath can achieve the same effect for those of us who live in the constant temperature of the indoors (Chapter 6).

27. Sleep hygiene

Insomnia is a vicious cycle. Sleep hygiene includes first-aid interventions that can reel that cycle in before it gets too off track (Chapter 7).

28. Cognitive behavioral therapy for insomnia

When sleep hygiene is not enough, this behavioral program can treat more intractable cases of insomnia. The American Academy of Sleep Medicine recommends it above sleep medications, and it has surprising benefits for depression as well (Chapter 7).

29. Antidepressant diet

This diet is simple enough for people with depression to follow, but powerful enough to have a significant antidepressant effect (Chapter 8).

30. Antidepressant apps

Apps offer therapy on the go, allowing clients to continue the work between sessions. This list highlights the select few that worked in clinical studies and are available to the public (Appendix).

part I

symptoms
and
causes

Using Diagnosis In Therapy

Therapy works best when clients turn away from their symptoms and build on their strengths. To do that, they first need to know what their symptoms are. Psychoeducation about those symptoms can be therapeutic in itself, providing hope, validation, acceptance, and direction.

1. **Hope.** Let clients know that their symptoms are part of a problem that is understood and treatable.
2. **Validation.** Emphasize that the client's problems are real. They aren't just lazy or making excuses.
3. **Acceptance.** When clients view their symptoms as something they have instead of who they are, it buffers them against a vicious cycle of self-blame.
4. **Redirect their energy.** Clients waste a lot of energy mulling over symptoms that they are innocent of causing and helpless to control. They stew over their symptoms, and even try to rope the therapist into this rumination, presenting them as problems to be solved. Most depressive symptoms can't be solved directly, but you can redirect your client's energy toward other areas that are more likely to bear fruit, as the following case example shows.

The chapters that follow will walk you through the major mood disorders, from symptoms to diagnosis. You'll see how major depression and bipolar disorder differ, and how they overlap. Within that overlap is a spectrum of symptoms, from depression to mixed states to mania. Through the collaborative tools in these chapters, clients can gain a better understanding of their problems.

Case Example | **Reggie**

Reggie had anhedonia, a symptom of depression that muffles all positive feelings. What bothered him most was his loss of affection for other people, and he could chastise himself over this for hours.

We had approached his isolation in therapy without success. His social life was like a barren land where nothing could take root, and working on it seemed to further his guilt and isolation. He opened today's session with a rant. "I must be an awful person. I'm antisocial and keep to myself all the time."

Instead of engaging with the rumination, I turned the conversation toward an area of his life that I sensed was untouched by depression. "How do you feel about your dog?" "Pretty good. Piper is the only thing that keeps me going, but I'm not a good dog owner. I rarely take him out for walks."

We developed a plan to take Piper on regular walks and Reggie was successful with this. Unlike his social life, his affections for Piper were intact, and we had something to build on. After a few weeks of these walks, his depression started to lift, and work on his social life became a little more productive.

The Mood Spectrum: Diagnoses in the *DSM-5*® Era

For many years, there were two major mood disorders in the *DSM*: bipolar I disorder and major depressive disorder. *Bipolar* means two poles: mania and depression. Major depressive disorder has only one pole – depression – which is why it's sometimes called *unipolar* depression. The problem is that nature is rarely so black and white, and a sizable minority of clients with depression don't fit neatly into those two categories. They've had some manic symptoms but have never had full mania. That lands them somewhere in the middle of the two extremes: not fully bipolar but not fully unipolar either.

This middle zone was first identified in the 1980s as the ***bipolar spectrum***. Over time, that spectrum has been absorbed into the *DSM*, beginning in 1994 with bipolar II disorder, in which frequent episodes of depression cycle with mild manic states called *hypomania*. The *DSM-5* expanded the spectrum further by recognizing that manic symptoms can happen in unipolar depression. This new diagnosis is called major depression with mixed features because the manic symptoms are "mixed" into the depression, and it represents about a quarter of clients with major depression.

Although depression and bipolar disorder fall along a continuum (Phillips & Kupfer, 2013), that continuum is not explicitly spelled out in the *DSM-5*, which remains a categorical system. Nonetheless, if we line up the mood disorders in the *DSM-5*, we can see an underlying spectrum. Capping the spectrum are the two original mood disorders: unipolar depression at one end and bipolar I disorder at the other. Manic symptoms increase in duration and intensity as we move from the unipolar to the bipolar side.

Identifying these mild manic symptoms helps predict how people will respond to medication. Sometimes antidepressants can worsen mood, and that risk depends on how long the hypo/manic* symptoms have lasted (see figure). It can also guide therapy. Some of the approaches in this book, like dark therapy and social rhythm therapy, work better for clients with manic symptoms.

Just how common is this middle spectrum? It's estimated that 40-50% of clients with depression are in the middle of the spectrum between the extremes of major depression and bipolar I disorder (Nusslock & Frank, 2011). Although all of these mid-spectrum clients have hypomanic symptoms, only half would be classified with a bipolar disorder – namely, cyclothymic disorder or bipolar II disorder – according to *DSM-5* criteria. The problem is that the classification of the bipolar disorders is a little arbitrary. From a scientific point of view, people in the middle of the spectrum are more alike than they are different. However, in the *DSM-5*, the presence of one symptom, such as rapid speech, may make the difference between a bipolar and a unipolar diagnosis. This wouldn't be such a big deal if the word "bipolar" didn't carry so much stigma.

Diagnosing the Middle Spectrum

The mood disorders in the middle of the spectrum bear little resemblance to bipolar I disorder with its full, out-of-control manias. For example, clients who have depression with mixed features may present with symptoms that resemble depression with a restless, irritable edge to it. Similarly, those with hypomania may present as a "normal" person who's having a *really* good day, with a touch of flightiness that could be mistaken for attention-deficit / hyperactivity disorder (ADHD). These clients don't think of themselves as having "two poles," so the word "bipolar" does not sit well with them. Most clients with bipolar II and other mid-spectrum disorders think of themselves as having chronic depression.

For clients in the middle of the spectrum, accuracy of diagnosis is a crucial first component in therapy, as being able to pick up on hypomanic symptoms helps steer the treatment team in the right direction. An accurate diagnosis facilitates the effectiveness of the medication plan and influences the therapy plan as well. For example, clients

---

* Throughout this book, I'll use the shorthand "hypo/mania" when referring both mania and hypomania.

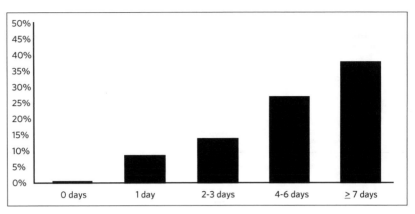

Risk of mood worsening on an antidepressant rises with duration of
hypomania (Angst et al., 2012)

Mood Spectrum Position	DSM-5 disorder	Depression?	Hypomania?	Mania?	Length of Depression	Length of Mania or Hypomania
Unipolar	Major Depressive Disorder	Yes	No	No	≥ 2 weeks	None
	Persistent Depressive Disorder	Yes	No	No	≥ 2 years	None
Middle Spectrum	Depression with Mixed Features	Yes	A least 3 hypomanic symptoms that overlap with the depression, but no full hypomania	No	≥ 2 weeks	The hypomanic symptoms are present for the majority of the depressive episode
	Depression with Brief Hypomania	Yes	Yes (brief)	No	≥ 2 weeks	< 4 days of hypomania
	Cyclothymic Disorder	Yes	Yes	No	< 2 weeks	Can be brief (< 4 days of hypomania) or longer
	Bipolar II Disorder	Yes (the main problem)	Yes	No	≥ 2 weeks	≥ 4 days of hypomania
Bipolar	Bipolar I Disorder	Optional (occurs in 90% of cases)	Optional	Yes	Varies	≥ 7 days of full mania

in the middle of the spectrum do better when they structure their day with regular routines that they keep at the same time, particularly with regard to sleeping, eating, and exposure to morning light and evening darkness. Ideally, the diagnosis they are given would naturally point them in that direction. The word "bipolar II" does not, so in my own practice, I explain it like this:

> *"The medical term for your depression is bipolar II, which is very different from bipolar I. For most people, 'bipolar' means bipolar I, or manic-depression. In your case, the word 'bipolar' is somewhat misleading. Bipolar II is really a form of depression, but one in which the depression keeps coming back. People with bipolar II cycle in and out of depression for many years and never have mania, while people with bipolar I cycle in and out of mania. It's the cycling that they have in common, not the mania, and there are things you can do to prevent that cycling.*
>
> *A more accurate word for your condition is **fragile circadian rhythm disorder**. Circadian rhythms regulate many of the symptoms you've been struggling with, like sleep, appetite, concentration, and energy. These rhythms are set by the body's internal clock, and that clock is a little broken in bipolar II disorder. In fact, many of the genes that cause bipolar II are involved in programming that clock."*

Fragile circadian rhythm disorder is not a real diagnosis, but it's a description that rings true for people whose moods are easily disrupted by seasons, sleep problems, and changes in their daily routines. It can also guide these clients toward the behavioral changes that will help them recover.

Moods and *emotions* are not the same, and mood disorders are not emotional illnesses. Energy is what defines the three types of mood episodes:
- Depression: low energy
- Mania: high energy
- Mixed states: a mix of high and low energy

Mood, Energy, and Emotion

Moods and Emotions

Mood disorders are not emotional illnesses. They certainly disrupt emotions – causing everything from anxiety to irritability to a complete inability to feel – but so do many other health problems. When it comes to diagnosis, emotions are a rough guide at best. For example, the most common complaint of people in a manic state is actually *depression* (Kotin & Goodwin, 1972). That may sound like a paradox, but consider the fact that mania makes people lose control over their own mind. It races in directions that they don't want to go and makes them do things they regret. Indeed, the pleasurable highs associated with hypo/mania are rarely seen in the office, or in life. After a few days, euphoric states become tinged with impatience, irritability, anxiety, and even mild paranoia.

Instead, energy is a more accurate and meaningful guide to mood. It is low in depression, high in hypo/mania, and up and down in mixed states. Depression is a low energy state that affects both the mind and body. Muscles feel weak and heavy, thinking is slow, and energy is drained.

When you think of mood in terms of energy, it becomes clear that the opposite of depression is not happiness. Rather, it's the high energy state of mania or, in its milder form, hypomania. Hypo/mania is a state of high energy and constant flux. That high energy causes the symptoms of hypo/mania to change rapidly, as if they are bouncing around like a ping-pong ball. Emotions are all over the place, shifting rapidly – or, in psychiatric terms, *labile*. In contrast, depression is more of a fixed state; there's not enough energy for the symptoms to move around. Although the high energy of hypo/mania can feel good, more often it makes people anxious, restless, and irritable.

Lastly, energy can jump up and down in a mixed state when depression and hypo/mania overlap. Agitation, irregular sleep, and heightened anxiety are the norm here. These "high energy" depressions are more severe than regular depression. They are mixed with desperation and impulsivity, which is why the risk of substance abuse and suicide are higher during mixed states than any other mood episode (Aiken, 2019).

It's very hard to change emotions, and that's not the goal of this book. Instead, you'll learn ways to help stabilize your client's energy by changing their environment, activity, and sleep patterns. Later we'll delve deeper into how to assess for these moods and use that diagnostic information to guide your treatment plans for the clients you serve.

Depression

Depression is a low energy state in which thoughts are slowed, motivation is low, and emotions are flat. It can feel like things are stuck, unchanging, as though every day is the same. Depression is not the same as sadness, which is a normal response to painful events. Rather, in depression, people experience overwhelming apathy, emptiness, loss of concentration, lethargy, and a sense of worthlessness that interferes with their ability to function.

Depression affects the brain much like medical illnesses affect the body, but there's one symptom of depression that makes it stand out from medical problems: self-blame. Depression can make people believe that the symptoms it causes are their own fault. For example, while pneumonia can also make people feel tired and sad, people with pneumonia usually don't think they're staying in bed all day because they are lazy.

Although depression is a real illness, it's easy for clients to forget that fact – in part, because the biological processes involved in depression cannot be seen or felt. Given this, when you're discussing depression with your clients, be mindful that depression makes people more sensitive to blame. Mild suggestions like, "You'd probably feel better if you got out of bed" can feel like verbal attacks. (At the same time, getting out of bed *is* a step they can take to feel better.) It's the perfect storm. So, what should clients (and you) do in that storm? Remind them to go easy on themselves. They're only human. It's not their fault that they have depression, but it is their responsibility to seek help and take an active role in recovery.

Before we talk about getting your clients out of bed, let's take a closer look at the ways that depression is affecting their life. Use the **Depression and Self-Blame** worksheet to see the extent to which a client's depression is causing them inordinate guilt. Give clients the **Depression Symptoms** worksheet to get a sense of what's going on in their mind and body. Follow that up with the **Patient Health Questionnaire-9** (PHQ-9) to determine the severity of their symptoms.

Depression and Self-Blame

The following are some of the ways that depression can cause people to blame themselves. Check how strongly you believe each statement:

I'm a burden to others.

not at all   not sure   fully believe it

I've let my family, friends, or coworkers down.

not at all   not sure   fully believe it

I don't try hard enough.

not at all   not sure   fully believe it

What other ways have you blamed yourself when you're experiencing depression?

_____

_____

_____

Have you felt blamed by others for the way that depression affects you? How so?

_____

_____

_____

Depression Symptoms

The following list includes several physical and mental symptoms of depression. Look through the list and check any symptoms that you've experienced in recent months. Are there any that you didn't know were caused by depression? Mark those with a star.

Mental Symptoms

☐ I'm sad or depressed.

☐ I'm anxious and panicky.

☐ I no longer enjoy anything.

☐ I give up easily.

☐ I can't concentrate.

☐ It's hard to hold a conversation.

☐ It's hard to get started on things. I don't know where to begin.

☐ I've lost my spiritual faith.

☐ I'm easily stressed.

☐ Little things make me feel rejected, criticized, or disliked.

☐ I don't have feelings for friends or family like I should.

☐ Food is tasteless.

☐ I've lost interest in sex.

☐ I feel numb and empty.

☐ Frightening or terrible images flash in my mind.

☐ I avoid and procrastinate a lot.

☐ I don't like myself.

☐ I'm indecisive.

☐ My mind is slowed down.

☐ I'm forgetful.

☐ I have trouble standing up for myself.

☐ Whenever I see the police, I have a dreadful sense that they'll pull me over.

☐ I feel like a failure.

☐ I'm easily overwhelmed by everyday hassles.

☐ I struggle with guilt and shame.

☐ I'm easily irritated.

☐ I put others needs above my own.

☐ It feels like I'm being punished.

☐ I doubt whether God could love or forgive me.

☐ I feel like a burden to others.

☐ I have no confidence.

☐ I feel powerless and incompetent.

☐ I'm stubborn and inflexible.

☐ It's hard to go with the flow and adapt to stress.

☐ I think I'd be better off dead.

☐ I don't take care of myself.

☐ I've withdrawn from everyone.

☐ Everything seems hopeless.

☐ I'm emotionally reactive.

☐ I can't stop worrying.

☐ I can't complete simple tasks.

☐ Nothing brings me pleasure.

☐ Time moves slowly.

☐ I think about past mistakes or bad memories a lot.

☐ I have a sense of dread like something bad is going to happen.

Physical Symptoms

- ☐ I'm tired. My energy is low.
- ☐ My muscles are weak or slowed down.
- ☐ I'm restless and tense.
- ☐ My appetite is high.
- ☐ My appetite is low.
- ☐ I have heavy feelings in my arms or legs.
- ☐ I have trouble falling or staying asleep.

- ☐ I wake up too early.
- ☐ I sleep too much.
- ☐ I never feel rested.
- ☐ I have headaches.
- ☐ My muscles ache.
- ☐ I feel constipated or sick to my stomach.

Which of these symptoms are the most difficult to live with? What problems have they caused?

_____

_____

_____

Rating Depression: The Patient Health Questionnaire-9 (PHQ-9)

The following is a widely-used rating scale for depression. Rate how frequently you've experienced these symptoms over the past week. Use this scale to track your weekly progress with the mood chart on pages 30-31.

Over the past week, how often have you been bothered by any of the following problems?

	Not at all	Several days	More than half the days	Nearly every day
1. Little interest or pleasure in doing things	0	1	2	3
2. Feeling down, depressed, or hopeless	0	1	2	3
3. Trouble falling or staying asleep, or sleeping too much	0	1	2	3
4. Feeling tired or having little energy	0	1	2	3
5. Poor appetite or overeating	0	1	2	3
6. Feeling bad about yourself – or that you are a failure or have let yourself or your family down	0	1	2	3
7. Trouble concentrating on things, such as reading the newspaper or watching television	0	1	2	3
8. Moving or speaking so slowly that other people could have noticed. Or the opposite – being so fidgety or restless that you have been moving around a lot more than usual	0	1	2	3
9. Thoughts that you would be better off dead, or of hurting yourself in some way	0	1	2	3

Add columns: _____ + _____ + _____

Total: _____

10. If you checked off any problems, how difficult have these problems made it for you to do your work, take care of things at home, or get along with other people?

| Not difficult at all | Somewhat difficult | Very difficult | Extremely difficult |

Scoring

Add your responses to questions 1 through 9 to arrive at your final score (from 0 to 27). Question 10 helps clarify if your symptoms are due to clinical depression. If your symptoms aren't causing a problem, then they may be a normal reaction to stress instead of clinical depression. The following cutoffs allow you to compare your score to the general population. These are based on averages, so it's not set in stone that your depression is mild just because you scored a 7:

PHQ-9 score	Depression level
0–4	None
5–9	Mild
10–14	Moderate
15–19	Moderately severe
20–27	Severe

Hypo/mania

Mania and hypomania are both high energy states that share the same symptoms but differ in degree, with hypomania being the milder form. Throughout this book, I'll use the shorthand "hypo/mania" when referring to both mania and hypomania. During hypomania, people can still put the brakes on, while in mania there's a greater loss of self-control. That means it's harder to rebound from the problems that mania causes, such as bankruptcy, job loss, divorce, or legal charges. Although hypomania causes problems as well, it tends to be things that people can overcome without too much trouble, like talking out of turn, arguing, overspending, or driving fast. The following table clarifies how those symptoms can manifest.

Hypo/manic symptom	How it looks in real life
Elevated energy	Motivated, driven, able to accomplish a lot without getting tired.
Elevated mood	Happy, excited, giddy, good humored, feeling a spiritual sense of connection.
Irritable	Impatient, reactive, short-fused, feeling people have it out for them, starting fights or arguments.
Hyperactive	Exercising or moving more, feeling restless, socializing more, making lots of plans or starting many projects.
Impulsive	Spending more money, driving faster, engaging in sudden travel, starting new relationships or projects, gambling, using drugs, hypersexuality.
Decreased need for sleep	Able to stay active despite sleeping less than 6 hours a day.
Increased confidence	Being more certain of their ideas or abilities, optimistic, self-important, or arrogant.
Distracted	Changing tasks frequently, thoughts shift from topic to topic, easily distracted by things around them.
Racing thoughts	Having lots of ideas, thoughts may be crowded or hard to keep up with, or so intense that they can't shut them off.
Rapid or pressured speech	People can't follow what they're saying. They interrupt a lot or talk over people.

Myths about Hypo/mania

Myth #1: Hypo/mania feels good

Intense pleasure, confidence, and spiritual bliss are symptoms of hypo/mania – but, unfortunately, they are the rarer of the bunch. More often, the elevated energy associated with hypo/mania makes people feel anxious, impatient, and out of control. "I felt infinitely worse [during mania] than when in the midst of my worst depressions," wrote Kay Redfield Jamison, a psychologist whose best-selling memoir describes her own experience with bipolar I disorder (Jamison, 1995).

Myth #2: People with bipolar disorder lose all self-control

Mania does make people lose self-control, but mania only happens in bipolar I disorder – and only one in 10 people on the mood spectrum have that form. Although it's rare, bipolar I disorder was the first form of bipolar identified back in 1980. Bipolar II disorder, the late comer, is the more common form, and the hypomanias that define it never rise to a level where all self-control is lost.

Myth #3: All clients with hypo/manic symptoms have bipolar disorder

About one in three people with non-bipolar depression have a few hypo/manic symptoms but do not have full hypomania. These symptoms may occur on their own or overlap with depression in a *mixed state*. However, these symptoms are too brief (fewer than four days in *depression with brief hypomania*) or mild (fewer than four symptoms in *depression with mixed features*) to count as full bipolar disorder. As illustrated in the following table, hypo/manic symptoms occur along a spectrum, from severe (bipolar I disorder) to none (pure, unipolar depression). These symptoms gradually decrease in severity from black to gray to white, and only the dark gray regions of that spectrum represent bipolar disorder.

Bipolar Disorders			Non-bipolar Depression		
Bipolar I	Bipolar II	Cyclo-thymic	Brief hypomania	Mixed features	Pure depression (no hypo/mania)

Myth #4: Clients know when they have hypo/mania

People can have hypo/mania without even knowing it. That's because the frontal lobes, which are involved in self-awareness, are turned down in hypo/mania. This is in contrast to depression, which actually turns the frontal lobes up, flooding the mind with negative self-talk and painful self-awareness.

Is Hypo/mania Ever Normal?

Most people have experienced hypo/manic symptoms in their lives. Energized, confident, euphoric... life would be pretty drab without them. The Swiss psychiatrist Jules Angst followed a large group of young adults over 20 years to see how the experience of these symptoms differed between people with bipolar disorder and those with no mental illness, the "normals." Although the symptoms were more numerous and longer-lasting in the bipolar group, many "normals" had hypo/manic symptoms as well, and there was no sharp dividing line between them. Hypo/manic symptoms were not always a blessing in the normal group. Those who reported them had greater rates of impulsivity, irritability, sleep problems, binge eating, and substance abuse. They were also more likely to have a family history of bipolar disorder (Gamma et al., 2008).

The following questionnaires can help determine if your clients have ever experienced hypo/mania. The **Hypomania Survey** includes symptoms that are common during hypomania but not necessarily diagnostic of it. It will give you a sense of how the experience affects their life. The **Hypomanic Check List-32** has more diagnostic utility. It was created by Jules Angst, who first developed the concept of bipolar disorder in the 1960s. Unlike the popular Mood Disorder Questionnaire,[†] which is geared toward bipolar I disorder, the Hypomanic Check List-32 is more sensitive for bipolar II disorder (Carvalho et al., 2015).

The symptoms of hypo/mania can be difficult for clients to recognize, as the episodes tend to be brief, rare, and are often forgotten. Given that clients may be unaware that they have experienced hypo/mania, it helps to have input from someone who knows them well, like a trusted friend or family member.

---

† Available online at www.sadag.org/images/pdf/mdq.pdf

Hypomania Survey

Hypomania has many faces. The words below came from people who've experienced it. Check any symptoms that you've experienced, either recently or in the past.

☐ My thoughts bounce around like a ping-pong ball.

☐ I clean, decorate, or organize all night.

☐ I have strong desires to reconnect with old friends or lovers.

☐ My attention shifts from one thing to another, and I never finish anything.

☐ I'm playful with words, often making puns or rhymes.

☐ I'm easily overstimulated.

☐ I'm flirtatious and seductive, but it feels like I'm playing a role.

☐ Buying things brings great pleasure.

☐ I blurt things out. No filter.

☐ My senses are heightened. Colors are brighter and sounds are louder.

☐ I can't turn my mind off.

☐ I spend too much money.

☐ My romantic interests are intense but change frequently.

☐ I'm full of plans, projects, and new pursuits.

☐ I strike up conversations with strangers.

☐ I overstep my bounds and disregard rules and authorities.

☐ I'm drawn to dramatic or high-fashion clothing.

☐ It feels like people are staring or laughing at me.

☐ I like to be the center of attention.

☐ I'm interested in everything and everybody.

☐ I speed or drive aggressively.

☐ I feel strong and invulnerable, resistant to illnesses and accidents.

☐ I do things to excess.

☐ I'm very assertive.

☐ I make sudden travel plans.

☐ I feel like people's comments are directed toward me.

☐ I have so many thoughts and ideas at once that it's hard to express them.

☐ Others are attracted to my confidence, energy, and enthusiasm.

☐ I feel a sense of oneness with others, like we have a lot in common.

☐ I'm physically restless.

☐ I suddenly change hair styles, color, or other fashions.

☐ I have greater mental clarity.

☐ I take risks easily.

☐ I see things, like shadows or bugs.

☐ I buy multiple copies of the same thing.

☐ I enjoy dangerous, risky, challenging, or emotionally intense activities.

☐ I'm easily distracted.

☐ I frequently change jobs, homes, friends, or hobbies.

- ☐ I feel overly certain about my own ideas.
- ☐ I'm much more interested in sex.
- ☐ I do things more quickly and easily.
- ☐ I have a stubborn, one-track mind.
- ☐ I go for days without sleeping or with much less sleep than usual but still keep active.
- ☐ I talk a lot, interrupt, and talk over people.
- ☐ I feel sped up inside.
- ☐ I get easily caught up in addictive things, like gambling, sweets, porn, or drugs.
- ☐ I have mystical experiences or visions.
- ☐ I'm driven to do something but don't know what to do.
- ☐ I give lots of presents.
- ☐ It's hard to wind down and sleep at night.
- ☐ The smallest things make me very enthusiastic.
- ☐ I'm so confident in what I do that I'm indifferent to criticism.
- ☐ I'm driven to get things perfect.
- ☐ It feels like I have extrasensory perception (ESP).
- ☐ Time moves quickly.
- ☐ I quit jobs or end relationships abruptly.
- ☐ My sense of taste and smell is vivid.
- ☐ People complain that I'm too noisy.
- ☐ I'm very impatient.
- ☐ People think I'm irresponsible.
- ☐ Sometimes I hear things, like my name being called.
- ☐ My emotions shift rapidly.

- ☐ I'm over-reactive.
- ☐ People can't keep up with me.
- ☐ I make major life decisions without much thought.
- ☐ I'm very confident and self-assured.
- ☐ I'm more extroverted and charismatic than usual.
- ☐ People think my speech is rapid or loud.
- ☐ I see connections in things that others miss.
- ☐ People think I'm exhausting or irritating.
- ☐ I have an irresistible urge to communicate by phone, letters, emails, or texts.
- ☐ I mistrust other people's intentions.
- ☐ I'm more optimistic.
- ☐ I feel vigorous, lively, and full of energy.
- ☐ I feel really good about my looks.
- ☐ I act without thinking.
- ☐ I have a sense of superiority, as though I have amazing abilities, talents, knowledge, or powers.
- ☐ I have multiple trains of thought. Sometimes it's hard to keep up with, but I can also multitask, like carrying on a conversation while my mind is on another track.
- ☐ I have intense enjoyment or appreciation of artistic works.
- ☐ I'm overly carefree.
- ☐ I'm particularly sensitive to shapes, forms, and harmony in nature.
- ☐ I get involved in other people's lives and feel like I can make decisions for them.

- ☐ I have urges to self-medicate to calm my nerves.

- ☐ I write long texts or emails.

- ☐ I'm drawn to bright colors or red hues.

- ☐ I'm the life of the party.

- ☐ I often see humor where others miss it.

- ☐ I spend a lot of time on social, political, or religious causes.

- ☐ I'm unusually vindictive and feel a need to even the score.

- ☐ I leave big tips.

- ☐ I exercise a lot or am more physically active.

- ☐ I feel like I'm losing control.

- ☐ I play devil's advocate and do the opposite of what people want me to do.

- ☐ I'm very artistic and creative.

- ☐ I cry and laugh at the same time.

- ☐ I binge on food.

- ☐ I'm very critical or sarcastic.

- ☐ I'm drawn to argument.

- ☐ I feel mentally sharp, brilliant, and clever.

- ☐ I often break out into song or dance.

- ☐ I daydream a lot and get lost in fantasy.

- ☐ I have a lot of difficulty seeing things from other people's point of view.

- ☐ I feel unappreciated because no one shares my optimistic or imaginative ideas.

- ☐ I want to decorate my body with tattoos, piercings, or makeup.

- ☐ I make inappropriate jokes.

- ☐ I can't turn my mind off.

Hypomanic Check List-32

At different times in our lives, everyone experiences changes or swings in energy, activity, and mood ("highs and lows" or "ups and downs"). The aim of this questionnaire is to assess the characteristics of the "high or hyper" periods.

1. First of all, how are you feeling today compared with your usual state?

Much worse than usual	Worse than usual	A little worse than usual	Neither better nor worse than usual	A little better than usual	Better than usual	Much better than usual
☐	☐	☐	☐	☐	☐	☐

2. Compared with other people, your level of activity, energy, and mood... (not how you feel today, but on average):

... is always rather stable and even.	... is generally higher.	... is generally lower.	... repeatedly shows periods of ups and downs.
☐	☐	☐	☐

3. Please try to remember a period when you were in a "high or hyper" state. How did you feel then? Check all the statements below that happen during a high or hyper state:

In such a "high or hyper" state:	Yes	No
I need less sleep.	☐	☐
I feel more energetic and more active.	☐	☐
I am more self-confident.	☐	☐
I enjoy my work more.	☐	☐
I am more sociable (make more phone calls, go out more).	☐	☐
I want to travel and/or do travel more.	☐	☐
I tend to drive faster or take more risks when driving.	☐	☐
I spend more money/too much money.	☐	☐
I take more risks in my daily life (in my work and/or other activities).	☐	☐
I am physically more active (sports, etc.).	☐	☐
I plan more activities or projects.	☐	☐
I have more ideas; I am more creative.	☐	☐
I am less shy or inhibited.	☐	☐
I wear more colorful and more extravagant clothes/makeup.	☐	☐
I want to meet or actually do meet more people.	☐	☐
I am more interested in sex and/or have increased sexual desire.	☐	☐
I am more flirtatious and/or am more sexually active.	☐	☐

In such a "high or hyper" state (con't):	Yes	No
I talk more.	☐	☐
I think faster.	☐	☐
I make more jokes or puns when I am talking.	☐	☐
I am more easily distracted.	☐	☐
I engage in lots of new things.	☐	☐
My thoughts jump from topic to topic.	☐	☐
I do things more quickly and/or more easily.	☐	☐
I am more impatient and/or get irritable more easily.	☐	☐
I can be exhausting or irritating to others.	☐	☐
I get into more quarrels.	☐	☐
My mood is higher, more optimistic.	☐	☐
I drink more coffee.	☐	☐
I smoke more cigarettes.	☐	☐
I drink more alcohol.	☐	☐
I take more drugs (sedatives, anxiolytics, stimulants, etc.).	☐	☐

4. Did the previous chart, which characterizes a "high," describe how you are?

Sometimes	Most of the time	I've never experienced such a "high."
☐	☐	☐
(If you mark this box, please answer all questions 5 to 9.)	(If you mark this box, please answer only questions 5 and 6.)	(If you mark this box, please stop here.)

5. What is the impact of your "highs" on various aspects of your life?

	Positive and negative	Positive	Negative	No impact
Family life	☐	☐	☐	☐
Social life	☐	☐	☐	☐
Work	☐	☐	☐	☐
Leisure	☐	☐	☐	☐

6. How did people close to you react to or comment on your "highs"?

Positively (encouraging or supportive)	Neutral	Negatively (concerned, annoyed, irritated, critical)	Positively and negatively	No reactions
☐	☐	☐	☐	☐

7. Length of your "highs" as a rule (on the average):

        ☐ 1 day   ☐ Longer than 1 week

        ☐ 2–3 days   ☐ Longer than 1 month

        ☐ 4–7 days   ☐ I can't judge/don't know

8. Have you experienced such "highs" in the past 12 months?

                ☐ Yes   ☐ No

9. If yes, please estimate how many days you spent in "highs" during the last 12 months:

        Taken all together, about _____ days

Scoring

If you marked "yes" to at least 14 statements in item 3, and those highs lasted at least four days, then it's very likely that you have had full hypomania (and possibly mania if the highs caused a major problem). The rest of the test does not count toward the score but can help you further describe those highs.

Hypomania: Input from a Trusted Companion

Sometimes, those around us can recognize our symptoms more easily than we ourselves can, and getting their input can be helpful in seeing the big picture. **This worksheet is intended to be filled out by someone you trust about your possible symptoms of hypomania**. This can be a friend, family member, or someone else who knows you well.

Has your friend or relative ever had the following symptoms in their life? Circle YES, even if they happened long ago, were brief, or seemed like they were due to external circumstances.		
1. Has there ever been a period of time when they were not their usual self and...		
...they seemed to feel so good or so hyper that you thought they weren't their normal self, or they were so hyper they got into trouble?	Yes	No
... they were so irritable that they shouted at people or started fights or arguments?	Yes	No
...they acted much more self-confident than usual?	Yes	No
...they got much less sleep than usual and seemed to not really miss it?	Yes	No
...they were much more talkative or spoke faster than usual?	Yes	No
...they had many ideas at once or their thoughts raced from topic to topic?	Yes	No
...they were so easily distracted by things around them that you had trouble following their train of thought?	Yes	No
...they seemed to have much more energy than usual?	Yes	No
...they were much more active or did many more things than usual?	Yes	No
...they were much more social or outgoing than usual; for example, telephoning friends in the middle of the night?	Yes	No
...they were much more interested in sex than usual?	Yes	No
...they did things that were unusual for them or that you thought were excessive, foolish, or risky?	Yes	No
...they spent money to the point that it got them or their family into trouble?	Yes	No
2. If you checked YES to more than one of the items above, have several of these ever happened during the *same period of time*?	Yes	No
3. How much of a *problem* did any of these cause – like being unable to work; having family, money, or legal troubles; or getting into arguments or fights?		

No Problem   Minor Problem   Moderate Problem   Serious Problem

Mixed States

Depression and hypomania are opposites: One is characterized by low energy, and the other by high energy. However, these moods can also overlap, and when they do it's called a *mixed state*. It would be nice if the ups and downs cancelled each other out. Unfortunately, they don't. Mixed states are painful, and the push and pull of these opposing energies creates anxiety, tension, and desperation. People describe feeling "tired and wired; restless; driven to do something but I don't know what to do."

The *DSM-5* does not include separate criteria for mixed states. Instead, it asks you to count the hypo/manic and depressive symptoms separately. The problem with this is that these symptoms create a different picture when they overlap in a mixed state, much like yellow and blue overlap to form green. For example, ask a client with mixed depression, "Do you have times when you don't need much sleep?" and they will answer "No." In truth, they do keep going with little sleep, but they feel that they need it, because they want to quiet their racing, anxious mind.

Similarly, ask a client in a mixed state, "Do you feel more confident than usual" and you'll get a big "No." Mixed states have all the insecurity of regular depression, but if you look closer, you'll see things that don't fit. Instead of being passive and deferential (like we see in depression), clients in a mixed state can be demanding, aggressive, and overly assertive. What does high energy look like when mixed with depression? Mixed states make people hyperactive, but in a disorganized and directionless manner. They set out to rearrange their furniture but end up moving it into random piles and creating a big mess.

The following table describes how hypo/manic symptoms can manifest in a mixed state:

Hypo/manic symptom	How it looks in a mixed state
Elevated energy	An uncomfortable, anxious energy that is commonly described as "wired, restless, crawling out of my skin."
Elevated mood	Emotions swing rapidly from one to another (e.g., oscillating between irritable, sad, anxious, despairing, and – rarely – giddy or happy).
Irritable	Angry, impatient, reactive, short-fused, feeling people have it out for them, starting arguments or isolating themselves to avoid other people.
Hyperactive	Pacing from room to room without a clear purpose, feeling agitated or tense, going on random walks or drives.
Impulsive	Engaging in reckless, destructive actions (e.g., suddenly leaving relationships or jobs, breaking things, driving aggressively). Sometimes, pleasure is pursued impulsively, in which case it feels like a desperate attempt to relieve the depression (e.g., overspending through "retail therapy," binge eating, addictive behavior, pornography).
Decreased need for sleep	Sleep is random; they may be up all night and asleep during the day. When their amount of sleep is decreased, they still feel like they need it, in part because sleep offers some relief from the terrible anxiety of a mixed state.
Increased confidence	They probably don't feel too good about themselves, but they may come across as demanding, pushy, or stubborn to others.
Distracted	Changing tasks frequently, disorganized, finding it hard to think, shifting thoughts from one anxious topic to another.
Racing thoughts	Their mind is crowded with depressive or anxious thoughts, imagining the worst-case scenario. It's hard to shut their mind off, particularly at night.
Rapid or pressured speech	There's an urgent, emotional tone to their speech.

Hypo/manic and depressive symptoms can overlap in many ways, so no two mixed states are the same. The ups and downs tend to fluctuate throughout the day. The depressive side is usually worse in the morning, while the hypo/manic symptoms enter at night, but there are many variations. The diagnostic criteria in *DSM-5* requires at least three hypo/manic symptoms during a depression to diagnose a mixed state.‡

Mixed states are important to recognize because they elevate the risks of suicide, self-harm, and substance abuse. While manic impulsivity drives people toward pleasurable pursuits, during mixed states the impulsivity is destructive. Instead of starting new relationships, they are more likely to destroy the ones they have, such as leaving a marriage or quitting psychotherapy in a fit of rage.

Mixed states help predict how people respond to medications. There's a greater risk that antidepressants won't work in a depression with mixed features, and mood stabilizers may be needed to help the agitated symptoms. Mixed states also tell us about what types of lifestyle changes will help your client's mood. In particular, mixed symptoms indicate that something is wrong with the hormones that set the biological clock, so the techniques presented later in this book, which help regulate that clock, will be particularly important.

There is not a good diagnostic test for mixed states as these symptoms are common in many disorders. They could be due to anxiety, addiction, borderline personality disorder, or post-traumatic stress disorder. When a client has classic mania, you're much more sure of what you're doing. During mixed states, the diagnosis is less certain. This is where the non-symptomatic markers of bipolar disorder come in handy (see *Beyond Symptoms* on page 27).

On that note, the **Rating Hypo/mania Scale** that follows is not meant to diagnose mixed states, but to track them. The scale allows clients to rate their hypo/manic symptoms, regardless of whether they occurred in a mixed or pure form. In essence, it combines hypo/mania and mixed states into one rating that can be tracked on a mood chart. Is anything lost in combining the two? Not really. Pure hypo/mania will still be recognizable by the lack of depressive symptoms on the other side of the mood chart. Mixed states and hypo/mania require the same interventions. Those include dark therapy, regulation of daily routines, and, on the medication side, mood stabilizers.

---

‡ In *depression with mixed features*, at least three hypo/manic symptoms need to overlap with depression, but the following symptoms are not allowed to count toward the diagnosis: irritable, distracted, and physically agitated.

Rating Hypo/mania

Hypo/manic symptoms look different depending on whether they are "mixed" with depression or occur on their own in "pure" form. The following scale describes the pure symptoms in plain text and uses *italics* for symptoms that are typical of the mixed version. Rate the frequency with which you have experienced these symptoms over the past week, regardless of whether they were pure or mixed. Use this scale to track your weekly progress with the mood chart on pages 30-31.

Over the past week, how often have you experienced any of the following symptoms, whether they bothered you or not?

	Not at all	Several days	More than half the days	Nearly every day
1. "Hyped up" or energized; or *feeling physically restless, agitated, or "wired" with anxious energy.*	0	1	2	3
2. Feeling unusually good; or *emotions that shift rapidly from one to another.*	0	1	2	3
3. Irritable, impatient, or argumentative.	0	1	2	3
4. More active, social, or sexual than usual; doing more projects or making more plans than usual; *or frequently shifting tasks, driven to do something but you don't know what to do.*	0	1	2	3
5. Acting on impulse or doing things that others might think are excessive, foolish, or risky. Examples include over-spending, sexual indiscretions, sudden travel, reckless driving, *suddenly starting or ending relationships or jobs, breaking things, violence, dangerous behavior, binge eating, and addictive behaviors.*	0	1	2	3
6. More confident, sure of your ideas, or self-important; *or demanding, pushy, or overly stubborn.*	0	1	2	3
7. Sleeping less than usual but still able to keep going during the day; *or irregular sleep patterns that swing from sleeping too much to being unable to sleep and up all night.*	0	1	2	3

8. More talkative than usual, interrupting others, or speech that is rapid, loud, or pressured.	0	1	2	3
9. Easily distracted, racing thoughts, or thoughts that jump from topic to topic.	0	1	2	3

Add columns: _____ + _____ + _____

Total: _____

10. How difficult have these symptoms made it for you to do your work, take care of things at home, or get along with other people?

| Not difficult at all | Somewhat difficult | Very difficult | Extremely difficult |

Atypical and Classic Bipolar

While the *DSM* focuses on the difference between bipolar I and II, there's another way to divide bipolar disorders that's just as relevant to treatment. While there's no official term for these types, some call them **classic** and **atypical**.

Classic bipolar is the textbook case. The hypo/manias tend to be euphoric, productive, and quick-witted state. Episodes of hypo/mania are clearly separated from those of depression, and the two rarely overlap in mixed states. The depression often occurs as though following the law of "what goes up must come down." When clients aren't in either of these episodes, they tend to have healthy personalities and are usually free of other mental disorders. Classic bipolar typically starts in the late teens, from age 15-20.

Atypical bipolar comes on earlier in life, at or before puberty, and tends to stick around longer. These are the clients who say, "I don't know what normal is." They cycle in and out of depression and hypo/mania, and those moods frequently overlap in mixed states. Anxiety and cognitive problems are common. Full recovery is rare, and many of these clients have personality problems that get in the way of that recovery. In fact, comorbid psychiatric disorders are common in this group, including anxiety, addictive disorders, bulimia, ADHD, obsessive compulsive disorder, and borderline personality disorder. Early childhood trauma, head injuries, and substance use are also more common in people with atypical bipolar.

From anxiety to addiction, most of the comorbidities in atypical bipolar respond better to therapy than medication. Furthermore, the medications that are used most often in those comorbidities are antidepressants, which can worsen bipolar symptoms. For those reasons, psychotherapy is particularly important in atypical bipolar.

In contrast to clients with atypical bipolar, clients with classic bipolar tend to have more personal strengths. They are more confident, action-oriented, intelligent, warm, and extroverted than their atypical cousins, and even have a little more than the average "healthy control" (Galvez et al., 2011). That poses a different problem in therapy: They don't think they need it. They also tend to stop their medication for the same reason. Action-oriented clients may resist insight-oriented therapy, but they will do well to at least learn the basic behavioral approaches to preventing bipolar disorder that are laid out in this book.

The following table outlines some of the key differences between classic and atypical bipolar disorder. Importantly, clients don't need to have all these features; what matters is which side predominates.

Feature	Classic Bipolar	Atypical Bipolar
Mania and hypomania	Euphoric (though can become irritable and impatient)	Depressive, anxious manias or mixed states
Mixed states	Rare	Common
Recovery	Episodes are separated by long periods of full recovery	Milder symptoms persist between episodes
Frequency	Rapid cycling is rare	Rapid cycling (≥ 4 episodes per year) is common
Comorbidities	Few major comorbidities	Comorbidities are common
Onset of bipolar	Age 15-20	At or before puberty

Personality	Normal or hyperthymic (high energy, natural leader)	Borderline and other personality disorders are common, as is cyclothymic temperament
Genetics	Family history of bipolar is more common	Family history is often mixed with various psychiatric conditions
Environmental factors	Less traumatic lives	Childhood trauma, head injury, and addictions are more common
Medication response	More responsive to lithium	More responsive to anticonvulsants and atypical antipsychotics

Beyond Symptoms

The symptoms of bipolar disorder overlap with many other diagnoses, which is part of the reason this diagnosis is so difficult to make. Post-traumatic stress disorder (PTSD) makes people irritable and impulsive. Generalized anxiety disorder causes racing thoughts, and ADHD is marked by distraction and hyperactivity. Complicating the issue of differential diagnosis even further, sometimes a client presents with multiple conditions on top of bipolar disorder. This is often the case in atypical bipolar, where comorbid anxiety, addiction, ADHD, bulimia, and trauma are the norm.

The way to peel through this confusion is to look at non-symptomatic signs that can point toward or away from a bipolar diagnosis. The following three signs significantly increase the chance that a client with recurrent depression is on the bipolar side of the spectrum.

1. **Family history.** Bipolar disorder is more genetic than unipolar depression, so a family history of bipolar raises the risk, particularly if it's in a first-degree relative, like a parent or sibling. However, it's rare to know the true diagnosis of a family member. Ask if other family members have had frequent episodes of depression that cycled with irritability, impulsivity, or out-of-control behavior, which might have been due to mania.

2. **Age of onset.** The average onset of bipolar disorder is 15-20 years, while unipolar depression tends to come on after age 30. To parse out a client's age of onset, ask them how old they were when they first had mood problems, not just when they first came to treatment, and inquire more about what those early symptoms were. If the answer is "all my life," then they may have one (or all) of these possibilities:
   * Early childhood abuse or neglect
   * Temperamental problems (dysthymic or cyclothymic temperament)
   * Atypical bipolar

3. **Poor response to antidepressants.** Antidepressants are helpful in a minority of bipolar patients (around 10-20%), but most respond in one of the following ways:
   * Mania: This response usually occurs within three months of starting the antidepressant.
   * Mixed states: This response is much more common, as most antidepressants are not powerful enough to flip depression into full, pure mania. Instead, they sprinkle manic symptoms on top of the depression. To the client, it feels like the volume is turned up on their depression, and they'll usually say that the antidepressant made them feel worse.
   * No response: Often, antidepressants prove ineffective for those with bipolar disorder, as 40-60% of people who don't respond to two or more antidepressants turn out to have bipolar disorder (Francesca, Efisia, Alessandra, Marianna, & Giovanni, 2014).

Mood Charting

A mood chart is a graphic timeline of depressive downs and hypo/manic highs. It was first used by Emil Kraeplin, the German psychiatrist who first described manic depression in the early 1900s. Later, it was revived at the National Institute of Mental Health to measure patterns of mood and treatment response. Since the advent of effective psychotherapies for bipolar disorder in the late 1990s, therapists have used mood charts to understand the interactions between mood, stress, and behavior change.

Mood charting is particularly helpful for medication providers, given that they see their clients less often than therapists do. Sharing that data at a medication visit can make a big difference. In fact, one study found that regular mood ratings doubled the rate of recovery from depression because the doctors had better information to base their decisions on (Guo et al., 2015).

When I first went into practice, I used mood charting with gusto, but I soon ran into problems. First, most mood charts require daily entries, and clients find that tedious. Some even complained that it was depressing to think that much about their mood. Second, many available charts ask for ratings of emotion rather than mood. Emotions, as we've seen, don't tell us much about whether mood is up or down. Given those issues, the chart in this book asks for *weekly* ratings and provides a detailed rating scale to assess the "ups" and "downs" more accurately. For clients, this takes the guesswork out; for providers, it gives us the information we need.

But are weekly ratings good enough? Generally, yes. What we're looking for on the chart is steady, long-term change. Clients are less likely to give up on treatment when they can appreciate the steady trend of progress on their chart, and many of the lifestyle changes in this book take a while to work. That delay is well-illustrated by a study of a bipolar-specific form of cognitive behavioral therapy for insomnia (CBT-IB) that focused on regular patterns of sleep, waking, and daily activity, much as this book does. In the first two months of the study, clients who undertook CBT-IB saw little change in their mood compared to a control group who received weekly psychoeducation about bipolar disorder. However, after six months, the changes were profound. Those in the CBT-IB group had an eight-fold reduction in the frequency of their mood symptoms (Harvey et al., 2015).

I've included a **Mood Chart** on page 31. Here are some ways you can use it in practice:

1. **Use the chart to enhance the motivational interview.** Mood charts add a visual element to the motivational interview, and help put the client and therapist on the same page. Both you and your client can look at the chart together and try to figure out what's working and what's not.

2. **Search for causes.** Clients often present with a new depression and have no idea where it came from. Depression, after all, does not inspire good problem-solving skills. Whenever mood has worsened, look through the chart for potential clues. Often, the cause has occurred weeks or months in the past.

3. **Examine seasonal patterns.** You'll pick up on winter depression and spring mania in some clients. Pay attention to the equinox around late September and mid-March. That's when the amount of daylight changes rapidly, which can be particularly destabilizing for clients with bipolar disorder.

4. **Identify rapid cycling.** Rapid cycling refers to four or more mood episodes in a year, which can include depression, hypo/mania, or a mixture of the two. It's often missed in practice because the changes are not very rapid (e.g., happening every few months), but they will stand out on a mood chart. Rapid cycling can result in clients being prescribed a lot of medications that they don't need, because every time they start a new medication, they cycle out of the episode. That gives the illusion that the medication worked, when in reality they would have cycled out of the episode anyway. Worse, antidepressants can cause rapid cycling, in which clients get better quickly after starting the antidepressant but then go on to have more and more frequent cycles. Other causes of rapid cycling include substance abuse, thyroid abnormalities, and irregular sleep patterns.

Clients usually know what helps them in the short term. It's the long-term view that's missing, and that's where therapy and mood charting fill a useful role. Treating mood disorders is a lot like finding the way out of a dense forest. The thorns are many, and the path is narrow, but you need to mark your trail along the journey to keep from going in circles.

Mood Charting Apps

There are plenty of apps that chart mood, but most ask clients to rate emotions rather than mood. One option that stands out from the crowd is the eMoods Bipolar Mood Tracker.

Mood Charting Instructions

Moods are like the weather. Symptoms may change from day to day, like the temperature, but you'd need to look at a weather map with months of data to know what type of climate you're in. That's what mood charting does. This paper-and-pencil technique was developed at the National Institute of Mental Health. It's practically free, but it tells us more about your diagnosis and treatment than an MRI of the brain. A mood chart is provided on the following page.

To use it, rate your high and low mood symptoms at the end of each week using your responses from the "Rating Depression" and "Rating Hypo/mania" scales (pages 11 and 24, respectively). **Shade the boxes to correspond with your total score on each rating scale (ranging from 0 to 27). Leave the boxes blank for a score of 0. For the lows, shade downward from the midline; for the highs, shade up. You can use different colors to represent the highs and lows.** The mood chart on the following page contains an example in the righthand column showing a March 8th rating with hypo/mania at 12 and depression at 17.

At the top of the chart, mark any medication changes under "Med Changes." In the "Life Changes" column, include major life events, stressors, and – importantly – when you started or stopped a therapeutic routine, such as exercise, diet, or any other suggestions in this book.

Client Worksheet

Weekly Mood Chart

	Example
Month/Weekday	3/8
Med Changes	Start Lexapro
Hypo/mania 25-27	
22-24	
19-21	
16-18	
13-15	
10-12	(shaded)
7-9	(shaded)
4-6	(shaded)
1-3	(shaded)
Depression 1-3	(shaded)
4-6	(shaded)
7-9	(shaded)
10-12	(shaded)
13-15	(shaded)
16-18	(shaded)
19-21	
22-24	
25-27	
Life Changes	Start walking routine

2

Rumination, Cognitive Problems, and the Affective Temperaments

The Missing Pieces in the *DSM-5*

Sometimes the symptoms that matter most are not even in the *DSM-5*. There's a reason for this. The *DSM-5* is a tool for diagnosis, not for self-understanding. It focuses on symptoms that improve diagnostic accuracy. In the process, it leaves out symptoms that are common to many diagnoses but may be very important to those who suffer from them. This chapter covers three areas that are largely missing from the manual: rumination, cognitive problems, and the affective temperaments. It will also shed light on normal mood and how to live with mood problems in the family.

Rumination

Rumination is a repetitive style of negative thinking. It is self-focused, and its effect is to pull a person inward, away from meaningful action and practical solutions. It's common in many disorders but diagnostic of none. Mania, depression, and anxiety disorders are all magnets for rumination. People with mood disorders often have ruminative tendencies that persist at a temperamental level, and that tendency is a risk factor for depressive relapse.

By addressing this nagging symptom, therapists can help clients achieve a fuller and more lasting recovery. Rumination-focused CBT (RF-CBT) is a therapy that does just that. Developed by Dr. Edward Watkins, RF-CBT views rumination as a habit. RF-CBT makes no attempts to challenge or change the *content* of ruminative thoughts. Instead, it aims to reduce the frequency of these thoughts through standard habit-change techniques:

1. Recognize what triggers rumination. These are the situations, thoughts, and feelings that make rumination more likely.
2. When triggers arise, intervene with actions that are incompatible with rumination before it gets out of control.

What actions are "incompatible with rumination"? The simplest answer is **absorbing activity.** These are activities in which a client participates fully and to which they devote their full attention. There's little room for rumination when the mind is fully engaged in a task, like knitting, playing basketball, or riding a bike. Chapter 5 reviews qualities that make an activity absorbing and gives ideas for these types of pursuits.

The Benefits of Rumination

Although rumination can be dysfunctional in nature, it differs from other habits, like nail biting, in that it also has a healthy side. Therefore, getting rid of it entirely isn't a good idea. Worry can help people prepare for the worst, self-criticism can catch mistakes, and mulling over a problem can generate solutions.

Indeed, clients with ruminative tendencies can be great problem solvers. Scientists, creative artists, and political leaders are included in their ranks. This dogged style of thinking may partly explain the higher rates of mood disorders that are seen in those fields. For example, consider Abraham Lincoln, who once said, "I walk slowly, but I never walk backward." That was Lincoln's response when he was criticized for taking too long to make a decision. Lincoln believed in looking at problems from every angle, and history had given him a problem that required that level of deliberation. However, it wasn't always this way for Lincoln. He suffered from depression throughout his life, including a period of suicidality in his early 30s. His ability to turn that ruminative tendency into a strength was hard won.

As Lincoln suggests, useful rumination moves toward a goal, decision, or action, while dysfunctional rumination walks backwards, goes in circles, and gets nowhere. The goal is to recognize when it's off track and put it to use when it's moving in the right direction. RF-CBT seeks to minimize dysfunctional rumination while still preserving its healthier side. How can you tell the difference? **Functional rumination moves clients toward action in the real world, while the dysfunctional type leads to more avoidance.**

In the full version of RF-CBT, clients learn other ways of engaging with their thoughts and feelings, such as mindfulness and compassionate thought. These move clients away from the harsh, logical, self-critical mode of rumination and into a more encouraging and accepting frame of mind. Although there's a lot more to RF-CBT than the pages of this book can hold, the following section includes the techniques that are easiest to adopt into therapy and that can yield big returns. Readers who are interested in RF-CBT in its entirety can turn to *Rumination-Focused Cognitive-Behavioral Therapy for Depression* (Watkins, 2016).

This section contains several worksheets to help clients break the habit of dysfunctional rumination. In particular, the **Rumination: Minding the Gap** worksheet is intended as a starting place to help clients see how rumination is affecting their lives. Clients can also use the **Useful vs. Dysfunctional Rumination** worksheet to help them differentiate between times in which rumination moved them toward their goal vs. pushed them away. The **Can You Turn It Off?** and **Rumination Scavenger Hunt** worksheets help clients identify their ruminative triggers and develop a plan for dealing with these triggers when they arise. These worksheets pair well with the exercises on avoidance and absorbing activity in Chapter 5.

Rumination: Minding the Gap

Do you stew with self-critical thoughts? Fret over unsolvable problems? Have a worried mind that you can't control? If so, you're not alone. This type of thinking is called *rumination*, and it's common in both depression and bipolar disorder. We've even narrowed down the part of the brain that's responsible for rumination: the *default mode network*.

Rumination takes many forms. It can involve over-analyzing situations, engaging in self-critical thoughts, stewing over problems, worrying, dwelling on painful memories or past mistakes, judging or evaluating oneself, and feeling pressured, overwhelmed, or rushed by responsibilities.

What fuels these thoughts? They often center on a gap that can't be filled. The mind feels pressured to fill the gap – to solve the problem or resolve the worry – but it can't. Still, it keeps trying, and with each ruminative thought it thinks it's getting closer, but the gap never closes. Here are some common sources of rumination and the gaps that fuel them:

Source	The gap is between
Uncertainty	What you're sure of... And what you want to be sure of
The past	What happened... And what you wish had happened
The self	The way you are.... And the way you wish you were
Physical and mental symptoms	The way you feel... And the way you want to feel
Unsolvable problems	What you want to fix... And what you can fix
Perfectionism	What you can accomplish... And what you want to accomplish

Think about times when you ruminated. What themes did you dwell on? What was the gap you were trying to fill?

_____

_____

_____

_____

How did the rumination affect your mood? Your energy?

_____

_____

_____

_____

Useful vs. Dysfunctional Rumination

It may seem counterintuitive, but rumination isn't always a bad thing. It can spur you on to solve problems, get things done, and recognize mistakes. When it's useful, rumination moves you toward a goal, decision, or action. Rumination only becomes dysfunctional when it is used to avoid action, such as stewing over everything that's wrong with your marriage instead of openly discussing those concerns with your spouse. Use this worksheet to differentiate between times when your rumination was useful and times when it was dysfunctional.

Describe a time when mulling over a problem led to *useful* action, plans, or solutions.

_____

_____

_____

_____

_____

Describe another time when ruminative thinking made you *avoid* taking action or confronting problems in real life.

_____

_____

_____

_____

_____

Can You Turn It Off?

It would be nice if there was a switch that could turn rumination off when it's up to no good. Unfortunately, reaching for that invisible switch only causes more rumination. Telling your brain to "stop thinking about my mistake at work" only reminds it of that embarrassing mistake.

Rumination is hard to stop because the brain finds it rewarding, even when it feels miserable. The brain actually thinks it's solving an important problem and doesn't want to give up. This is a trick of the imagination, but the brain doesn't know any better. The ruminative brain may be imagining a confrontation with the people who've wronged you, replaying old regrets with different endings, or preparing for problems by conjuring all that could go wrong in the future. To the brain, all this is real, and it thinks it's making progress.

The ruminative brain is like a child who won't come down for dinner because she's engrossed in a project. "Just one more thing mom, I'm almost done," she says, but dinner gets cold and she never reaches the end.

The off switch doesn't work, but there is a way to turn down the mental chatter. Rumination is a habit, and the first step in changing a habit is to recognize the triggers that set it off. It's easier to break out of it early in the game, before it spirals out of control. This principle is the same with other habits, like overeating. Once that bag of potato chips is open, it's hard to resist them, so it's better to intervene at an earlier stage. For example, you could avoid the kitchen when you're at risk for a binge, such as late at night, when you're alone, or when you're stressed. The same approach works with rumination.

The checklist that follows asks you to identify the situations, thoughts, and feelings that put you at risk for rumination. By becoming more aware of these triggers and intervening before they get out of control, you'll start to break free from the vicious cycle of rumination.

Internal Triggers

Which subjects tend to lead to rumination when you think about them?

- ☐ The future

- ☐ Conflicts, mistakes, or upsetting events from the past

- ☐ Uncertainties, doubts, or imperfections

- ☐ Wondering about other people's intentions

- ☐ Comparing yourself to others or to an ideal

- ☐ Asking "why" questions or pondering the meaning of things

- ☐ Analyzing mistakes or situations that went wrong

- ☐ Loss, including unfulfilled dreams, grief, and broken relationships

- ☐ _____

- ☐ _____

- ☐ _____

Which of these emotional states trigger ruminative thoughts?

☐ Feeling rejected, wronged, or misunderstood by others

☐ Being bored or tired

☐ Experiencing physical pain or tension

☐ Feeling disorganized or pressured

☐ _____

☐ _____

☐ _____

External Triggers

Which of these situations trigger ruminative thoughts?

☐ When it's early in the morning

☐ When it's late at night

☐ When I'm alone

☐ Sitting and doing nothing

☐ Driving

☐ Checking social media, texts, messages, or emails

☐ Being alone in public, surrounded by strangers

☐ Withdrawing from people after getting upset

☐ Dressing, grooming, or shopping for clothes or cosmetics

☐ _____

☐ _____

☐ _____

Over the next week, go on a scavenger hunt for your triggers. Every time you have a bout of unhelpful rumination, record the thoughts, feelings, and situations that triggered them using the **Rumination Scavenger Hunt Chart** on the next page. Once you have the pattern down, you can start to intervene in the early stages.

The best way to intervene is to do something that fully occupies your mind so that it's hard to ruminate. **Absorbing activities** have that quality. They are different for everyone. They may be physical, like crafts, gardening, or sports; mental, like a board game or a good book; or social, like walking or dining with a friend. (See Chapter 5 for additional ideas on absorbing activities.)

Rumination Scavenger Hunt

Each time you ruminate, record the following: *Date and Time* (When did it happen?), *Place* (Where were you when it happened?), *Duration* (How long did it last?), *Situation* (What was going on, or what were you doing, just before it happened? Were you alone or with others?), *Emotion* (What was your emotional or physical state just before it happened?), and *Subject* (What were you thinking about that spiraled into rumination?).

Date & Time	Duration	Place	Situation	Emotion	Subject
12/2, 10pm	2 hours	Home office	Shopping for Christmas gifts online	Anxious, tired, pressured	Remembering all the bad Christmases I've spent alone. Thinking: "Did I pick the right gift?" "Do my friends really like me?" "Will they remember me this Christmas?"

Cognitive Symptoms

In 2013, an article in the *New York Times Magazine* went viral. It was a personal story by Linda Logan, a talented woman whose life had been derailed by bipolar disorder. Her concern was not the mania, depression, or psychosis she had lived through but something else: "the self." She called on doctors and therapists to "ask about what parts of the self have vanished and… help figure out strategies to deal with that loss."

Why did her words strike a nerve with so many clients? The parts of the self that she found missing reflect a common problem that is rarely addressed in treatment: the cognitive symptoms of mood disorders. "I lost my sense of competence… Word retrieval was difficult and slow… Clarity of thought, memory, and concentration had all left me. I was slowly fading away." These losses followed her even after she was told she had recovered. "I still don't have full days—I'm only functional mornings to mid-afternoons."

Mood disorders don't just change the way people feel. They also disrupt memory, attention, and concentration, and those problems can persist long after the mood symptoms have gone away. In fact, many people on psychiatric disability for a mood disorder have few of the symptoms that define those disorders. Instead, it's the cognitive problems that continue to get in the way (Goodwin & Jamison, 2007). That disability isn't limited to the workplace. Relationships are equally affected. Cognitive problems rob people of the roles that Freud thought of as "the cornerstone of our humanness" – to love and work (Erickson, 1993). It's no wonder Ms. Logan called it a loss of self.

What causes these problems? Mood episodes create small changes in the brain that take a while to repair. The brain is not damaged, but its cells have shrunk back and have fewer connections, like a tree with fewer branches. As a result, clients often run into trouble because they only have a few ways of reacting to stress. "It seems like the only way I deal with problems is to run away or get angry."

The following table describes how cognitive symptoms can manifest and continue to interfere with functioning even after mood symptoms have lifted.

Cognitive symptom	How it looks in real life
Attention	"I'm distracted, can't follow a movie."
Memory	"I forget what I went in the room for." "I have trouble finding words or remembering people's names." "I repeat conversations… it's embarrassing!"
Executive functioning	"I have a poor sense of time – I'm always late." "I'm overwhelmed by complex tasks, like cleaning my house, shopping for groceries, or paying bills. I don't know where to start." "I'm impulsive. I make rash decisions, jump to conclusions, and say things I regret." "I'm indecisive – I feel paralyzed by difficult decisions and have to turn to others for help." "My boss is so unfair. She keeps changing the rules on me."

The rating scale on the following page will help you get a sense of how well your client is functioning.
To interpret the score:
0-11 = non-impaired
12-20 = mild impairment
21-40 = moderate impairment
> 40 = severe impairment

Functioning Assessment Short Test (FAST)

To what extent are you experiencing difficulties in the following areas?

		No difficulty	Mild difficulty	Moderate difficulty	Severe difficulty
Autonomy	Taking responsibility for a household	0	1	2	3
	Living on your own	0	1	2	3
	Doing the shopping	0	1	2	3
	Taking care of yourself (physical aspects, hygiene)	0	1	2	3
Occupational Functioning	Holding down a paid job	0	1	2	3
	Accomplishing tasks as quickly as necessary	0	1	2	3
	Working in the field in which you were educated	0	1	2	3
	Managing the expected work load	0	1	2	3
	Occupational earnings	0	1	2	3
Cognitive Functioning	Ability to concentrate on a book or movie	0	1	2	3
	Ability to make mental calculations	0	1	2	3
	Ability to solve a problem adequately	0	1	2	3
	Ability to remember newly-learned names	0	1	2	3
	Ability to learn new information	0	1	2	3
Finances	Managing your own money	0	1	2	3
	Spending money in a balanced way	0	1	2	3
Relationships	Maintaining a friendship or friendships	0	1	2	3
	Participating in social activities	0	1	2	3
	Having good relationships with people close to you	0	1	2	3
	Living together with your family	0	1	2	3
	Having satisfactory sexual relationships	0	1	2	3
	Being able to defend your interests	0	1	2	3
Leisure	Doing exercise or participating in a sport	0	1	2	3
	Having hobbies or personal interests	0	1	2	3

_____ + _____ + _____

Total = _____

Cognitive Symptoms: Some Facts

Cognitive symptoms are quite common in mood disorders: 30-60% of people who've been through significant mood episodes have cognitive problems, even after those episodes have gone away. It's validating when clients learn that these symptoms are real and common. Despite their worst fears, it's not an early sign of dementia. The following are some helpful messages to convey to your clients to normalize any concerns they may have about their cognitive symptoms:

1. **Recurrent mood episodes are the most common cause of cognitive symptoms.** Cognitive problems become more common as mood episodes build up. Each episode stresses the brain, shrinking the connections between the nerve cells that allow them to function. The best way to restore cognition is to prevent new episodes. When the brain is free from symptoms of depression and bipolar, it can heal. That healing takes time, around six to 12 months. Exercise, sleep, and diet are the top ways to improve cognition, and these are detailed more in Chapters 5 through 8.

Top ways to improve cognition	
Exercise	45 minutes every other day of light aerobics, like brisk walking (Chapter 5)
Sleep	Deepen sleep quality, darken lights before bed, and treat insomnia (Chapters 6 and 7)
Diet	A Mediterranean-style diet (Chapter 8)

2. **Medications are usually not the cause.** Clients don't tend to notice their cognitive problems in the depths of depression. As their mood lifts and they take on more complex tasks, they become more aware that their mind is not working as well. At that point, they are likely to blame their medication. Cognitive side effects are very rare with antidepressants, though they can occur with high doses of mood stabilizers, antipsychotics, and sedatives, like benzodiazepines. However, these side effects are usually mild compared to the cognitive symptoms that mood disorders cause. Reducing medications is risky. Some medications actually improve cognition, and coming off medications can cause new episodes that further erode cognitive functioning. Clients should work closely with their provider to address this concern.

3. **It is not necessarily ADHD.** Cognitive problems are so common in mood disorders that it's not necessary to invoke another diagnosis to explain them. However, the two can coexist, and about 10-20% of people with mood disorders also have ADHD. The cognitive problems that ADHD causes are usually more prominent in childhood and improve with age, while those that are due to a mood disorder worsen as people age and the episodes build up.

4. **It is not a sign of early dementia.** Cognitive symptoms are more prominent after middle age, leading many clients to fear the worst. It is a great relief to learn that these are not a sign of early dementia. At best, the symptoms will improve. At worst, they'll remain stable, but they won't go significantly downhill like they do in dementia.

5. **Practice and compensation can help.** Functional remediation is a form of psychotherapy that treats the cognitive symptoms of mood disorders. It builds on a long history of rehabilitative therapies that have successfully helped people with strokes, head injuries, and schizophrenia. It works through two strategies: *remediation* and *compensation.* Remediation aims to sharpen cognition through practice, while compensation gives clients tools to compensate for cognitive problems that don't improve.

Remediation Strategies

Clients can build back their cognitive skills through regular practice. These exercises should be challenging enough to keep their attention, but not so difficult as to be overwhelming. Here are some ideas.

1. **Skill building.** Learning a sport, craft, or musical instrument can help improve attention and memory. Games that build on mental dexterity, like table tennis or bowling, can help as well. These benefits also extend to more active video games, such as Wii Sports and Wii Fit (Chao et al., 2015).

2. **New activities.** Ask clients what activities they've given up on, like cooking, shopping, cleaning, or socializing. Have them rank these from easiest to hardest, and then have them start taking on one activity through daily practice.

3. **Cognitive training programs.** Although some companies have made exaggerated claims about the efficacy of digital brain-games, they do have real benefits and are useful in functional remediation therapies for mood disorders (Hill et al., 2017). For best results, clients should practice these games two to three times a week in 30- to 90-minute sessions. Luminosity is the most popular app but is not the best researched and was actually fined $2 million by the Federal Trade Commission for false advertising. Well-researched programs include:

   • BrainHQ (www.brainhq.com)
   • Nintendo's Big Brain Academy
   • Cognifit (www.cognifit.com)
   • Dual N-Back game (free at www.brainworkshop.sourceforge.net)

4. **Analog games.** For clients who prefer the real world, there are plenty of non-digital game options that accomplish the same brain-training goals without the need for a digital device. Those include playing cards, word games, board games, sudoku, jigsaw puzzles, as well as dexterity games like table tennis.

Compensation Strategies

Even more effective than remediation strategies are strategies that help clients compensate for their cognitive difficulties. Part of the reason that compensation strategies are more effective is that they translate into real-life gains and have a direct effect on the bottom line: functioning (Torrent, 2013). Some compensation strategies include:

1. **An old-school planner:** Paper planners work better than digital planners because they engage visual memory with a broader view of the weeks and months. They also activate physical memory through the process of writing on the page. A good planner will have a month view and a day view for appointments, as well as a daily to-do list. Clients can scratch off their to-do list as the day goes on and carry forward any tasks that are left undone.

A Few Good Planners

• Top picks: Simple Elephant Planner and Panda Planner. Designed with mental health in mind, these include mood-boosting features like a gratitude journal.
• For a simple, affordable option: Blue Sky.
• For a classic, professional look: Moleskin, Lemome, and Ink+Volt.

---

2. **Strategies for attention:** Clients can improve their ability to pay attention at work by reducing external distractions, allowing adequate time for the task, and scheduling regular breaks. When reading, they

should pause to summarize the material to themselves. If the reading is dull, they can find ways to apply it to their lives. It is also helpful when clients reward themselves after completing a task, such as with a bite of dark chocolate or a visit to their favorite website. Lastly, clients can facilitate attention by staying hydrated. Mental performance improves when people drink water while they work.

3. **Strategies for memory:** To compensate memory problems, clients can organize their living space so that similar things are stored together. For example, they can store breakfast items in the same area of the kitchen or keep their wallet and keys in a bowl that's close to the door. Clustering items together in such a manner makes it easier to remember where they are. To keep up with appointments, birthdays, and daily tasks, they can use reminder systems like alarms, calendars, and apps.

4. **Task management:** The brain handles complex tasks by intuitively breaking them down into smaller steps. When that process fails, simple tasks like cleaning the bathroom, preparing dinner, or shopping can seem impossible. The solution is to replace that intuitive mechanism with a paper and pencil exercise:

  a. Have clients choose a task they've been avoiding that needs to get done.

  b. Then, ask them to write down in detail all the steps that are necessary to complete the task.

  c. Next, instruct clients to sort those steps so the ones that are most important, or that need to be done first, are at the top.

  d. Finally, starting at the top, have them complete each step, one at a time.

That exercise takes time, but it is better than procrastination, which is the alternative response to tasks that feel overwhelming. Your clients may not get as much done as they did when their thoughts were quick and clear, but at least they won't avoid everything. With practice, it will start to become second nature.

Temperament and Mood

Temperament is the biological side of personality. It refers to individual differences in reactivity and self-regulation that impact a person's development (Rothbart, Ellis, & Posner, 2004). Temperament is something that we're more or less born with. For example, all babies are born with different ways of responding to the world; some tend to be calm and easygoing, whereas others are fussier and more prone to frustration. These differences are stable through time and play a central role in:

*   How much sleep we need

*   How much we avoid danger or seek out new situations

*   How sociable we are

*   How much we persist vs. how easily we let go

*   How reactive we are to stress

Around 50% of people with mood disorders also have a distinct pattern of traits called the **affective temperaments**. These four affective temperaments are hyperthymic, dysthymic, irritable, and cyclothymic. Although two of the affective temperaments – depressive and cyclothymic – are recognized as disorders in the *DSM*,[*] this is not how they were originally conceptualized. Rather, they are *predispositions* to mood disorders. Unlike disorders, these temperaments can exist without causing distress or impairment.

---

* In 2013, dysthymic disorder was merged with chronic depression in a new diagnostic category: persistent depressive disorder.

Affective Temperament	Mood It's Linked To	Common Features
Depressive	Depression	Self-critical, "glass half-empty," avoidant, worried, hard-working, realistic
Hyperthymic	Hypomania	Energetic, confident, extroverted, charismatic, impatient, hot-headed, impulsive
Irritable	Mixed states	Quick tempered, skeptical, suspicious, dissatisfied, assertive
Cyclothymic	Rapid cycling of all moods	Traits from the other three temperaments cycle frequently, from energized to sluggish, extroverted to withdrawn, and passionate to disinterested. This cycling leads to anxiety, insecurity, and instability in relationships and work – but also to creativity, empathy, intuition, and spontaneity.

Although the affective temperaments can make people vulnerable to new mood episodes, they also carry unique strengths. The challenge in therapy is to help clients find productive channels for those strengths so their predispositions don't turn into major episodes. Much of that work involves guidance in managing work and relationships.

An understanding of temperament can also help clients avoid over-medication. Some psychiatrists have argued against the aggressive prescription of medications for temperament, cautioning doctors to respect individual differences and to elicit the desirable aspects of the patient's predisposition (Akiskal & Akiskal, 2011). The following sections discuss the four affective temperaments in greater detail, including their strengths and limitations.

Depressive Temperament

People with a depressive temperament are characterized by worry, brooding, and a sensitivity to rejection. They tend to put the needs of others above their own, which paradoxically can strain relationships.

Although the glass may be half-empty for people with a depressive temperament, research actually confirms the relative accuracy of their worldview. It turns out that the average person sees the world through rose-colored glasses and is a little more confident than the facts would support. For example, most people believe that their driving skills are better than average, as is their intelligence, parenting abilities, likeability, etc. However, statistically speaking, we can't all be above average!

In this respect, people with depressive tendencies have a more accurate view of themselves and the world around them. Hence, they are better able to anticipate dangers, identify problems, and approach life with admirable humility.

Limitation	Strength
Self-doubting, non-assertive	Humble, thoughtful
Anxious, worried	Realistic
Indecisive, avoidant	Cautious, prudent
Sensitive to rejection	Empathic, considerate, sensitive to others' pain
Little pleasure in life	Hard-working, conscientious, ethical
Non-spontaneous, difficulty adjusting to change	Dependable, consistent, fair-minded
Low energy, high need for sleep (>9 hours/day)	Patient, persistent

Hyperthymic Temperament

Hyperthymic is Greek for *elevated mood*, so it is no wonder that people with hyperthymic traits are natural leaders and lovers of life. They are action-oriented, energetic, and decisive – and their confidence and charisma attract others. Although the hyperthymic temperament is associated with a variety of strengths, it does have its downsides. In particular, their propensity for novelty seeking can lead to impulsive, pleasure-seeking behaviors that are often a source of marital breakdowns or – in public figures – scandalous headlines. The hyperthymic temperament is closely related to hypo/manic moods. Some, but not all, people with these traits have close family members with bipolar disorder.

Limitation	Strength
Arrogant, self-assured, egotistical	Confident, decisive, a natural leader
Risk-taking, impulsive, reckless	Action-oriented, optimistic, cheerful
Controlling, overbearing, domineering, meddlesome	Influential, involved, interested in others
Overindulges in food, drink, or sex	Lover of life, spreads joy to others
Unfaithful, unreliable, making spur of the moment plans that can't be followed through or promises that can't be kept	Spontaneous, fully engaged in the moment
Talks over people, socializes to the point that it's exhausting to others	Friendly, extraverted
Though warm and engaging, can also be insensitive and unempathetic	Thick-skinned, able to take insults in stride like "water off a duck's back"
Lacking in self-reflection, which makes it hard to learn from mistakes	Easy going, comfortable, not bogged down by self-conscious worries
Impatient	Active, energetic, lots of interests
Can turn into insomnia in middle age	Decreased need for sleep (<6 hours/day)

Irritable Temperament

People with an irritable temperament have to walk a fine line. They need other people but also find them irritating. Isolation is a big risk for irritable types, so they need to hold on to those they respect and trust. Those qualities are not easily earned, as this type tends to be guarded and suspicious of other people's intention. On the other hand, they are great fighters. They aren't afraid to make waves or question authority. They can speak truth to power and fight for the causes they believe in. If they can keep their irritable side in check, the skepticism that comes with this temperament can lead to success in journalism, science, or law. Careers in forensics, law enforcement, the military, or security are also a good match.

The irritable temperament corresponds closely to mixed states, where depressive and hypo/manic symptoms overlap. Like those in mixed states, people with this temperament often feel restless, anxious, and edgy.

Limitation	Strength
Irritable, hot-headed, quick to anger	Assertive
Mistrustful, suspicious of others	Skeptical, "nobody's fool," scientific
Jealous	Protective, loyal to their inner circle
Conflicts in relationships, social isolation	Able to take important stands that others are not comfortable making; original, iconoclastic, independent
Easily dissatisfied, complaining, sarcastic	Honest, frank, not afraid to point out real problems

Cyclothymic Temperament

Cyclothymic is Greek for *cycles of mood*, and people with a cyclothymic temperament have frequent ups and downs in their mood, both with or without stress. At various times in these cycles, they may exhibit traits from any of the other three temperaments, but what marks cyclothymia is the inconsistent shifting between them. That inconsistency makes cyclothymic clients feel anxious and insecure, unsure of how they'll be from one day to the next. The brighter sides of this temperament may draw people into their circle, but conflict seeps in as others find out they can't depend on them. Their work history is often inconsistent. "I could do well on any job for a few months, but then I'd fall apart." Their interests are broad, but they can become a "Jack or Jill of all trades but master of none."

People with cyclothymia are very attuned to their environment. This can feel "overstimulating," but it is also an extraordinary gift. Music, art, cosmetology, and culinary pursuits are natural callings, but cyclothymia can be an asset in less creative fields as well. Like the proverbial canary in a coalmine, a hotel manager with cyclothymia may be the first to notice that the lighting is off or the temperature is not right. That attunement helps them thrive in customer service jobs, as does their natural warmth and empathy. Cyclothymic clients benefit from a flexible work environment, but they shouldn't shy away from jobs that require structure, as that can have a stabilizing effect on their mood.

Cyclothymia is closely related to bipolar disorder, particularly the rapid-cycling form of the disorder where various moods change frequently. Although cyclothymia has been recognized since the mid 1800s, there is little public awareness of this common temperament. Its many faces can also lead to diagnostic confusion. For example, the impulsive, restless, and distracted nature of cyclothymia can resemble ADHD, or it may be mistaken for an anxiety disorder. Cyclothymia is also a common cause of substance abuse.

Limitation	Strength
Inconsistent, unreliable	Spontaneous, flexible, open to new experiences, creative
Rapidly shifting moods	Adaptive. They have learned how to cope with many moods and can relate to a broad range of people
Emotionally reactive, sensitive to rejection	Engaged and responsive to others, able to feel deeply and passionately
Sensitive, easily overwhelmed or over-stimulated	Highly attuned to the sensory world, which can lead to artistic gifts and success in music, culinary arts, cosmetology, and the hospitality industry
Tendency to self-medicate with alcohol, drugs, caffeine, or nicotine	Tend to seek professional help when needed and make good use of therapy
Falls in and out of love too easily, impulsively starts and ends relationships	Able to rebuild their social network when things break down
Often have to cover up negative moods, which can lead to habitual lying or the feeling that "no one knows the real me"	Able to put on a mask when needed, to "fake it 'til they make it"
Overly trusting of others; easily drawn into fads, cults, or deceptive marketing schemes	At other times, have the healthy skepticism that comes with experience

Bipolar Disorder, Cyclothymia, and Borderline Personality Disorder

The difference between bipolar and borderline personality disorders is a source of much debate. Both camps are concerned that misdiagnosis will rob clients of the proper treatment: mood stabilizers in the case of bipolar, and psychotherapy in the case of borderline personality disorder. These disorders do share common features, but almost all of that overlap is due to cyclothymic temperament. Clarifying that fact drains a lot of the energy out of this debate, in part because psychotherapy is the main treatment for both. There are no controlled medication trials in cyclothymic disorder, but controlled studies do support psychotherapy (Fava et al., 2011).

The seed of this overlap can be found in the early descriptions of borderline personality disorder. Borderline personality disorder first appeared in *DSM-III* in 1980, but in the early drafts of that manuscript it went by a different name: cycloid personality. The description of "cycloid" reads like a mix of borderline and cyclothymia. "Irregular energy levels" with "intense, variable moods," where depression predominates but is interspersed by brief periods of "elation... dejection, anxiety, or impulsive anger" (Millon, 1996, p. 658). In her classic text on dialectical behavior therapy, Marsha Linehan wrote that this description of cycloid personality was "in many ways similar" to her own theory of borderline personality disorder (1993, p. 10).

	Borderline Personality Disorder	**Cyclothymic Disorder**
High Overlap	Affective instability due to marked reactivity of mood (e.g., intense episodic depression, irritability, or anxiety lasting hours to days)	Rapid mood swings that cycle between depression, irritability, anxiety, and excitation over days to weeks
	Unstable relationships that shift from idealization to devaluation (splitting)	Relationships that vacillate from glowing adoration to hateful paranoia
	Unstable identity	Insecure identity; frequent changes in beliefs, religions, and social groups
	Impulsivity	Impulsivity
	Intense anger	Intense anger
Some Overlap	Frantic efforts to avoid real or imagined abandonment	Intense romantic attachments and sensitivity to rejection
	Recurrent suicidal behavior, gestures, threats, and self-injury	Elevated risk of suicide and self-injury
Less Overlap	Chronic feelings of emptiness	May occur if there is a significant history of trauma or neglect
	Transient, stress-related paranoid ideation or severe dissociative symptoms	Paranoia can occur during severe mood episodes, and dissociation may be part of the picture if there is a significant trauma history

Despite their similarities, borderline and cyclothymia diverged when *DSM-III* was released in 1980, as did the experts who studied them. Although arising from two different camps, that research has arrived at similar findings. Both conditions are high in neuroticism and rejection sensitivity, and low in agreeableness and conscientiousness.

They also share a paradoxical overlap: Both are high in the opposing traits of harm avoidance and novelty seeking (Aiken, 2019). What does that paradox look like in real life? It's a dangerous mix of anxiety and impulsivity. While most anxious clients go out of their way to avoid harm, borderline and cyclothymic clients can be fearless in their impulsive attempts to relieve anxiety. Substance abuse, self-harm, and "frantic efforts to avoid abandonment" are among the disastrous results.

This overlap is not 100%. Cyclothymia is a risk factor for borderline personality, but it does not always go to that extreme, nor is it the only road to borderline personality. Other forces are clearly at play here, most notably trauma. Cyclothymia is just one piece of the puzzle, but clarifying its edges can help inform psychotherapy.

Effective therapy for cyclothymia is similar to that for borderline personality, with an emphasis on cognitive behavioral techniques, acceptance, and skill building. It also aims to stabilize circadian rhythms through regular patterns of activity and sleep. Circadian rhythm abnormalities are also common in clients with borderline personality, and the approaches in this book are starting to prove helpful for that disorder as well (Bromundt et al., 2013).

Assessing the Affective Temperaments

On the following page is a worksheet that you can use to assess for affective temperaments in the clients with whom you work. Called the **Temperament Evaluation of Memphis, Pisa and San Diego-Auto Questionnaire** (or TEMPS-A), this scale has been validated in 27 studies spanning 15 countries and involving over 20,000 subjects (Elias et al., 2017).

The scale is divided into four parts, one for each temperament, but I've obscured the titles to avoid biasing the client. They are: (1) Depressive, (2) Hyperthymic, (3) Irritable, and (4) Cyclothymic. Since temperament exists on a spectrum, there are no official cut-off scores for any category. Rather, look for temperaments in which the client endorses more than half of the items, which indicates they possesses those traits to some degree. If they check more than 75% of the items, they probably have that temperament. If a client checks multiple items across *all* the temperaments, then cyclothymic temperament, which can cycle into all of those faces, is a likely choice.

TEMPS-A Temperament Scale

Use the following scale to rate how well each of these different traits describe you. Check "yes" if that trait has characterized you for at least two years and you had it to some degree before age 21. Don't focus on how you feel right now when answering. Rather, look for traits that describe your personality over many years.

Part One	Check if "Yes"
I have always blamed myself for what others might consider no big deal.	
I'm the kind of person who doesn't like change very much.	
In a group, I would rather hear others talk.	
I often give in to others.	
I feel very uneasy meeting new people.	
My feelings are easily hurt by criticism or rejection.	
I am the kind of person you can always depend on.	
I put the needs of others above my own.	
I would rather work for someone else than be the boss.	
Part Two	**Check if "Yes"**
I'm usually in an upbeat or cheerful mood.	
Life is a feast which I enjoy to the fullest.	
I'm the kind of person who believes everything will eventually turn out all right.	
I have great confidence in myself.	
I often get many great ideas.	
I am always on the go.	
I can accomplish many tasks without even getting tired.	
I love to tackle new projects, even if risky.	
Once I decide to accomplish something, nothing can stop me.	
I am totally comfortable even with people I hardly know.	
I love to be with a lot of people.	
I have abilities and expertise in many areas.	
Normally I can get by with less than 6 hours of sleep.	
Part Three	**Check if "Yes"**
I am a grouchy (irritable) person.	
I am by nature a dissatisfied person.	
I often feel on edge.	

I often feel wound up.	
I often get so mad that I will just trash everything.	
When crossed, I could get into a fight.	
People tell me I blow up out of nowhere.	
When angry, I snap at people.	
I can get so furious I could hurt someone.	
I am so jealous of my spouse (or lover) that I cannot stand it.	
I am a very skeptical person.	
Part Four	**Check if "Yes"**
I often feel tired for no reason.	
I get sudden shifts in mood and energy.	
My moods and energy are either high or low, rarely in between.	
My ability to think varies greatly from sharp to dull for no apparent reason.	
I can really like someone a lot and then completely lose interest in them.	
I often start things and then lose interest before finishing them.	
My mood often changes for no reason.	
I constantly switch between being lively and sluggish.	
I sometimes go to bed feeling great and wake up in the morning feeling life is not worth living.	
I go back and forth between feeling overconfident and feeling unsure of myself.	
I go back and forth between being outgoing and being withdrawn from others.	
I feel all emotions intensely.	
The way I see things is sometimes vivid, but at other times lifeless.	
I am the kind of person who can be sad and happy at the same time.	
I daydream a great deal about things that other people consider impossible to achieve.	
I often have a strong urge to do outrageous things.	
I am the kind of person who falls in and out of love easily.	

Living Beyond Mood

"I don't know what normal is" is a common concern for clients with mood disorders, particularly those with the affective temperaments. I myself don't know what it is either, but working in this field has given me a good sense of what mental health is. It's the ability to change and adapt flexibly to life. In that work, it helps to draw on a client's strengths.

People with mood disorders have a slight edge when it comes to certain strengths. I've listed some of them below. Understanding these strengths validates what many clients know intuitively: Their suffering may be great, but so is their potential to contribute to the world. Listen carefully, and you'll find that clients with mood disorders have learned effective ways of living with mood problems on their own. They become avid runners, specialized scholars, creative artists, or master gardeners. They turn to pursuits that get them "out of their head," and do so with a dogged determination that the rest of us lack.

Clients often forget their strengths in the midst of a mood episode, which is where David Seligman's work on positive psychology comes in. Dr. Seligman has found that people are happiest when they engage in pursuits that draw on their strengths. For example, consider a young man who finds his job as a grocery bagger depressing. His strengths include high social intelligence, but he is low in persistence and self-regulation. Drawing from this knowledge, he makes a plan to put his strength to use by engaging each customer in conversation on the job. In turn, the hours go by faster and the tasks feel less grueling.

Through his research in positive psychology, Dr. Seligman has distilled 24 unique character strengths. The following **24 Character Strength Survey** will help your clients evaluate and identify their own character strengths. They can also take a free test for character strengths at www.authentichappiness.sas.upenn.edu. The strengths inventory is particularly useful when planning meaningful activities with clients, which we'll do in Chapter 5.

Strengths Associated with Mood Disorders

Empathy	Intelligence
Realistic thinking	Linguistic talents
Leadership ability	Extroversion and warmth
Creativity	

24 Character Strength Survey

People tend to underrate their strengths, especially if humility is one of them. For each of the following character strengths, rate how well each trait describes you when you are not in a mood episode. Think back to those better days. How did you spend your time then? What strengths did you use? How would people who know you well describe your strengths?

Curiosity

You are curious, interested, and questioning. Fascinated by learning and exploring. The process of discovery is just as enjoyable as the end result. You are open to new experiences and seek them out.

rarely   sometimes   very often

Self-regulation

You are disciplined, balanced, and have good self-control. You think before you act and don't let your emotions run your life.

rarely   sometimes   very often

Integrity

Honest in words and deeds, you live your life in a genuine and authentic way. People see you as "real" or "down to earth." You inspire trust and take responsibility for your own emotions and actions.

rarely   sometimes   very often

Leadership

You can motivate and organize people to get things done. In groups, you make everyone feel included and work to resolve conflicts. You are focused, action-oriented, and help your team achieve its goals.

rarely   sometimes   very often

Vitality

Life is an adventure, and you approach it with passion. Enthusiastic, energetic, lively, vigorous, and active. You pour yourself into things whole-heartedly.

rarely   sometimes   very often

Perspective

Others look to you for wisdom and advice. You see things in perspective and don't sweat the small stuff. You may not think of yourself as wise but your friends do.

rarely	sometimes	very often

Fairness

You treat all people the same and are guided by principles of equality, justice, and fairness. You seek facts and avoid assumptions. You strive to give everyone a fair chance and to keep biases or emotions from influencing your decisions.

rarely	sometimes	very often

Forgiveness and Mercy

You are forgiving and understanding. You give people a second chance and are guided by mercy, not revenge.

rarely	sometimes	very often

Prudence

You are careful and cautious in your actions, well prepared for any risks that may lie ahead. You avoid saying or doing things that you might come to regret.

rarely	sometimes	very often

Gratitude

You appreciate the people in your life and the good things that happen to you. Even when things don't turn out the way you wanted, you find something to be grateful for instead of dwelling on regrets. You don't take things for granted and take time to express your thanks to others.

rarely	sometimes	very often

Love

You are good at giving and receiving love. You care for those close to you and allow them to care for you. You form long-term, close relationships with people and enjoy sharing life with them and confiding in them.

rarely	sometimes	very often

Bravery

You do the right thing even in the face of danger, difficulty, and opposition from others. You act on your convictions and do not shy away from threats.

rarely	sometimes	very often

Social Intelligence

You have people skills and emotional intelligence. You adapt well and can fit in with many types of people. You pick up on social cues, communicate well, and know how to make others comfortable. You have good intuitions about other people's motives, feelings, and needs.

rarely	sometimes	very often

Love of Learning

You love to learn new things and develop new skills, whether in school or on your own. You have many of the strengths described for curiosity, but also have the rigor of a scholar, working hard to deepen your understanding of subjects. You practice regularly to develop mastery of new skills.

rarely	sometimes	very often

Humility

You have a realistic view of your strengths and weaknesses, and don't tend to think you are better than others. You don't seek out fame or attention. You share credit and let your accomplishments speak for themselves.

rarely	sometimes	very often

Kindness

You are generous, nurturing, and compassionate to others. You notice when others are in need and are happy to lend a hand without expecting something in return. You are kind and considerate to friends and strangers alike.

rarely	sometimes	very often

Persistence

You enjoy completing things and can persevere through the difficult and tedious parts of tasks in order to get them done. You are focused and diligent, working hard to do things on time and get them done right.

rarely	sometimes	very often

Hope

You believe that people can build a better future. Even when things don't go well, you maintain an optimistic outlook and don't let it get you down.

rarely   sometimes   very often

Humor

Light-hearted, playful, and good humored. You can be a tease, but mostly you enjoy bringing laughter and smiles to others.

rarely   sometimes   very often

Appreciation of Beauty and Excellence

You are moved by beauty and excellence in art, nature, science, or athletics. You appreciate what it takes to achieve that excellence. You have a sense of wonder and awe.

rarely   sometimes   very often

Creativity

Inventive, original, and able to think outside the box. You are always looking for new ways to do things, whether in the arts, athletics, science, or finding solutions in the workplace.

rarely   sometimes   very often

Open-mindedness

You are not set in your ways and are able to change your mind when new evidence comes to light. You examine your assumptions, think things through, and don't jump to conclusions. You are good at critical thinking and can see many sides to things.

rarely   sometimes   very often

Citizenship

You work well as a member of a group or team. You are loyal to the groups you are a part of and value their rules and customs as your own. You are dependable, always doing your share and working hard for the success of the team.

rarely   sometimes   very often

Spirituality

Life has meaning and you seek to find the right path in that journey. You have faith in a coherent set of beliefs and are guided by a sense of purpose beyond yourself. You have a spiritual practice and may have had deep spiritual experiences.

rarely   sometimes   very often

Mood in the Family

The family is never far from the room when working with mood disorders, and it can help to bring them in. When all the psychotherapy studies on bipolar disorder were stacked up for review, one thing stood out: Outcomes were better when the family was involved in the work (Chatterton et al., 2017). This doesn't mean that the family has to be at every session, but bringing them in for education can make a difference (with the client's permission). Top areas to cover include:

1. Education about the illness to reduce blame
2. Healthy boundaries
3. Problem-solving skills for specific areas of conflict
4. Communication skills
5. Emergency preparedness

That last item is particularly relevant for the manic episodes associated with bipolar I, but it is also important to prepare families for crises involving suicide, substance abuse, and intense conflict.

Who is the Client?

Family therapy for mood disorders differs from traditional family therapy in that there is an identified client. This has ethical ramifications because the therapist's allegiance is to the client, not the family. Usually there's no conflict here, as what's good for the family is good for the client and vice versa. However, exceptions exist, such as when family members decide that getting a divorce or cutting off their relative is necessary for their own sanity. It's best to clarify your role before those dilemmas arise.

Another quandary that comes up when working with families is confidentiality. This issue can be handled early on by allowing the client to decide what information they'd like shared with family members and signing the appropriate consent. Of course, it is important to make clear to the client that there are exceptions to confidentiality in the case of an emergency. HIPAA privacy guidelines allow therapists to break confidentiality when doing so is necessary to avoid suicide, violence, or other serious risks.

Families often want to keep secrets from the client, and it's best to clarify your stance on this before they call and say, "There's something I need to tell you about [the client], but I don't want you to share it with them." Your obligation in these situations is to do what's in the client's best interest, and keeping secrets is usually not a good foundation for therapy. Technically, anything that a relative shares becomes part of the client's medical record, and under HIPAA law, clients have access to that record, so keeping secrets isn't feasible from a legal position either.

Expressed Emotion

Much of the research on family therapy for mood and other psychiatric disorders draws from work on *expressed emotion*. Though the concept of "expressed emotion" sounds like a good thing, it's not. Rather, expressed emotion refers to critical comments, hostile attitudes, and over-involvement that relatives exhibit toward the family member who is the identified client. Importantly, the presence of expressed emotion in the family is consistently linked to higher relapse rates in schizophrenia, bipolar disorder, and depression.

Expressed Emotion	Definition
Critical comments	Specific negative comments about the client
Hostility	A belief that the client can control the symptoms of their disorder but chooses not to. The client is seen as the cause of all the family's problems.
Over-involvement	Over-protectiveness, enmeshment, poor boundaries, self-sacrifice, excessive praise or blame

Critical Comments and Hostility

Most families understand that criticism and hostility can be hurtful, but they may not appreciate how mood disorders heighten the sensitivity for these interactions. A simple comment such as, "Did you exercise today?" can sound like a harsh attack to someone who is experiencing depression. People with mood disorders are also more sensitive to facial expressions and body language, and that sensitivity can remain even after they've recovered. They tend to misread neutral faces as critical, and fearful faces as angry.

Over-Involvement

This aspect of expressed emotion is hard to give up because it's a natural and loving reaction to someone with a mood disorder. Over-involved families try to take over the client's life to protect them from the consequences of their disorder. Fearing academic failure, they discourage their daughter from returning to college. Fearing suicide, they refuse to leave their son home alone. They are frequent attendees at appointments and dispensers of medications. However, people with depression already suffer heightened guilt, helplessness, and poor interpersonal boundaries. Over-involvement further stresses those systems. The result is a client who has little initiative or feels guilty for all the worry they bring to their family.

These families overestimate how much control they have over their relative's mood. Since moods fluctuate on their own, this over-involved style will seem to work *on occasion*. When it works, the over-involved behavior is reinforced. That type of random reward, known as *intermittent reinforcement,* creates habits that are difficult to break. Just as a gambler gets hooked on a slot machine that randomly turns out a win, so the family gets hooked on over-involvement, always watchful for signs of progress or decline in their relative. The reality, however, is less exciting: There isn't much that relatives can do to significantly alter the course of a mood disorder.

In addition, over-involved families are often very educated about the client's illness. That knowledge is helpful, but not in the way they imagined. Their interactions with the identified client tend to center around the diagnosis and all of the symptoms that it causes. While it helps to understand those symptoms, it doesn't help to pay too much attention to them. Family members can't change symptoms, and trying to change them only leads to frustration. **Instead, family members should focus their attention on everything their relative does that's not consistent with their mood disorder.** For example, rather than talking about how the client overslept, notice the times that they get up and make breakfast.

Over-involved families will have to accept some setbacks as they allow their relative more responsibility. It is important to normalize these setbacks and to encourage families to go easy on themselves, as well as their relative. Families should foster independence when it's feasible and lower their expectations when it's not. Tell the family, "Don't do anything for him that he can reasonably do himself. I know that's a hard call to make, because there's a risk that it won't go well if he takes it on himself. In the past, you've been erring on the side of caution, stepping in whenever his abilities are in doubt. That will prevent mistakes, but it also takes away opportunities to learn. Now that he's in therapy, he can make use of those opportunities, so I'm asking you to err on the other side and allow some mistakes to happen."

Expressed emotions are harmful because they activate the stress-response system. Too much activation worsens mood disorders, but the issue is one of frequency. A little activation now and then is not going to cause much harm. Shifting the frequency toward positive interactions and away from stressful ones will go a long way. In other words, there's a biological rational behind the comforting message that families need to hear: Perfection is not the goal.

Coping with Mood Problems in the Family

Living with mood problems in the family can feel like a constant crisis. Stress hormones surge for the family and client alike, and it's hard to think clearly in that state. Families wonder how to react, how to help, and whether their relative is doing all of this on purpose or is driven by symptoms that they can't control.

It's important to remind family members that there is not a lot they can do to change someone who is in the midst of a mood episode. It's hard enough to change people when they're not having mood problems. Still, it's likely that family members will continue to argue with a manic relative or try to motivate a loved one who is depressed. To help them break this habit, advise them to focus their efforts on changes that we know are helpful, as doing more only frustrates the problem.

The following handouts describe helpful and harmful ways of interacting and coping within families. In many ways, human interactions function like medicine for a mood disorder: Some styles of communication stabilize brain chemistry, while others cause it to flare up and get in the way of recovery. Therefore, as you discuss these ways of relating, family members should keep in mind that it's not about what's "right and wrong" or "good and bad." It's about what works for the brain.

Helpful Interactions

1. Emotional Warmth and Empathy

Warm, accepting, and compassionate body language has a healing effect on the brain. It can include simple empathic statements like, "I see your point" or "I know what you mean," or more specific comments like, "It must be hard to go through the motions each day when you're depressed." Empathy doesn't mean that you agree with what someone is feeling – just that you *understand, or at least want to understand,* what they are feeling. It does not involve changing or judging them.

These gentler emotions are admittedly hard to come by during a crisis. If you feel unable to exhibit warmth and empathy, practice acting the *opposite* of your emotions. A simple visualization can help you do this. For example, just as an athlete imagines the ball going through the goal, picture someone who exudes warmth and calm. This could be a favorite celebrity, relative, minister, or teacher. Although you may feel like an actor at first, as the saying goes, "Fake it 'til you make it."

2. Positive Comments

While it helps to know the signs and symptoms of a mood disorder, it doesn't help to point them out. Rather, pay attention to what your relative *can* do. Notice improvement. Admire their struggle. Notice how they came to dinner, instead of reminding them that they stayed in bed all day. Notice the healthy parts of your relative because what you shine a light on is what will grow. Use language that accepts things the way they are without judging it, trying to change it, or getting into motivations and causes.

3. Optimism About the Illness

Your loved one may forget that recovery is possible in the midst of an episode. Be careful that you don't lose this awareness and that you openly express hope. Remember how your relative was before the episode, and communicate optimism that they'll be that way again.

Harmful Interactions

1. Critical Comments

Critical comments are often well-intentioned, but they stress the brain, particularly when someone is depressed. Avoid expressions that find fault, pass judgment, or point out problems. Watch for the word "should" in your mind and in your words. Try not to communicate that things "should" be different; they aren't.

Critical comments often come about when families try to solve a problem that can't be easily solved. Mood disorders don't respond well to ordinary problem solving, and trying to fix an unsolvable problem just creates frustration for all.

Of course, you'll still need to discuss problems, but reserve that for a regular, scheduled family meeting. Without this kind of structure, people can feel as though they are never safe from criticism and attack. During your meeting, use a neutral, "just-the-facts" tone. Avoid hot-buttons that tend to spiral into conflict. These buttons are different for everyone, but some common ones are talking about people's intentions or how things affect you emotionally. It's okay to talk about how things affect you, but keep that short and simple.

2. Scrutinizing Mood

Everyone gets emotional, whether they have a mood disorder or not, but trying to figure out whether your relative's emotions are "normal" or due to their mood disorder is neither practical nor helpful. Treat their emotions as though they are real and valid. No one wants to hear, "Did you take your medicine today?" whenever they get angry.

At the same time, families have insight into symptoms that their relative may not see. When things are calm, ask your relative how *they* would like you to share your observations. One way to do this is to write your observations down in a brief paragraph that your relative can bring to their next doctor's appointment and to avoid bringing it up at other times.

3. Trying to Win or Resolve Arguments

Too much talk stresses the mind, particularly if it's already worn down by a mood episode. Make an agreement with your relative to stay apart if either of you get too hot-headed. Usually, that means going into separate rooms. Decide on a signal for this time out, like hanging a scarf on the doorknob. In addition, avoid trying to resolve fights in the evening. There's no telling when that will end, and it's more important to preserve sleep. The rested brain is much better at negotiations and compromise.

4. Over-Involvement

Over-involvement is a natural and loving reaction to someone who is depressed. It means you want to protect them, help them, and take over the areas of their life that are falling apart. It's often driven by understandable fears, like suicide, school failure, or non-compliance with medication. Over-involvement may work from time to time, but in the big picture it makes things worse.

The problem with over-involvement is that it can keep your relative from owning their problems. It's also stressful. People with depression already feel intense guilt and helplessness. Over-involvement magnifies those problems and makes them feel guilty for all the worry they put their family through.

Now, you might be thinking, *"What if they won't get out of bed unless I wake them? What if they'll miss their appointments unless I drive them, or skip their homework unless I do it with them?"* There's no easy answer to these questions, but keep these guiding words in mind: Don't do anything for your relative that they could reasonable do themselves.

That motto is different from that which many families live by, which is: Do everything for your relative that they might not be able to do themselves. In contrast, this new motto asks you to err on the side of *not* doing things. You won't get it right every time, and there will be situations where you need to step in because the consequences are too serious or dangerous. That's okay. It's the frequency that matters. Following this principle as *often* as you can will make a big difference. Stepping back and giving them space will hasten their recovery.

5. Hostility

Hostility comes from the belief that your relative isn't doing enough to control their symptoms or doesn't really want to get better. These beliefs start out as thoughts like:

> *"He wouldn't be like this if he tried harder."*
>
> *"She doesn't want to get better."*
>
> *"He just wants an excuse for his behavior."*

Nearly everyone who's lived with a mood disorder in the family has had those thoughts. The trick is to keep them from sticking. Let them pass through you, just as you let so much else pass by throughout the day: the random chatter of strangers, advertisements on TV, and the sound of a dog barking. If you pay them too much attention, these thoughts can multiply into beliefs that are hard to let go of, such as:

> *"She may have a disorder, but she can control herself a lot more than she does. Whenever her friends come over, you can guarantee she's pleasant and perky as can be."*

All mood disorders react to their environment. The brain changes visibly in new situations and around different people. This is even true in neurologic illnesses like Parkinson's disease. Although people with Parkinson's can barely move, they will suddenly rise up and walk when they see a striking image, like a series of black and gold lines on the floor. However, that's not a reliable cure for Parkinson's. Eventually, the novelty wears off and they are back in the chair. The same phenomenon occurs when a person with depression is visited by friends: Dopamine spikes in their brain and, for a little while, they may not even seem depressed. However, if they were to move in with those friends, it would be a different story.

Where to Draw the Line

Does this mean you need to lie down and accept everything your relative does? Not at all. The message is just that words rarely solve the problems that mood disorders bring. Families need to plan ahead for dangerous or destructive behavior. This involves action, not words – and your relative should have a strong voice in that plan.

Problems to anticipate include violence, suicidal behavior, substance abuse, overspending, and fights that impact children in the home. Hospitalization is not the only solution. Consider temporarily living apart, locking away guns or extra medication, and allowing family members to contact the treatment team or come to an appointment.

The Long-Term View

If the advice in this handout sounds hard to follow, it's not – it's actually impossible! No one can get it right all the time. Fortunately, it's good enough to adjust the ratio: Raise the warmth and positivity, and decrease the anger, criticism, and tension. When you can't do that, insert a long pause by going into separate rooms.

Stick with the basics. Trying to do more than what is in these handouts tends to backfire. Recovery is slow, and it takes patience and some bravery to make it through. Don't forget to reward yourself along the way. You'll need a healthy dose of warmth and positivity as well.

3

Causes of Mood Disorders

Breaking Down the Causes of Mood Disorders

Trevon: *"I'm much more depressed the last few weeks. I know what it's about. There's just been a lot of conflict in my marriage."*

Therapist: *"That's hard. You've been doing so much work to prevent depression, exercising every day and…"*

Trevon: *"No, I actually gave up exercise two months ago. But that's not why I'm depressed. I was feeling fine until the last few weeks."*

The brain is slow to change, and the seeds of depression are often planted months before the episode starts. The mind is more concerned with recent events, and the depressed mind is inclined to see the negative in them. Like most marriages, Trevon's was a mix of good and bad. Little had actually changed in his marriage, but through the lens of depression it looked drastically different. He was depressed *about* his marriage, but what actually *caused* the depression was giving up aerobics two months before.

Psychologist James McCullough observed that chronically depressed clients have a striking inability to discern cause and effect. They may not even recall things in the order that they occurred, a blind spot that makes it hard to learn from mistakes and solve problems. Over time, they get caught in a web of problems, are unable to see their way out, and blame external factors in a way that leaves them helpless to change.

Dr. McCullough used that insight to develop the cognitive behavioral analysis system of psychotherapy (CBASP), one of the first effective therapies for chronic depression. Although CBASP requires skills that are beyond the scope of this book, his insight reminds us not to take everything the depressed mind puts forth at face value.

Mood episodes are, to paraphrase Freud, overdetermined. In this chapter I'll review what we know about those causes.

Depression and Chronic Stress

Acute stress rarely causes depression. Instead, it more often motivates action and problem solving. For example, the sudden loss of a job can jolt a client with depression out of withdrawal and into a search for employment. Acute stress also helps people gain perspective. Minor conflicts shrink in the face of a major stress. Chronic stress is a different story. When efforts to solve a problem are met with repeated failure, depression is a natural outcome. Generally, it takes about three to nine months for an unrelenting stress to cause depression, depending on how much resilience there is on reserve.

The key to preventing depression is not to avoid problems, but to focus on those that are solvable. Working on a solvable problem is a good antidepressant. It focuses the mind, motivates action, and builds a sense of competence. Much of the work of therapy involves helping clients divert their time and energy away from unsolvable problems and toward the ones that can be solved.

The difficulty is when an unsolvable problem is too important to ignore. For example, illness in a child, demoralization at work, or unending marital conflict. These problems can overpower the mind and cause clients to ruminate about them every waking hour. One solution is to reduce the client's exposure to the problem. That is, what is the minimal amount of time they need to devote to the issue in order to manage it on a day-to-day basis? For the rest of the time, clients need to find activities that are absorbing enough to counter the magnetic pull of the ongoing stress (see Chapter 5).

Mania, Mood Instability, and Daily Rhythms

While the slow build of chronic stress is a common cause of depression, it's rapid changes that tend to destabilize hypo/manic moods, particularly changes in daily rhythms. That includes sleep, sunlight, and daily activity. People with bipolar disorder are especially sensitive to these disruptions, but they affect clients with unipolar depression as well. Both groups are prone to circadian disruptions, and signs of this disturbance are:

- Being more active at night and having trouble falling asleep
- Difficulty waking up and getting moving in the morning

People with these disrupted rhythms feel better when they stick to a regular schedule. However, when their routines are thrown off – such as starting a new job or vacationing in a faraway time zone – it disrupts their biological clock. The result is a rapid destabilization of mood, usually within days to weeks of the circadian stressor. In bipolar disorder, this typically begins with hypo/mania. That flame soon turns into a mixed state, and then darkens further into a depression.

The Germans have a word for routines that stabilize mood – *zeitgebers* – which translates to "time givers." Zeitgebers are the daily activities that instill a sense of time as the day flows from morning to night. These events trigger hormonal changes that set the biological clock. **Sleep, light, and darkness are the most important zeitgebers, but anything that causes hormonal changes can disrupt the body's internal clock and destabilize mood.**

For example, the postpartum period after childbirth is the highest risk period for mood problems in a woman's life, particularly for those with bipolar disorder. Fathers, too, are at high risk during that period due to the disruptions to sleep and daily routines that a newborn brings.

Rapid changes in sunlight are among the most potent mood destabilizers. These changes are most dramatic around the spring and fall equinox in September and March. In some parts of the world, the change is gradual, but when the light shifts quickly, it can destabilize mood, causing hypo/mania or depression. Similarly, both the brightness of the full moon and the gravitational changes of the lunar phases have been implicated in mood cycles (Wehr, 2018).

Even "good stress" can cause mood destabilization because the hormones that run the body's internal clock can be shaken by stresses good and bad. For example, planning a wedding, becoming pregnant, going on vacation, and buying a house are all examples of positive life stressors that can trigger new episodes in bipolar disorder.

Helping Clients Get to the Root Cause

In order to help clients with mood disorders get on the road to recovery, it is important to work with them to identify what is causing their symptoms. The two worksheets that follow encourage clients to consider a broad range of causes for their depression and bipolar disorder, which can then be sorted into solvable and unsolvable problems. As a therapist, you must carefully choose which problems to work on because success, however small, is an important ingredient in recovery. Look for problems that are important and motivating to the client, and that draw on their strengths.

Top Causes of Depression

Depression has many causes, and understanding them can clear the path to recovery. Common causes of depression are included on the following list. Read through them and check off any items that apply to you, including any that you've been through in the past year.

Stress and Relationships

☐ **Continuous stress.** Stress usually doesn't cause depression at first, but when problems go on too long (like months), and efforts to fix them keep failing, depression is a common result.

☐ **Trauma.** Trauma is an extraordinarily stressful event that involves a serious threat of death or injury. It can also include seeing that happen to someone else. Both recent and past traumas can cause depression.

☐ **Early childhood stress.** When children are neglected or abused by their early caregivers, it can lead to long-standing depression.

☐ **Major life transitions.** Changes that bring new roles and responsibilities can cause depression, particularly when they affect relationships. Examples include a new job or promotion, a recent move, graduation, retirement, or becoming a new parent.

☐ **Conflicts in relationships**

☐ **Grief and loss**, including the death of a pet

☐ **Shame.** Stressors that are associated with shame or a loss of status (e.g., job loss, school failure, bullying, marital infidelity) have a strong tendency to cause depression.

☐ **Social isolation**

Mental Health

☐ **Incomplete recovery.** People stay out of depression longer if they recover fully. When mild symptoms remain, they can build up into full episodes, much like a small weed can take over a garden.

☐ **Stopping treatment too soon.** How long you need to stay on medication depends on your diagnosis, but the minimum is six months after completely recovering. Psychotherapy should also continue after recovery, at least until the gains made become steady habits on their own.

☐ **Insomnia and nocturnal activity.** Irregular or poor sleep is a risk factor for depression. So is being active in the late hours and sleeping in during the day.

☐ **Anxiety and avoidance.** Anxiety can make people avoid opportunities, and depression tends to set in gradually as life becomes more restricted by that avoidance. It's the avoidance, not the anxiety, that causes the depression.

☐ **The wrong diagnosis.** Antidepressants often don't work well in people who have bipolar depression or hypo/manic symptoms. There are other types of depression that respond better to particular antidepressants (see page 70).

☐ **Other mental health problems** can cause depression, and recovery is slower if they're not addressed. Examples include:

    ☐ Addiction and substance use

    ☐ Anxiety disorders (e.g., social anxiety, panic, excess worrying)

    ☐ Post-traumatic stress disorder (PTSD)

    ☐ Attention-deficit/hyperactivity disorder (ADHD)

    ☐ Personality problems, like borderline personality disorder

    ☐ Obsessive compulsive disorder (OCD)

    ☐ Autism spectrum disorders

Seasons

Some people experience seasonal shifts in their mood. Fall and winter are the most common times for depression, although other patterns can occur. During which seasons does your mood tend to be worse?

☐ Winter

☐ Spring

☐ Summer

☐ Fall

☐ No pattern

Genetics

☐ **Family history of mood problems.** Depression and bipolar disorder tend to run in families, and understanding your family history can point the way toward recovery. If a medication worked well for your family member, it may work for you as well. This is particularly true for lithium.

Physical Health

☐ **Weight.** Antidepressants don't work as well if your body mass index (BMI) is over 30. (You can google "BMI calculator" to calculate yours.)

☐ **Chronic pain.** This is a two-way street. Unrelenting pain causes depression, and depression makes people more sensitive to pain.

☐ **Chronic health problems.** Living with a chronic medical condition that impairs quality of life (e.g., multiple sclerosis, cancer, renal failure, Parkinson's disease) increases the risk of depression.

☐ **Recent surgery, infection, allergies, or other inflammatory states.** When they body is under attack, whether from infectious bacteria or a surgeon's knife, it mounts an inflammatory response. That inflammation is a necessary form of self-defense, but it is also a cause of depression.

☐ **New medications.** Depression is listed as a side effect to many medications, but this is difficult to know for sure and depends on the person. For example, birth control medicine, statins, and pain medicines may improve or worsen mood. Some medications with strong links to depression include: steroids (e.g., prednisone), isotretinoin, opioids, beta-blockers, interferons, acyclovir, some antibiotics (e.g., fluoroquinolone types like cipro), and any medicine that causes fatigue.

☐ **Poor diet.** Eating too many fried or processed foods, simple sugars, and saturated fats raises the risk of depression about 30%.

☐ **Lack of activity.** Aerobic exercise treats depression as well as an antidepressant.

☐ **High altitude living.** Lower levels of oxygen at higher altitudes can cause depression.

☐ **Other health problems.** The list of health problems that are linked to depression is long, but most of those associations are not very strong so it's best to consult with your doctor before drawing conclusions on this one. Some of the better-known causes are:

　☐ Thyroid or endocrine disorders

　☐ Head injury

　☐ Neurologic or brain illnesses (including stroke)

　☐ Sleep apnea

　☐ Low blood count (anemia)

　☐ Vitamin deficiencies (e.g., B- and D-vitamins, folate)

Women's Health

☐ Childbirth in the past six months

☐ Recent or current menopause

☐ Worsening of mood around the menstrual cycle

Work

☐ Nightshift work

☐ Long commutes. Work commutes over 30 minutes (one-way) raise the odds of depression, particularly if the travel is by car.

☐ Long work hours. Routinely working over 11 hours a day doubles the risk of depression.

☐ Feeling bullied or shamed at work

☐ Job loss or financial stress

Other

☐ _____

☐ _____

☐ _____

Subtypes of Depression

Atypical Depression

Symptoms of atypical depression include:

- ☐ High appetite
- ☐ Tiredness or oversleeping
- ☐ Heavy feelings in the arms or legs
- ☐ Mood that is highly reactive to stress or rejection

Melancholic Depression

Symptoms of melancholic depression include:

- ☐ Low appetite
- ☐ Waking up early in the morning
- ☐ Severe slowing or agitation in the muscles
- ☐ Mood worse in morning
- ☐ Mood that feels different from ordinary sadness (it may feel physical, or like an intense dread)
- ☐ Unshakable negative thoughts
- ☐ Mood that reacts very little to life events whether good or bad

Top Mood Destabilizers

The following list contains some of the most common events that destabilize mood, particularly in bipolar disorder. Check any that have happened within the past three months, even if you think they weren't relevant to your current symptoms.

Sunlight, Sleep, and Daily Routines

☐ Loss of sleep

☐ Changes in sleep schedule, including shift work

☐ Insomnia

☐ Rapid changes in sunlight (e.g., between February-April or September-November)

☐ Traveling across more than two times zones

☐ Change in physical activity, especially stopping exercise

☐ Change in daily routines (e.g., the *timing* of meals, sleep, social, or work activities)

☐ Change in the frequency of family get-togethers

☐ Change in church or spiritual activities

Health

☐ Changes in medical health

☐ Changes in female hormones (e.g., pregnancy, childbirth, menstruation, menopause, or birth control pills)

☐ Head injury

☐ Consuming more high fructose corn syrup (e.g., from sweets, juice, breads, or sodas) or nitrated meats (e.g., beef or turkey jerky, Slim Jim's, hot dogs, bacon, salami, or pepperoni)

Medications and Drugs

☐ Coming off mood stabilizers

☐ Starting medications that can destabilize mood (e.g., antidepressants, stimulants, steroids, testosterone, weight loss medications, and pain medications)

☐ Changes in psychiatric medications

☐ Starting new supplements, particularly St. John's Wort, SAMe (s-adenosylmethionine), dehydro-epiandrosterone (DHEA), rhodiola rosea, or L-Glutamine

☐ Changes in recreational drug use (e.g., alcohol, pain medication, nicotine, caffeine, steroids, as well as the "harder" stuff)

Recent Positive Stress

- ☐ Job or school change, including new responsibilities, promotions, or change in work hours
- ☐ New romantic relationships
- ☐ Moving or changing residences
- ☐ Holiday, vacation, or trip
- ☐ House guests
- ☐ Parties, big events, or celebrations
- ☐ Birth of a new family member
- ☐ New achievement or financial success
- ☐ Other positive stress: _____

Recent Negative Stress

- ☐ Relationship or work conflict
- ☐ Grief, including loss of a pet
- ☐ Relationship loss, including divorce and separation
- ☐ Job loss or financial setback
- ☐ Legal problems
- ☐ Trauma. This is an extraordinarily stressful event that involves serious threat of death or injury. It can also include seeing that happen to someone else.
- ☐ Other negative stress: _____

Other

- ☐ _____
- ☐ _____
- ☐ _____

part II

an
antidepressant
lifestyle

Introduction to an Antidepressant Lifestyle

Interventions

Now that you understand the symptoms and causes of mood disorders, it's time to turn to interventions. In particular, this book focuses on lifestyle interventions that clients can put into action outside of the therapy session. I've collected these interventions in Part II of this book, with these criteria in mind:

1. **They work.** By "work," I mean that they've been put to the test in research, preferably through a controlled trial in the real world.

2. **They are simple.** "Simple" is based on my experience as a practicing psychiatrist, psychotherapist, and director of a center for mood disorders. It's there that I fine-tuned these chapters with the help of around 100 therapists, psychiatrists, and nurse practitioners. As we tested them out with over 20,000 clients, I noticed that some of the techniques had few takers, while others were adopted with minimal persuasion. It's those that made the final cut.

3. **They are often overlooked in practice.** Many of these interventions have been overlooked because they were developed outside the traditional schools of psychotherapy. Environmental psychology, sleep medicine, nutrition, exercise, and music therapy have all developed effective treatments for mood disorders. Those treatments can be readily integrated into traditional therapy.

Motivation is in short supply during depression. The art of this work is in guiding clients toward the changes they are ready to make, and the ones that will make the biggest difference. That art involves a few steps, which are outlined in the following sections.

Step 1: Diagnostic Assessment

The first step in developing an effective treatment plan with your client is to determine where they fall on the mood spectrum. Part I of this book should give you a good idea of whether your client falls on the bipolar or the unipolar side of the mood spectrum. Why does this matter in therapy? Clients on the bipolar side will benefit more from the circadian rhythm approaches in this book, particularly if they are having hypo/mania, mixed states, or rapid cycling. Two interventions that are uniquely suited to those bipolar phases are:

1. Dark therapy for mania and mixed states (Chapter 6)
2. Social rhythm therapy (Chapter 5)

Prevention is another reason to make this distinction. The kinds of triggers that clients need to be mindful of are different for bipolar and unipolar disorders.

Step 2: Biopsychosocial Assessment

The next step is to gather information about the client's life that's relevant to their mood disorder. This includes information about stressors, relationships, strengths, and weaknesses. It also includes the client's diet, physical activity, and sleep, with particular attention to their environment and activity before bed and just after waking. The worksheets on the "Top Causes of Depression" and "Top Mood Destabilizers" presented in Chapter 3 can prompt this conversation.

When working to disentangle the underlying causes of your client's mood disorder, the assessment needs some structure to it. Many of the causes are not intuitive, and if asked open-ended questions, most clients are likely to tell you what they are depressed about rather than what caused their depression. The timeframe is important to keep in mind. Causes of depression tend to start three to six months before the episode, while hypo/mania tends to be triggered by disruptions in routines over the past few weeks.

As you go through this assessment, make a list with the client. Try to get a feel for areas in which they'll have the best chance of succeeding. What have they tried on their own so far? How did it work? What factors does the client think are contributing to their problems, and which ones are they motivated to change?

Step 3: Present Options

Once you've identified the factors that are causing or perpetuating the episode, the solutions follow intuitively. For example, a fast food diet suggests a nutritional approach. A sedentary lifestyle points to brisk walking or forest therapy, and oversleeping calls for brisk awakening or the dawn simulator. Behavioral activation (Chapter 5) is particularly helpful in shifting clients away from ruminative thinking. The chapters that follow present you with a variety of options to choose from.

From this work, gather a short list of lifestyle changes that the client can pick from, like a menu. Choose the changes that they are most motivated to tackle, most likely to succeed in, or are likely to make a significant difference. Present them as lifestyle changes with an emphasis on their benefits and ease of adoption. Usually, I'll ask the client to pick just one to work on, but if they fight me on it, I'll easily settle for more. The point is to make this a success. No need to overwhelm them with changes they can't make.

Step 4: Monitor Progress

There are many ways to monitor progress, but what matters most is that the client has someone to be accountable to. That's you. They need a way to show you how well they are sticking to their goals at each session. A calendar, daily checklist, or the mood chart on page 31 can all serve that purpose.

I reserve time at the beginning of each session to review this progress, praising success and approaching setbacks in a neutral but interested tone. I'm very curious to know what got in the way of achieving those goals and how the client feels about it. Avoid communicating disappointment or criticism, and bear in mind that mood disorders can make clients read those messages even when they're not there. You want to ally yourself with the client's goals, as opposed to straying too far down your own path. Empathy can keep things on course.

Next is planning and troubleshooting. If the client is having trouble reaching their goals, and problem solving doesn't yield solutions, it's best to lower the bar or change approaches. Instead of walking in the forest daily, how about three days a week? If it's just too far for the client to drive there, then change to something else on the lifestyle menu.

If a client is succeeding, I'll wait a few weeks before adding something new in. It takes time for those changes to become a habit.

Finally, you'll want some way to measure mood while they built these new habits. While the mood chart is ideal, some clients find it too cumbersome. Alternatively, they can rate their overall wellbeing on a scale from 1 to 10, or come up with their own target measure such as "If this works for you, what do you hope to see different in the way you feel?"

Have the client rate whatever item you've agreed upon at the beginning of each session. If you're not using the mood chart, graph the ratings visually as you go. Some of the changes in this book take months to work, while others take weeks. Clients with depression are slow to recognize progress and quick to give up on things that are working. I'll frequently hear that the changes they've made are "doing nothing," when the lines on the graph tell a very different story.

Therapy with a Biological Basis

There are many biological pathways that lead to mood disorders, and several are behind the lifestyle interventions in this book: circadian rhythms, neurohormones, and neuroplasticity.

Circadian Rhythms

Circadian rhythms are physical and mental changes that follow a daily cycle, including sleep, appetite, and energy. It's no coincidence that those are the key symptoms of mood disorders, as circadian rhythms are usually disrupted in depression and bipolar disorder.

The largest confirmation of this link comes from a study that measured daily activity levels in 91,000 adults. Those with high activity levels at night and low activity levels in the day were more likely to develop depression or bipolar disorder when followed up on two years later. Happiness, wellbeing, and concentration were also linked to these circadian disruptions. These associations remained strong after controlling for other potential causes, like gender, alcohol and tobacco use, obesity, childhood trauma, and other psychosocial stressors (Lyall et al., 2018).

This finding raises the intriguing possibility that mood might improve by shifting activity to the morning hours and quieting it at night. That is the basis for social rhythm therapy, which is an effective treatment for bipolar disorder that informs this book. It also may explain a surprising finding in psychotherapy: that behavioral interventions for insomnia don't just improve sleep, they improve depression as well (Cunningham & Shapiro, 2018).

Light and darkness are the most direct ways to stabilize circadian rhythms, and controlling these environmental cues treats depression, bipolar disorder, and insomnia. *Chronotherapy* relies on these techniques and uses simple devices to help clients regulate their light and dark exposure. We'll explore those techniques throughout this book, including dawn simulators for depression and blue-light blockers for sleep and bipolar disorder.

Neurohormones

The brain is a well-protected organ. The skull defends it against external injury, and a tight meshwork called the *blood-brain barrier* protects it from internal threats, like toxins and infections. That leaves a problem: How can the brain communicate with the body if it's locked up behind a tight barrier? As a solution, a few select chemicals are allowed to move through this barrier, and it's through these *neurohormones* that the brain and body coordinate. Essentially, neurohormones are the mind-body connection.

Cortisol is a neurohormone that lets the brain know it's under stress. Normally, it rises in the morning, promoting alertness and energy, and falls during the day. It also rises during times of stress, activating the brain's stress-response system. During depression, however, cortisol gets stuck on red alert, and its levels remain high throughout the day. It's as though the body is under constant stress – and, indeed, the same flat-line levels of elevated cortisol are seen during chronic stress, PTSD, and other anxiety disorders.

All this cortisol takes a toll on the brain and the body. On brain imaging scans, there is visible shrinkage in the hippocampus and amygdala, which form the brain's memory and mood centers, respectively. Chronic cortisol elevations also impair people's ability to manage stress by altering the connections between the brain's mood center and its action/planning center (e.g., the frontal lobes) (Sharpley, 2010).

Restoring the normal rhythms of cortisol is an important part of treating depression, and here's the surprise: Psychotherapy accomplishes that task even better than medication. Stabilization of cortisol has been seen after CBT, psychoanalysis, and mindfulness training, as well as exercise, yoga, a healthy diet, and music therapy (Anderson & Wideman, 2017; Riley & Park, 2015; Trappe, 2010). Similarly, research has found that when people with bipolar disorder learn how to regulate their daily routines, their cortisol levels drop down from red alert and revert to the daily rise-and-fall that is a mark of good health (Delle Chiaie et al., 2013).

Neuroplasticity

The brain grows new connections when people learn new skills, and psychotherapy is no exception. This phenomenon was first demonstrated in the early 1990s with exposure therapy for obsessive compulsive disorder, and it has since been established with cognitive and interpersonal therapies for depression, insomnia, social phobia, panic disorder, schizophrenia, and PTSD (Peres & Nasello, 2008).

This phenomenon is known as *neuroplasticity*, and it refers to the brain's ability to reshape itself throughout life, forming new connections and repairing ones that have been broken down by stress. Brain cells connect through dendrites, which reach out like limbs on a tree. However, stress, cortisol, and depression cause those dendrites to shrink back.

Most successful treatments for depression enhance the growth of those dendrites by increasing *neuroprotective agents.* These are naturally occurring compounds that trigger the growth and repair of brain cells. Brain-derived neurotrophic factor (BDNF) is the most well-known among them, but there are many others, including B-cell lymphoma 2 (bcl-2), nerve growth factor (NGF), and various antioxidants.

Neuroprotective agents decline during mood disorders, rendering the brain unable to repair itself. Psychiatric medications and psychotherapy reverse that trend. As a result, the brain slowly grows new connections over weeks and months, which is part of the reason that these treatments take a while to work. Lifestyle approaches, like aerobic exercise and the Mediterranean diet, also have significant neuroprotective effects.

The Do-It-Yourself Mood Spa

7:30 a.m.	Awake with the sunrise
8:00 a.m.	Breakfast: tea, berries, and yogurt
8:30 a.m.	Stroll by the ocean
10:00 a.m.	Yoga
11:30 a.m.	Lunch: grilled chicken and walnut salad
1:00 p.m.	Mindfulness class
2:00 p.m.	Forest hike
3:30 p.m.	Aromatherapy massage
5:00 p.m.	Dinner: roasted ginger salmon, arugula salad, chocolate walnut tart
6:30 p.m.	Hot spring and cold plunge pools
8:00 p.m.	Reading and harp music by the fireside
10:00 p.m.	Sleep

That's a typical schedule at a luxury spa, where people spend thousands of dollars to de-stress in tranquility. Every item on this list also has antidepressant properties, and there's a story behind that coincidence. In the 19th century, people went to beautifully landscaped retreats to recover from depression. They gardened, exercised, took therapeutic baths, and lived by a simple, regular schedule.

Those institutions bear little resemblance to the psychiatric hospitals of today, where brief stays on locked, indoor units are the norm. This shift began after the discovery of antidepressants in the 1960s. For clients, these medications were life-changing. For insurers, they were an excuse to cut funding for recreational and environmental therapies. As those approaches fell out of hospital life, spas started taking them over. The spas of today bear some resemblance to the best psychiatric asylums of yesteryear.

The problem is that antidepressants don't work well in the wrong environment. Lifestyle factors can double their effects, and we now know what some of those factors are. They follow the rhythms of the day, from sunrise to sundown, much like the spa schedule listed above. In the chapters that follow, behavioral steps that improve mood are spread out along a 24-hour cycle, ranging from morning (Chapter 4), daytime (Chapter 5), to evening (Chapter 6). Throughout these chapters, the emphasis is on:

1. What the client is doing
2. What time they are doing it
3. The environment they are doing it in

As you read through these steps in the next chapters, think of it as a do-it-yourself (DIY) luxury spa. Compared to a weekend at Canyon Ranch, it costs pennies on the dollar.

4

Morning

The goal in the morning is to quickly shift from sleep to wakefulness. Traditionally, this is achieved through a loud alarm clock and a big cup of coffee. Clients with depression may not feel fully awake until midday. The techniques in this chapter highlight behavioral and environmental techniques to get the brain moving, including:

- Brisk awakening
- Dawn simulation
- Judicious use of caffeine
- Activating music
- Aromatherapy with activating scents
- Air ionization

All of these techniques are safe and feasible to use in a therapy practice. Two require devices (dawn simulators and air ionizers), and specific product recommendations are included.

Brisk Awakening

Why is it so hard for clients to get out of bed when they're depressed? The answer isn't laziness. It's actually a little-known symptom of depression called *sleep inertia*. Sleep inertia occurs when the brain is jolted from deep sleep to full awakening. The result is a groggy state of mind and a brain that isn't fully awake.

Sleep inertia happens to most people, depressed or not. Depression just makes it last longer, so instead of 15 minutes, it drags on for hours. *Brisk awakening* is a technique that improves this groggy state. It also treats depression, so it is worth trying even if clients wake up with a spring in their step. The main idea is to rise quickly out of bed at regular times each morning. The specific steps involved are (1) establishing a regular wake time, (2) establishing a morning routine, and (3) engaging in an energizing activity in the morning. These steps are discussed in further detail on the client worksheet on the following page.

Brisk Awakening

What does it help?

Concentration, alertness, energy, depression, insomnia, and bipolar disorder.

How long does it take to work?

Clients should see gradual progress over one to four weeks, and even more benefit after three to six months.

The research

In a controlled study of bipolar disorder, brisk awakening reduced the duration of sleep inertia by 50% (Kaplan et al., 2018). When paired with CBT-insomnia, it improved sleep and reduced overall mood symptoms in bipolar disorder eight-fold (Harvey et al., 2015).

How does it work?

Brisk awakening improves alertness by shifting brainwaves into the faster frequencies. Waking up at regular times helps insomnia by setting the biological clock. Starting the day with an energizing activity raises dopamine and other antidepressant neurotransmitters.

Brisk Awakening

Brisk awakening is a technique that involves rising out of bed at the same time each day. This is hard to do when you're depressed. The following are the steps involved in brisk awakening:

1. Wake up and start your day at a regular time

Officially, the day starts when you get out of bed and stand upright. The nervous system shifts into high gear when you stand up, causing blood to pump more intensely so you don't faint. Those changes also set the biological clock, so if you wake up – and stand up – at the same time each day your energy, sleep, and mood will improve. "At the same time" actually means give or take 15 minutes. That's the margin of error that the biological clock can tolerate.

2. Morning routine

Establish a few routines to help you stay out of bed, like:

- Open the curtains and turn on the lights

- Disable the snooze button

- Make the bed

- Shower and dress (put on shoes!)

- Other:

  _____

  _____

  _____

3. Energizing activity

Start your day with activities that make you feel more energized and alert. Energizing activities get you going and keep you going. Perhaps you are already doing these things in the evening, such as surfing the web or decorating the house all night. If that's the case, just move them to the morning, and save the passive, relaxing, wind-down activities for the hour before bed. The following are all qualities that characterize an energizing activity:

- It involves standing, moving, or changing positions, rather than sitting or lying down.

- You get absorbed or caught up in it.

- It's slightly addictive. The more you do it, the more you want to do it.

- It peps you up a little instead of leaving you drained.

- It's interactive instead of passive.

- It's something you look forward to.

What's energizing to one person can be draining to another, so take these examples with a grain of salt and think about what works best for you:

- Step outside and move around for 15 minutes

- Aromatherapy (mint, lemon, geranium, juniper, rosemary, and sage are activating)

- Make a cup of coffee or tea

- Make breakfast

- Take a cold shower or wash your hands and face with cold water (this improves wakefulness by causing blood vessel constriction)

- Get a head start on work or chores

- Get some sunlight or turn on bright lights

- Call a friend or talk with the people you live with

- Play energizing music, like dance, gospel, or exercise tunes (for a calmer effect, try nature sounds with a morning feel, like chirping birds)

- Sing, dance, or play a musical instrument

- Stretch

- Garden

- Take care of pets

- Go for a drive or run errands

- Other:

_____

_____

_____

For Your Next Session

Over the next week, check the box for each step of brisk awakening that you completed.

	Mon	Tue	Wed	Thurs	Fri	Sat	Sun
Woke at a regular time (_____ a.m.)							
Got out of bed upon awakening							
Made the bed							
Engaged in energizing activity							

Brisk Awakening: Troubleshooting

"Nothing energizes me."

Depression can make it hard to feel energized. If everything you do feels the same, think of things that once felt energizing when you weren't depressed, or choose from the list on the previous page. Brisk awakening can work even if you don't feel the energy, it may just take longer.

"It's hard to get up."

If you find that you are having difficulty getting up in the morning, try some of the following techniques:

1. Use a dawn simulator to wake up (see page 86).

2. Use a lively alarm clock (see page 88).

3. Make it a game. Keep a timer next to your bed to track your progress. Each morning, start the timer when you wake up, and stop it when you get out of bed. See if you can beat your record. Ideally, you'll be out of bed within a minute of waking.

"I set my alarm extra early because it takes me a while to get up."

Although it's tempting to deal with morning fatigue by sleeping in a little longer, that second round of sleep can disorganize brainwaves in ways that cause even more grogginess when you wake up again. When it comes to sleep, focus on quality, not quantity.

Dawn Simulator

A dawn simulator creates a virtual sunrise in the morning. It works while the client sleeps and treats sleep inertia by gradually lifting the brain from deep sleep to full awakening. Additionally, these devices treat winter depression by providing a needed dose of light on gray winter mornings. Dawn simulators pair well with brisk awakening. Although they help clients with depression, bipolar disorder, and insomnia, normal folks benefit from them as well. People tend to use less caffeine and have better energy and alertness when awoken by a dawn simulator.

The following client handout describes how to use a dawn simulator and lists products to choose from. An important point to emphasize to clients is that they should wake up gradually with the device, over 30 to 120 minutes. If it wakes them up too early, have them move the light away from the bed. If it doesn't wake them up at all, bring it closer.

Dawn Simulator

What does it help?

Dawn simulators improve energy, depression, and concentration. They reduce the duration of sleep inertia by 50%. Though they are not as powerful as a lightbox, they did improve winter depression in five small controlled trials. In one study, they helped people in recovery from alcohol abuse stay sober.

How long does it take to work?

The antidepressant effects build gradually over two to six weeks, though it can improve energy and alertness right away.

How does it work?

Dawn simulators improve wakefulness by suppressing melatonin and raising cortisol in the morning. These neurohormones are involved in depression and set the body's internal clock.

Dawn Simulator

It's not natural to wake up to sound. Loud alarm clocks jolt people out of deep sleep, leaving the brain in a groggy state called *sleep inertia*. The brain was designed to wake up to a sunrise. A steady increase in morning light lifts the brain from deep sleep to light sleep and into full awakening.

If your bedroom has small or north-facing windows, you may not be getting enough sunlight to wake up, especially in the winter months. Depression is common in winter, and lack of morning light is part of the cause. A *dawn simulator* improves this problem by creating a virtual sunrise in the bedroom. It works while you sleep, gradually turning on over 30-120 minutes.

Choosing a Product

Dawn simulators are not regulated by the Food and Drug Administration, so it can be difficult to know which model is best. A good resource is the Center for Environmental Therapeutics, which is a non-profit group that tests light therapy devices. Their latest recommendations are on their website (www.cet.org,). A consumer group that makes recommendations is www.sunriseclocks.org.

A good product will turn on gradually and peak with a bright light (at least 250 lux). There are models with built-in lamps, timers that connect to an existing light, and smart bulbs that turn on gradually. The built-in lamps offer a reliable source of light and use long-lasting LED bulbs. Timers are cost effective and allow people to keep their current lamp, but they only work with dimmable bulbs and need at least 75 watts. Smart bulbs will fit into an existing lamp and can be programmed to turn on gradually.

There are also apps that can convert a cell phone into a dawn simulator by slowly turning on the phone's flashlight. These have the advantage of being inexpensive and portable, but they don't emit enough light to improve mood. Still, some light is better than none. The following chart provides some good options in each category.

Dawn Simulators	
Lamps with timers	These options have the best research support. Their built-in LED bulbs are long lasting and emit a spectrum of light that is comparable to sunlight. 1. Nature Bright PER2LED: Recommended by the Center for Environmental Therapeutics, $50-90 2. Philips Morning Wake-Up Light HF3500, HF3510, and HF3520: Recommended by the National Sleep Foundation, $97 3. Lumie Bodyclock: Tested in clinical research, $225
Timers for existing lamps	These options work with an existing lamp but require dimmable bulbs: 1. LightenUp (windhovermfg.com), $20-40 2. SunRise Controller BioBrite, $40-50
Smart bulbs	Smart bulbs can be programmed to turn on gradually through a smart phone (e.g., Phillips Hue, $200)
Apps	Apps are inexpensive and portable but may not be bright enough to help depression. Make sure to use an app that turns on gradually (e.g., Rise & Shine, Lichtwecker).

How to Use It

The dawn simulator should wake you up at the time you set, when the intensity of the light peaks. If it wakes you up too soon, move it away from your head. Bring it closer if it doesn't wake you up at all. Waking at a regular time improves mood and sleep, so it's best to have the dawn simulator turn on at the same time each day, give or take 15 minutes.

Dusk Simulation

Some dawn simulators can also create a virtual sunset. In theory, this simulated dusk might improve insomnia, but this idea has never actually been tested. What does improve insomnia is warm, yellow light in the evening. The PER2LED simulator doubles as a yellowish reading lamp for use in the evening.

Philips Morning Wake-Up Light®

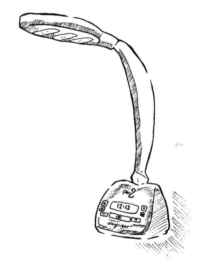

PER2LED by Nature Bright®

Dawn Simulator: Troubleshooting

"I still can't get out of bed."

Sleep inertia can be hard to break through. Position the lamp close to your head and use a high-wattage bulb if it doesn't wake you up. You can also pair it with a lively alarm clock that makes you get out of bed to turn it off. Once you're out of bed, try the ideas listed on the "Brisk Awakening" worksheet to keep you going. The following chart provides some ideas for lively alarm clocks:

Lively Alarm Clocks	
Clocky, Tocky, Blowfly	These alarm clocks run or fly away as they sound off, requiring you to get up and chase them down.
Smart Alarm Mat	An alarm that only turns off when you get out of bed and stand on a mat.
Shape Up Dumbbell Alarm Clock	A dumbbell-shaped alarm that will get you moving. It only shuts off after you've completed 30 curls.
IQ Alarm by Yanko	This alarm requires you to answer a few brain teasers before shutting the alarm off.
Smiley Alarm	Start your day with a smile. This app uses facial recognition software and only turns off the alarm if you smile. Research shows that smiling, even when it's forced, improves mood.
Sleep If U Can, Alarmy, Morning Routine	These apps require you to get up and photograph objects in your house to shut off the alarm.
Alarm Clock Xtreme, Mathe Alarm Clock, Puzzle Alarm	These apps require you to solve puzzles before turning off.
Wake N Shake	This app only shuts off the alarm when you vigorously shake the phone.

Coffee Or Tea?

To beat depression, the answer is tea. Drinking three cups of tea a day lowers the risk of depression by 37%, and the benefit doubles when you go to six cups a day. That's what a team of researchers concluded after analyzing 11 studies involving nearly 23,000 people (Dong et al., 2015). The results apply to green and black teas, but not herbal teas, which lack real tea leaves from the *Camellia sinensis* plant. The mood-lifting effects of tea are not just due to caffeine. Tea has several ingredients that protect brain cells: catechins, flavonoids, polyphenols, and L-theanine.

Where does this leave the coffee drinker? The news there is also good, in moderation. Coffee prevents depression, but only up to a maximum of 1.75 metric cups a day (about one mug). After that first mug, the benefits level off, and too much coffee (over two mugs a day) increases the risk of depression. These guidelines are based on caffeinated coffee and were distilled from 12 studies involving nearly 340,000 people (Grosso et al., 2015).

Moderating Caffeine

Small amounts of caffeine are helpful for mood, regardless of the source, but too much can increase the risk of depression. The safe upper limit is 300 mg/day. Let's look at how that limit translates to daily cups ("cups" here refers to the measuring cups used in baking):

Beverage	Max metric cups/day
Brewed Coffee	2
Latte or mocha	2.5
Espresso	0.5
Instant Coffee	5
Brewed black tea	6
Brewed green tea	10
Bottled tea	8
Cola	6
Energy drink	1.5
Energy shot	0.3

Drinking half a cup of coffee every few hours (again, that's a metric cup!) is about all that's needed to improve alertness. Any more may just go to waste, or cause anxiety and addiction. Indeed, anxiety is such a common side effect of caffeine that anyone with anxiety ought to try cutting out caffeine for two weeks to see if it improves (slowly lower it down to prevent withdrawal headaches). Another strategy is to switch to tea, which has ingredients that balance out the anxiety-provoking effects of caffeine.

Timing is also important. Any caffeine after 2:00 p.m. can worsen mood by disrupting sleep.

Other Health Benefits

Coffee and tea have physical health benefits as well. Both lower the risk of diabetes, dementia, cancer, liver problems, and heart disease. However, just as with mental health, tea is the safer option for the body. The high caffeine content of coffee can worsen some heart conditions, and even decaffeinated coffee contains acids that can worsen heartburn. Moreover, tea has an ingredient that balances caffeine's tendency to elevate blood pressure and anxiety: L-theanine.

Sweeteners reverse those health benefits, particularly artificial sweeteners. Although they have zero calories, artificial sweeteners cause weight gain and diabetes. They inflame the body and alter brain chemistry, which is why they are more likely to cause depression than natural sugars (Guo et al., 2014).

How to Lower Caffeine

If clients have insomnia, anxiety, tremors, dry mouth, heartburn (reflux), or high blood pressure, then they may do well to lower their caffeine intake. However, they shouldn't stop right away, as that can cause withdrawal symptoms. Those symptoms begin about 12-24 hours after their last drink, and include headaches, irritability, fatigue, muscle aches, and mental fogging.

Clients should lower their caffeine intake slowly, reducing the dose every two to three days by the amount in the chart below. If they have withdrawal symptoms, then slow down further. Drinking plenty of water and getting good sleep and exercise will further ease the withdrawal.

Beverage	Lower by
Coffee	¼ of a cup every 2-3 days
Soda	½ a can every 2-3 days
Energy drinks	¼ a can every 2-3 days
Tea	½ cup every 2-3 days

Morning Playlist

Music definitely affects the brain. Listening to Mozart improves cognitive performance and calms seizures, and electronic binaural beats help energy and focus (Maguire, 2017). When using music with your clients, consider how it affects their *energy*, not just their emotions. Remember: Energizing activity in the morning improves depression, so songs that get clients moving are a good addition to their morning routine.

Music in the Morning

What does it help?

Listening to music helps alleviate depression and increases energy. Music therapy has also been used successfully for anxiety, concentration, pain, and stress.

How long does it take to work?

The effects of energizing music are immediate, but the benefits for depression continue to build over several weeks.

The research

Listening to music improves depression, and the benefits are even greater when people play a musical instrument on their own (regardless of how good they are). That's the conclusion of 26 controlled studies (Leubner & Hinterberger, 2017).

How does it work?

Pleasurable music influences the limbic system, an area of the brain involved in mood and emotion. It raises brain-derived neurotrophic factor (BDNF), which helps brain cells grow and strengthen. Music may even influence how genes are expressed. That research isn't definitive, but it suggests that music can activate the genetic code in ways that alter dopamine, a neurotransmitter involved in motivation. Music also calms stress signals, as listening to pleasurable music lowers cortisol, improves immune function, and reduces anxiety by stabilizing the autonomic nervous system (aka the "fight or flight" system) (Howland, 2017).

There are lots of playlists on the internet that clients can use to generate ideas. For ambient music, they can try binaural beats in the beta and gamma range. If music is too distracting, have them make a playlist of morning nature sounds, such as birds chirping in a forest. The following **Morning Playlist** handout also includes a sample morning playlist that clients can use.

Morning Playlist

Put Your Records On, Corinne Baily Rae

Best Day of My Life, American Authors

Beauty in the World; I Try, Macy Gray

Girls Just Wanna Have Fun, Cindi Lauper

Three Little Birds; Coming in from the Cold, Bob Marley

Smile, Uncle Kracker

Happy, Pharrell Williams

Lean on Me; Lovely Day, Bill Withers

Can I Kick It, A Tribe Called Quest

Don't Stop Believin', Journey

Send Me on My Way, Rusted Root

Take on Me, A-ha

I'm a Believer, The Monkees

Love Shack; Roam, The B-52's

Praise You, Fatboy Slim

Walkin' on Sunshine, Katrina and the Waves

Brown Eyed Girl, Van Morrison

Shout, Isley Brothers

I Get Around; Do it Again; Wouldn't it be Nice, The Beach Boys

Groove is in the Heart, Deee-Lite

Beautiful Day; Where the Streets Have No Name, U2

Rise Up, Andra Day

Good Day, Nappy Roots

I Will Survive, Gloria Gaynor

Come Dancing; Better Things, The Kinks

The Circle of Life, The Lion King

I Feel Good, James Brown

These are Days, 10,000 Maniacs

Hold on Tight, Greg Holden

Hey Ya!, Outkast

Hey Soul Sister, Train

Can't Stop the Feeling, Justin Timberlake

Everyday People, Sly & the Family Stone

I Can See Clearly Now, Johnny Nash

Bubbly; Goldmine, Colbie Caillat

You Got It, Roy Orbison

Sunshine, Matisyahu

Down Under, Men at Work

Uptown Funk, Mark Ronson & Bruno Mars

Love Train, The O'Jays

On Top of the World, Imagine Dragons

Stronger (What Doesn't Kill You), Kelly Clarkson

Karma Chameleon, Culture Club

Up, Up, and Away, Kid Cudi

Dancing in the Streets, Martha and the Vandellas

Vacation, The Go-Go's

It's Amazing, Jem

Wake Me Up Before You Go-Go, Wham!

Centerfield, John Fogerty

Raise Your Glass, Pink

Faith, George Michael

Everyday, Buddy Holly

Sweet Persuasion, Brett Dennen

Ten Feet Tall, Afrojack

Sweet Caroline, Neil Diamond

Wotless, Kes The Band

Back in the Highlife; Higher Love; While You See a Chance, Steve Winwood

Zol!, BLK JKS

My Shot, Hamilton Cast

Pick Yourself Up, Nat King Cole & George Shearing

Tubthumping, Chumbawamba

Stayin Alive, The Bee Gees

Money on My Mind, Sam Smith

Pumpin Blood, NONONO

Cecilia, Simon & Garfunkel

I'm Gonna Be (500 miles), The Proclaimers

MMMBop, Hanson

Dance Tonight, Paul McCartney

Come on Eileen, Dexys Midnight Runners

How Will I Know, Whitney Houston

Just Like Starting Over, John Lennon

Respect, Aretha Franklin

You Can Call Me Al, Paul Simon

Nothing's Gonna Stop Us, Starship

Right by Your Side, Eurythmics

All About that Bass, Meghan Trainor

Break My Stride, Matthew Wilder

I'm Still Standing, Elton John

Upbeat Movie Soundracks (e.g., *Mama Mia, Grease, Footloose, Dirty Dancing*)

Streaming Playlists

Try these energizing playlists on your streaming service:

- Spotify: *Have a Great Day, Mood Booster, Good Vibes*

- Apple Music: *Get Happy, 100 Most Uplifting Songs Ever*

- Google Play Music: *Confident, Energetic*

Or search for these keywords: dance, exercise, happy, positive, mood, uplifting, energy, energizing, worship, or gospel.

Troubleshooting

"I can't stand happy songs."

You're not alone. While some people find that positive lyrics distract from negative thoughts, others find them grating or anxiety-provoking. The aim is to find music that gets you moving, not happy music. If the lyrics make you more depressed or anxious, try instrumental tracks (search for binaural beats in the beta and gamma range) or nature sounds (search for "morning forest," "nature sounds," or "outside broadcast recordings"). Or, try no music at all.

The Mozart Effect

A particular piece by Wolfgang Amadeus Mozart has forever changed how we view music and the brain. In 1993, Mozart's *Sonata for Two Pianos in D Major K. 448* was found to improve cognitive performance. The same piece was later shown to have a calming effect on seizures. That raises the question: Can specific types of music have a curative effect on the brain?

The songs on the previous handout playlist are meant to get you moving in the morning because physical activity in the early hours has antidepressant effects. But what if music can also treat depression? Studies suggest that the answer is yes. Music that brings you pleasure, or brings up positive memories, has been proven to improve mood. To get that effect, create a playlist that triggers positive emotions, and listen to it for about an hour a day.

It's best to find the tunes that are right for you, but you can also pull from the list of classic music that psychologists have used in studies of depression. Those are:

- Mozart, *Sonata for Two Pianos in D Major K. 448*

- Mozart, *Piano Sonata No 16 in C Major K. 545*

- J.S. Bach, *Italian Concertos, Badinerie*

- G.F. Händel, *The Arrival of the Queen of Sheba*

- Arcangelo Corelli, *Clavier Sonatas*

- Claude Debussy, *Preludes*

- Pieces from the album, "*The Most Relaxing Classical Album in the World...Ever!*"

Morning Air

Scent and Mood

The nerves in the nose connect directly to the brain's memory and emotion centers, the *hippocampus* and *amygdala*, respectively. That explains why familiar scents make us reminisce, like the aroma of antique wood that sets off memories of grandmother's house.

Scents also alter neurotransmitters, which can either stimulate energy and concentration, or induce relaxation and sleep. Scents with stimulating properties include mint, lemon, geranium, juniper, rosemary, and sage. By using aromatherapy, clients can capitalize on this mind-nose connection to improve their mental functioning. The following are several ways that clients can integrate aromatherapy into their morning routine:

- Use an aromatherapy diffuser. These can be connected to a plug-in timer so it turns on before they wake up.
- Use scented oils, sprays, candles, or bath products.
- Grow some potted mint in the kitchen.
- Infuse water with mint leaves, orange, or lemon peel.
- Eat fresh oranges or grapefruit in the morning. These fruits contain flavanols that improve brain health and reduce depression.
- Make a morning cup of mint or citrus tea.

Morning Temperature

A gradual rise in temperature helps the brain wake up. Sleep doctors recommend sleeping in a colder room (60-65 °F – yes, that cold!) and programming the thermostat to rise in the hour before waking. Smart beds can raise the temperature automatically or cool it with a fan, but these cost a few hundred dollars (e.g., BedJet, Bed Fan).

Antidepressant Air Ions

There's something special about the air around a waterfall, at the beach, or in a forest after it rains. The humidity in those places creates oxygen ions that give off that fresh, clean scent. Air ionizers are machines that do this indoors. They are sold as air purifiers because oxygen ions remove dust, mold, allergens, and cigarette smoke.

Air ionizers can also be used treat depression. If that sounds hard to believe, you're not alone. Researchers were originally so skeptical of air ionizers that they were first used as a placebo in studies of depression. To their surprise, the placebo air ionizers actually worked. Five clinical trials confirmed those observations (Perez et al., 2013).

Air ionizers are particularly good at treating winter depression. The dry, winter air is depleted of oxygen ions, as is indoor air. Heating and air conditioner units and dehumidifiers remove these antidepressant ions form the air.

Although we know that air ionizers treat depression, no one is sure how they do it. One reason may be because ionized air improves circulation throughout the body. As air purifiers, they reduce allergies and inflammation, both of which are known causes of depression.

Purchasing a Device

A good air ionizer needs to produce enough negative ions to treat depression. It also needs to minimize ozone, which is a dangerous byproduct of some devices. A research team at Columbia University tests available devices, and their recommendations are available at www.cet.org (type "*air ionizer*" in the search box). As of this writing, they recommend the *NaturAir Ionizer* and the *Wein VI-2500 High-Density Ionic Air Purifier*.

How to Use the Ionizer

In the original studies regarding the efficacy of air ionizers, people sat next to the ionizer for 90 minutes in the morning. However, an easier method has been developed that works while clients sleep. By plugging the ionizer into a wall timer, it can be programmed to turn on 90 minutes before clients wake up and to turn off when they awake. Clients should make sure to use a timer that won't wake them up with a loud click (e.g., the Digital Programmable Timer Socket Plug Wall Home Plug-in Switch Energy-Saving Outlet, available on Amazon). They can also just leave the ionizer on throughout the night, as there are no known risks with ionization.

Clients should place the ionizer on a sturdy surface (two to three feet from their head) and aim it so the ions flow in their direction. To maximize the flow of negative ions, it should sit at least two feet from a wall and at least three feet off the floor, as walls pull the negative ions away.

Clients should also keep the ionizer as far away from electronic devices as possible, even if they are turned off. That includes computers, smartphones, clocks, radio, lights, and TVs. At least six feet is a good distance. Electronic devices pull the ions away from the human body, even if the device is in our hands. LED screens can also be damaged if they are too close to an ionizer for too long.

"Over time, a gray film may develop on objects around the ionizer. This is from the build up of small pollutants that fall from the air when "zapped" by the ions. This film can be wiped off with any cleaning solution.

It is normal for static electricity to build up while the device is running. To prevent shocks, clients should avoid touching the ionizer directly unless it's off. They can turn it off by unplugging it, or by pressing the off button with a non-metal object, to further avoid shocks.

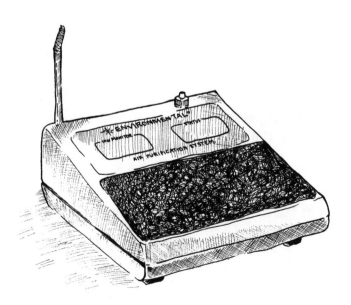

Wein VI-2500 Air Ionizer®

5

Daytime

The morning routine aims to wake up the brain, and the goal in the evening is to prepare for rest. That leaves about 12 hours left in the day. How should clients spend that time? What activities will ward off depression and, for those on the bipolar spectrum, stabilize mood?

While the answer is different for every client, there are some general principles to guide the way. In this chapter, we'll look at those principles, taking cues from a therapy that works well in depression – behavioral activation – and another that stabilizes mood in bipolar disorder – social rhythm therapy.

The first part of the chapter focuses on the *type* of activities that clients engage in, with particular attention to those associated with avoidance and its opposite, approach. The second part of the chapter focuses on the *timing* of these activities, particularly those that help set the biological clock.

Antidepressant Calendar

When working with a client who is depressed, it's important to understand how they spend their day. Though that sounds straightforward, it rarely is. Guilt, shame, and avoidance cloud these discussions, which often leave you with no more than a vague sense of what's going on. That's where the antidepressant calendar comes in.

The goal here is to get down to specifics. The calendar asks clients to record their daily activities in half-hour chunks. They begin by simply noticing what they are doing throughout the day, without making any changes to their behavior. As they become more aware of how they spend their time, they start to see that they are making choices each moment of the day and that these choices, in turn, affect their mood. The following sections discuss the different steps involved in this technique.

Step 1: Just Look at What's Happening

How do you motivate someone with depression to keep a calendar? At the beginning, don't suggest that you'd like to see any improvement. That's too intimidating. Instead, tell the client that the daily calendar is intended to help you understand the extent of their depression. Give them permission to lay it all out, warts and all.

If the client returns the calendar with a lot of blank space and says, "I did nothing all day," help them understand that depression can make people *feel* like they're doing nothing, but that feeling is not necessarily true. For example, did they sit and ruminate? Lay in bed? Think about the future? The past? All of these behaviors, which may seem like "nothing," actually involve doing *something*.

Step 2: Identify Approach and Avoidance Behaviors

As you read through the calendar, ask the client how each activity affected their mood. Try to understand whether the activity was an example of approach or avoidance. Avoidance can feel better in the short term but has long-term costs. While clients can usually identify the short-term gains of staying in bed with a bowl of ice cream, they may not be in touch with the costs. Ask questions to reveal those costs, which might include missed opportunities, social isolation, and unfinished tasks.

Although avoidance brings immediate relief, tolerance soon develops to that benefit. When this occurs, it leads clients to turn up the knob on avoidance. For example, people with agoraphobia begin by avoiding large stores and busy roads, and then avoid leaving the house altogether. Initially, this avoidance causes their panic to go down, but when it returns, they may avoid leaving their bedroom. Soon the panic is just as bad in their bedroom as it was at Walmart, but this doesn't motivate them to give up the strategy. At this point, the avoidance has become habitual, even though the rewards that first entrained it are no longer present. We see similar patterns in addictions that persist long after the pleasures they provided are gone. These are difficult cases. A turning point often comes when the client realizes that avoidance is no longer working like it used to and is actually making them more anxious in the big scheme of things.

It is important to note that there is nothing inherently wrong with avoidance. It is a strategy that has its pros and cons. Therefore, the goal is not to eliminate it entirely, but to help the client become more aware and purposeful in how they use it. Sometimes, avoidance is the best move, such as when more time is needed to make a decision.

Step 3: Time for Change

As clients get acclimated to the antidepressant calendar, the goal is to have them gradually increase approach behaviors – the ones that move them closer to action – and reduce the avoidant ones. To do this, the therapist should ask clarifying questions that help them make connections between their approach behaviors and their mood. How did the client feel before, during, and after these approach behaviors? How did they expect the activity to turn out? What was the actual outcome? Did they anticipate it with anxiety, and was it as difficult as they expected?

The aim is to shift the client's perspective from the immediate, emotional effects of the activity toward the longer-term gains. Depression makes people more sensitive to anxiety and less sensitive to pleasure and reward. That makes this work difficult. Talking about how good it would feel to go out for a swim may fall on deaf ears. The client is probably more in touch with the anxiety they would have as they drove to the pool. Therefore, the goal of this technique is not to convince clients that approach activities feel good. Rather, it's to get them to try out new experiences so they can judge these activities for themselves based on *real-world* outcomes, rather than the imagined outcomes in their head.

Step 4: Schedule Antidepressant Activities

Finally, have clients keep a list of activities that improve their life, lift their mood, or are pursued in the mode of approach rather than avoidance. Then, ask the client to start scheduling these activities in advance. Some activities have particular antidepressant effects. Qualities to look for include:

1. **Absorption.** Absorbing activities provide relatively quick rewards, as they tend to pull clients out of their depressive thoughts. Mindfulness achieves similar ends, but it can be difficult to learn during depression. In contrast, absorbing activities offer a quick path to a mindful state.

2. **Values-based actions.** Actions that are in line with the client's values have long-term benefits in depression. Anxiety, inertia, and all the things that get in the way of action are easier to tolerate when the action serves a greater purpose. These values need not be grand and are often close to home, such as family and pets. Values help clients get out of their head, so look for ones that transcend the self. Values-based action is important because it's sustainable. Pleasurable pursuits are quickly given up when they lose their thrill, but meaningful activity is maintained long after the thrill is gone.

3. **Self-transcendence.** As you talk with clients about what is good for them and what makes them feel better, you may run into an invisible wall. Depression makes people feel worthless, like they don't deserve to feel better. It's a little masochistic. This is where values-based actions are particularly helpful. Rather than done for the self, they are done for a greater good. Again, these values don't have to be grand. If asking a client how they felt after they took their dog for a walk gets you nowhere, ask if it was good for the dog.

4. **Strengths-based actions.** Another area to look for is activities that draw on the client's strengths. These are often innately rewarding. The "24 Character Strength Survey" is useful here.

5. **Activities that challenge depressive thoughts.** CBT uses many techniques to change depressive thinking, and one of the most effective is testing those beliefs out in the real world. Someone who believes they will fail at everything will find that this belief is challenged when they successfully organize their closet. It takes some careful questioning to help clients see the disconnect between their thoughts and the reality of their lives. Depressive thoughts are often detached from the real world, floating in a cloud of abstractions and globalizations. The goal is to bring them down to earth, into the nitty-gritty details, where they can be challenged in the real world.

Client Handout

Antidepressant Calendar

"Nothing." That's how people with depression usually answer when asked what they do all day. But is it really possible to do nothing? Probably not. Depression makes people *feel* like they're doing nothing, but that feeling may not be as true as it seems. Even surfing the internet is doing something. So is lying in bed. Depression can also convince people that they have no power to make decisions – that things just happen to them and they play no role in the events of their lives. Sound familiar?

This exercise will help you notice what you're doing throughout the day. From that knowledge, we'll work to understand how those actions affect you and build a lifestyle that will lessen depression. But that's getting ahead of things. For now, start off the first week by just *noticing* how you spend your time – without changing anything.

Week 1: Look at what's happening

For the first week, record how you actually spend your time each day. You can use the daily calendar provided on page 102, which is broken into half-hour chunks. The goal is to leave no blanks or "nothings." Thinking is an activity, so if you are lying in bed and worrying, write "in bed worrying."

Week 2: Look for antidepressant action

During the second week, think about the main reason behind the things you do. Common ones are:

1. "I enjoy it."

2. "It's a responsibility I have to take care of."

3. "It's a step toward something better in my future."

4. "It's part of my beliefs and values."

5. "I was avoiding uncomfortable feelings or a difficult situation."

The first four reasons are called *approach* because you're moving toward something, while the last one, #5, is called *avoidance*. Depressed days are often filled with avoidance, but approach is an antidepressant. Use a colored marker to highlight the half-hour blocks where you were in approach mode. If you can't figure out the reason, or it's a mix of approach and avoidance, we'll talk more about it in session.

Week 3: What's the outcome?

During the third week, continue to record your activities and the reasons that drive them. In addition, make a rough guess of how each activity influenced your mood or your life using the following coding system:

+: Improved my life or mood

–: Worsened my life or mood

+/–: Mixed results – it did some good, some harm

?: Unsure

It's okay if there are a lot of activities marked as "unsure." Depression can make everything feel the same, both the positive and the negative. If that's the case, think about how the activity affects your life rather than how it makes you feel. Talking to your child's teacher about their school problems probably won't lift your mood, but confronting it instead of avoiding it is likely to improve your life. Give that one a "+".

Weeks 2–4: Advanced planning

By now you should have a list of activities that improve your life, lift your mood, or are pursued with approach rather than avoidance. The section on "Antidepressant Activities" (p. 123) will help you add to that list and give you a few things to sample. Now it's time to start planning them.

For the upcoming week, add a few activities from that list to your calendar. Start slow, and add just enough activities so you can complete them without getting overwhelmed. If you can't keep up, add less. If you're checking off your list with ease, add more.

The calendar will also help you tackle complex tasks that you've been avoiding. First, break the task down into smaller steps. Then, add those steps in one at a time. For example, let's say you have been putting off getting the sink repaired. First, schedule a time to research and find a list of plumbers. Then, schedule a time to call the plumbers and find out who can do the job for the right price. Finally, schedule a time for them to come and fix it.

Troubleshooting

"It's too much to do."

Most people don't complete the whole calendar. That's okay. You can still make progress if you do it half-way.

"I can't think of anything to schedule."

In the beginning, it's good to choose random things to schedule as you experiment and find out what works for you. The section on "Antidepressant Activities" will give you some ideas.

Daily Calendar

DATE:	Activity	Avoidance or Approach?	Outcome (+,-,+/-,?)
7:00 a.m.			
7:30 a.m.			
8:00 a.m.			
8:30 a.m.			
9:00 a.m.			
9:30 a.m.			
10:00 a.m.			
10:30 a.m.			
11:00 a.m.			
11:30 a.m.			
12:00 p.m.			
12:30 p.m.			
1:00 p.m.			
1:30 p.m.			
2:00 p.m.			
2:30 p.m.			
3:00 p.m.			
3:30 p.m.			
4:00 p.m.			
4:30 p.m.			
5:00 p.m.			
5:30 p.m.			
6:00 p.m.			
6:30 p.m.			
7:00 p.m.			
7:30 p.m.			
8:00 p.m.			
8:30 p.m.			
9:00 p.m.			
9:30 p.m.			
10:00 p.m.			
10:30 p.m.			
11:00 p.m.			
11:30 p.m.			
12:00 a.m.			

Opposite Action

All of the symptoms of mood disorders are also part of everyday life. Who hasn't experienced anger, fatigue, or impulse shopping? The question is: When do these symptoms become a disorder? The answer depends on whether it naturally goes away on its own. In normal life, there are mechanisms in place to self-correct these symptoms so they don't get out of hand. That is, they are *self-resolving*. When it's part of a mood disorder, the symptom creates a self-perpetuating cycle. That's part of the reason that the *DSM-5* requires seemingly arbitrary durations to diagnose an episode: Two weeks for depression, one week for mania, and four days for hypomania. The intent is to avoid pathologizing symptoms that might be part of the normal ebb and flow of life. However, after a certain point, it becomes less likely that symptoms will resolve on their own and more likely that intervention is necessary. Consider the following examples of self-resolving vs. self-perpetuating depression:

1. **Self-resolving depression**

    Nate was turned down for a promotion on Friday and came home feeling pretty down. He retreated to his room and hid under the covers. The next day he overslept, didn't eat much, and generally avoided people. After a few days of this behavior, he started to feel a little stir crazy and called a friend. They went out for an enjoyable night, and Nate returned with a new perspective on his problems. The next day he felt like his usual self again.

2. **Self-perpetuating depression**

    Nate was turned down for a promotion on Friday and came home feeling pretty down. He retreated to his room like he did in the previous story, but this time something was different. After a few days of hiding away, his mood sank even lower than before. The thought of facing the world was now unbearable. He stopped returning phone calls and then felt guilty for not returning them, which made him avoid human contact even more. If this pattern of avoidance continued for at least two weeks, then we would say that Nate is clinically depressed, and he may need outside help to break the cycle.

A different kind of self-perpetuating cycle fuels hypo/mania, and this one tends to spiral out of control over a few days instead of few weeks. While avoidance is a common fuel for the vicious cycle of depression, in hypo/mania, it's lack of sleep that usually perpetuates the problem, as these two examples illustrate:

1. **Self-resolving hypo/mania**

    Nate came home excited after getting a promotion at work. He went out to celebrate and then stayed up late browsing online for fishing gear. He got little sleep and felt restless and wired the next day. That evening, he got online again to purchase the gear, but decided to sleep on it first. He turned on calming music, kept the lights dimmed, and went to bed. The next day he talked with his wife about their finances, and after she reminded him of the high interest loan they needed to pay off, he decided it was best to leave the gear in his wish list.

2. **Self-perpetuating hypo/mania**

    Nate came home excited after getting a promotion at work. He went out to celebrate and then stayed up all night browsing online for fishing gear. With little sleep, he felt restless and wired the next day. He organized his garage and stayed up even later, this time buying the gear. After a few days of this behavior, he was agitated, argumentative, and sleeping little. When the gear arrived, his wife complained, but he couldn't pause to understand her point of view. They had a blow-out fight.

Breaking the Cycle

You can help clients prevent these vicious cycles by intervening early with *opposite action*. This technique involves doing the opposite of what our emotions are telling us to do. For depression, the opposite action might be to confront difficult situations and take direct action, rather than avoid them. For hypo/mania, opposite action might mean slowing down and getting rest instead of burning the midnight oil. Use the following worksheet with your clients to help them prevent mood episodes through opposite action.

Breaking the Cycle Through Opposite Action

Mood episodes start with small symptoms that spiral out of control. One way to keep them from spiraling into a vicious cycle is to do the opposite of what your emotions are telling you to do. For example, depression drives people to give up, withdraw, and avoid action, while hypo/mania makes people stay up late, argue excessively, and act on impulse. Those behaviors, in turn, add fuel to the fire. The solution: to act the opposite of your mood.

Think about a recent time when you experienced early warning signs of a mood episode. What actions would have worsened the problem? Was there an opposite action that might have reversed it? Use the chart below to describe the situation, your mood, and an opposite action that might have turned things around. A couple of examples have been provided to get you started.

Situation	Discovered that a friend was spreading gossip about me
My mood or emotions	Rejected, hopeless, down
Actions my mood was driving me toward	Withdraw to the bedroom and stew over what people think about me
Opposite action	Go out with a friend to talk the problem over

Situation	Went on a date with someone I really like
My mood or emotions	Excitement, anticipation, can't wait to learn more about her
Actions my mood was driving me toward	Stay up late, read through her social media posts, call friends to share
Opposite action	Dim the lights, stretch, drink Chamomile tea and go the bed

Situation	
My mood or emotions	
Actions my mood was driving me toward	
Opposite action	

Avoidance

Avoidance is a driving force in the vicious cycle of depression. That cycle usually plays out in the following manner:

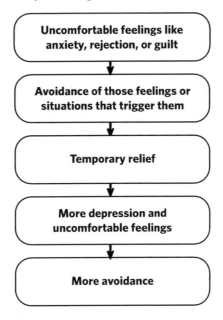

How do you tell if a client is avoiding? For example, consider a client who complains a lot. Are they doing it to avoid taking responsibility for their problems, or are they asserting their needs in a healthy way? **It's the reason behind the behavior, not the behavior itself, that marks avoidance.** Avoidant actions are done to ward off unwanted feelings or situations. They move people away from something, rather than toward it.

In the previous section on Opposite Action, we looked at how the cycle of avoidance played out for Nate when he was turned down for a promotion. Now let's look at how to break out of the avoidance cycle. Paradoxically, the first step is to accept the problem.

1. **Accept avoidance.** Avoidance can be a good thing. We all avoid, and sometimes it's the wisest option, such as when more time is needed to make a decision or to let our nerves cool down. Other times, it's a guilty pleasure. Either way, the point is for clients to be kind to themselves and to let go of any guilt around avoidance. The goal is not to get rid of avoidance, but to reduce its frequency. Avoidance is easier to recognize once someone has accepted it. Then it's not such a big deal, which helps with step two.

2. **Recognize avoidance.** Once someone has accepted their avoidant behaviors, they can start to recognize when they're engaging in avoidance and figure out whether it's serving a useful purpose.

As you do this work, keep in mind that clients are not likely to be spontaneous or direct about their avoidance. Look for vague generalities, like "I just want to get away from all the tension." Encourage them to be more specific. What is the tension? Who is it with? When does it happen? When did it start? What does the client do, say, or think to get away from it? Vague, intellectualized, and abstract thinking can be a form of avoidance, in which case getting into the gritty details is the opposite action. The details can be painful and bring up feelings of shame, but they are also the tools of effective problem solving. They give you and your client something concrete to work with.

The following two worksheets are intended to help clients recognize their avoidant behaviors, including whether they are helpful or unhelpful. The **Recognizing Avoidance** worksheet contains a sample list of actions that are often, but not always, motivated by avoidance. The **Avoidance Scavenger Hunt** worksheet asks clients to keep a running list of all the ways that they avoid.

Recognizing Avoidance

Avoidance is what people do to get away from something, whether it's an uncomfortable feeling or a difficult situation. Avoidance can either be helpful or unhelpful, depending on the purpose it serves and the outcome it leads to. For example, avoidance can work well for a short-term problem, where avoiding the issue gives you time to develop a solution. In contrast, if a problem has been going on for a long time, and avoidance just perpetuates it further, then it's probably not the helpful kind.

Use the checklist to identify the types of avoidant behaviors you have engaged in. Then, answer the questions at the end of this worksheet to see how avoidance has impacted you, both the helpful and the unhelpful kind.

Common Forms of Avoidance

Check the examples of avoidance that you often engage in:

☐ Staying in bed

☐ Staying at home

☐ Avoiding conflict, confrontation, or self-assertion with people

☐ Worrying, obsessing, or stewing over problems

☐ Not taking on new challenges or risks

☐ Avoiding situations that require you to take on responsibility

☐ Withdrawing from people

☐ Hiding your true thoughts or feelings from others

☐ Avoiding situations where you might feel evaluated or judged (e.g., sports, music, exams, job interviews)

☐ Worrying, over-analyzing, or daydreaming as a distraction from problems that you really need to face

☐ Seeking reassurance from other people to avoid feeling uncertain

☐ Putting off difficult decisions

☐ Thinking about things you need to do instead of doing them

☐ Complaining about problems in ways that don't lead to solutions

☐ Using food, drugs, alcohol, or sedatives to numb emotions

☐ Suppressing emotions or trying to keep from thinking about painful subjects

☐ Avoiding activities that you used to enjoy

☐ _____

☐ _____

☐ _____

☐ _____

When Avoidance Serves a Purpose

Here are a few examples where avoidance is helpful. Check any that you have recently engaged in:

- ☐ **Emotional avoidance** (e.g., suppressing emotions so you can focus better on a classroom lecture or work project)

- ☐ **Delay** (e.g., putting off a decision because you need more time)

- ☐ **Avoiding independence** (e.g., looking to others for reassurance when you are uncertain or need to connect with them for support)

- ☐ **Avoiding conflict** (e.g., withdrawing from an argument so you can cool down and revisit the issue more thoughtfully)

Think about a time when avoidance worked for you. Describe it with as much specific detail as possible.

_____

_____

_____

_____

_____

Now, describe a time when avoidance made things worse, using specific details. Even though it didn't work, did the avoidance provide any short-term emotional relief?

_____

_____

_____

_____

_____

_____

What made these two situations different?

_____

_____

_____

_____

_____

What are you worried will happen if you reduce avoidance? Are there emotions or problems that will come up? List as many as you can. For example, this can include anxiety, embarrassment, rejection, conflict, failure, or loss.

_____

_____

_____

_____

_____

Avoidance Scavenger Hunt

Over the next week, jot down specific times when you intentionally used avoidance. For each example, record what you did and how it turned out. An example has been provided below to get you started.

Date	What did you avoid?	What did you do instead?	Did it work?
Ex. 2/20	Managing bills	Distracted myself by organizing the apps on my phone	No

Approach

Avoidance is a hard habit to break. It is rewarding because it quickly reduces anxiety and creates a feeling of safety, even if that feeling is only an illusion. The best way to stop a habit is to replace it with something else. In this section, we'll look at ways to help your clients replace avoidance with its opposite: *approach*.

According to psychologist Edward Watkins, approach refers to "trying to embrace life and what you can get out of it, rather than trying to get through it with as little pain as possible" (2016, pp. 316-17). Approach moves people toward experiences instead of away from them. Those experiences could be positive (such as planning a weekend hike) or negative (such as confronting a coworker who puts all of their work on others' plates). Although most of life's experiences are a mix of positive and negative, they *feel* more negative during depression. Those feelings take time to change. The way to get there is to help clients change their *actions* first. Feelings change later.

Shifting from avoidance to approach carries short-term costs, like anxiety, but it also brings long-term rewards, such as less depression and a better life. As you do this work, look for ways to help clients manage those short-term costs and appreciate the long-term gains. The following section contains several worksheets that you can use with clients to help them get out of the habit of avoidance and into the habit of approach.

Approach

What does it help?

Depression and anxiety.

How long does it take to work?

By taking on a few approach activities each day, clients should start to see improvement within one to two weeks, and greater changes after two to six weeks. Consistency is what matters. It's better to do a few small things each day than to tackle a big task every now and then.

The research

The approach strategy comes from *behavioral activation,* an effective therapy for depression. It is the "B" in cognitive behavioral therapy (CBT), but works as well as the full CBT program. In severe depression, behavioral activation outperforms CBT (Dimidjian et al., 2006).

How does it work?

Approach draws people toward experiences. These new experiences change the brain, causing nerve cells to sprout and grow more connections. Those connections improve communication between the brain's emotion center (the amygdala) and planning center (the frontal lobes). That translates to less depression and better stress management. Behavioral activation also changes the part of the brain involved in rumination: the default mode network. When this network quiets down, people pay more attention to positive events in the outside world and less attention to the negative thoughts and emotions that stir inside their head (Yokoyama et al., 2018).

Approach Action

Approach is the opposite of avoidance. It moves people toward action and new experiences instead of away from difficulty. The following chart contains a list of common approach actions. For each one, think about a time that you used this action and write an example of what you did in the second column. Use more recent examples when possible, and skip over any that don't apply to you. Finally, use the third column to describe the outcome of your approach action. Did it make things better, worse, a mix, no difference, or are you unsure?

Approach Action	What did you do?	Outcome
Taking direct action		
Asking other people for help or support		
Asserting your opinion		
Taking on risks or uncertainty		
Trying something new to see how it goes		
Making a decision		
Taking on a new responsibility		
Expressing your feelings to other people		
Socializing		
Planning an activity		
Putting a solution into place		
Learning a new skill		
Allowing yourself to experience feelings		
Remembering a difficult or painful event in full detail		
Speaking clearly with eye contact		
Other:		
Other:		
Other:		

Approach Scavenger Hunt

Over the next week, look for times when you were tempted to avoid but instead went for the approach. Take note of these examples throughout the day, and at the end of the day, write one of them down. Choose the action that you're most proud of, that turned out the best, or that was the most challenging. We'll talk about them at your next session.

Date	What were you tempted to avoid?	What did you do?	Did it work?
Ex. 2/20	Managing bills	Organized them into low, medium, and high priority	Yes

Avoidance Makeover

Do you have a list of things you've been avoiding? Whether you've been collecting them through the "Avoidance Scavenger Hunt" worksheet or just storing them up in your head, this exercise will help you make that list more manageable. Start with one item. Choose one that you're really motivated to overcome, or just choose one that's easy to tackle, and write it below.

_____

_____

What's the main reason you've been avoiding this task? Match that with one of the reasons in the following chart, and try out the solution to the right of that reason. Do you have lots of reasons to avoid it? That's great – then it will match with many solutions, and you can use them all.

Reason to avoid	Solution
It's overwhelming	
I don't know where to start	1. Break it down into smaller steps
It's too complicated	
I don't know how to manage it	
I'm no good at it	2. Practice and prepare
I've never done it before	
I'm afraid I'll mess up	
What if I'm embarrassed or look bad?	
I'm worried it won't turn out well	3. Focus on the process, not the outcome
It makes me too nervous	
It's too difficult	
I don't have it in me	4. Imagine how you'll feel when it's behind you
It's probably not worth the effort	

Now let's look at those four solutions in more detail.

1. Break it down into smaller steps

Some tasks are so overwhelming that you don't know where to begin. If that is why you've been avoiding it, bring it into session and we'll break it down into smaller, manageable steps.

_____

_____

_____

_____

_____

2. Practice and prepare

Perhaps you are avoiding because you're out of practice or unprepared for the task. For example, job interviews are difficult for anyone, and most of us don't have much experience with them. You can better prepare by anticipating the questions that may be asked (an internet search helps here) and practicing your answers with a friend or in front of a mirror.

Are there specific ways you could prepare for the task? If the answer is "yes," then put the item on the back burner and focus on practice and preparation until you feel ready to take it on.

_____

_____

_____

_____

_____

3. Focus on the process, not the outcome

Are you avoiding something because you're worried about how it will turn out? In that case, the solution is to focus on the *process* of doing it rather than the outcome. This means accepting the possibility that it won't go well. "It's not whether you win or lose, it's how you play the game" or, for the creatively inclined, "It's art for art's sake."

Thoughts like "Am I good enough?... Am I doing it right?... Am I succeeding?" can distract you from actually doing it. Take socializing, for example. It's hard to hold a conversation when you're thinking about how you're coming across. Few outcomes are fully within our control, and being liked is not one of them. Social mingling is full of dead-ends, but if you focus instead on the process of making small talk, then you'll enjoy it more and eventually find the good friends you seek.

Is the task you've been avoiding one that would be easier if you focused on the process? Does anxiety get in the way of doing it? What specifically are you afraid will happen? Is it really as bad as it seems? How realistic or likely is it to happen? Write your answers here.

_____

_____

_____

_____

_____

Now, imagine doing the task for its own sake. What would that look like?

_____

_____

_____

_____

_____

4. Imagine how you'll feel when it's behind you

Does lack of motivation keep you from taking it on? Do you dread the negative feelings you'll have when you first start doing it? Instead, imagine how you'll feel when it's done. How will life be different? What opportunities will it open up? Will it clear up some mental space that you've been using up with worry and guilt over the procrastination?

_____

_____

_____

_____

_____

On the other hand, perhaps you're avoiding it for a good reason. Perhaps this isn't the right time, and life would be worse if you tried to tackle it now. If you think this task is better left undone, write down your rationale here.

_____

_____

_____

_____

_____

Putting it into Action

Have you found a task that you're ready to take on? Use these final two steps to make it happen:

1. Schedule it on your calendar at a specific time and place.

2. Whether it's an ongoing task, like cleaning the kitchen, or a complex one, like building a social life, make it a routine. Set aside a regular time and place to do it each day.

Turning Avoidance into Approach: Troubleshooting

Avoidance is hard to change. If you have thoughts that get in the way of that change, write them down and bring them to your next session. Some common examples that get in the way are listed below.

"I'm avoiding because there's nothing I can do about it."

If there's really nothing to be done, then you may be using healthy avoidance. Trying to fix an unsolvable problem only causes stress and frustration. Instead, work on something else while you put the issue on hold. What if there's nothing else to work on? Try the steps in "Crisis Survival" on page 120.

"I avoid things I can't tolerate. I panic and can't do it."

Make a list of all the feelings that get in the way of doing it. Then, look through the list and circle any feelings that you still have *even when you're avoiding the task*. How well is avoidance working to keep those negative feelings away? Bring the list to your next session and we'll look for other ways to manage those intense emotions. Meanwhile, try approaching something that's easier to tackle.

"It's not worth it to change."

How has avoidance affected your life and your relationships? How does it affect your self-worth? How much time and mental energy does it suck up? Write your answers down and bring them to your next session.

Surviving a Crisis

Crisis survival is one of the dialectical behavioral therapy skills that often comes in handy when working with clients who have mood disorders. Rates of trauma are two to three times higher among people with bipolar disorder than they are in the general population, and major crises are both a cause and a consequence of depression (Neria et al., 2008).

A crisis is a major stress that can't be readily fixed or easily ignored. The first response to a crisis is to try to solve it. *Crisis mode* is an active, energized state that is the opposite of depression. However, if the crisis goes on too long and solutions can't be found, a depressive state sets in.

Behaviorists call this state "learned helplessness" or a "defeat scenario." It happens when someone is faced with a constant stress, such as chronic pain, unemployment, or caretaking for a parent with dementia. Like first responders at an accident, the ruminative mind gears up to solve the problem, but it can't. Undeterred, it presses on, until exhaustion, depression, and a global sense of helplessness sets in.

The result is a new state of mind, entirely different from the motivated, energized state that sought solutions. This mind can no longer see possibilities, even if they were to arise. This is grimly illustrated by the animal model of learned helplessness where a mouse is randomly shocked while trapped in a cage. Unable to escape, it eventually gives up and hunkers down on the floor. Later, the walls of the cage are removed, but the mouse, now in a state of depression, doesn't even try to get out.

The lesson here is that repeated failure is a set up for depression. When a solution can't be found, it's time to change the game.

Step 1: Look for Solutions

When clients present with a major stressor, the first step is to figure out which aspects can be resolved and which cannot. This isn't easy work with a client who is depressed. They will have trouble seeing where the walls in their cage have cracks and may feel invalidated or even threatened by too much optimism.

Crises create a style of thinking that is narrow, reactive, and inflexible. That is great for dodging bullets, but not for solving problems. Ask your client questions that help broaden their perspective and analyze the concrete details of the crisis. This will help them shift toward the problem-solving style of thinking described in this table:

Crisis Style	Problem-Solving Style
Narrow, tunnel vision	Broad, views the problem from multiple angles
Reactive	Weighs options before acting
Vague, abstract, over-generalizing	Like a good reporter, gathers facts and specifics
"All over the place," distracted by "putting out fires"	Sees the problem as a story, with cause and effect laid out along a linear timeline
Catastrophizing	Grounded in the present moment, while aware of future possibilities both good and bad
Rigid	Flexible

Step 2: Accept Your Emotions

Emotions flare during a crisis, and it does little good to try to change them. Instead, encourage the client to adopt a mindful, accepting approach to them. If that doesn't work, move quickly to the distraction skills of Step 3. Mindfulness is difficult during times of crisis.

Step 3: Improve the Moment

What if the mouse in that cage had a companion to support it? An exercise wheel to run on? Or a box of fine cheese? Look for ways that clients can improve the moment as they go through a crisis. This takes some creativity. I always keep the example of Jim Quillen's time in solitary confinement in my mind (below). Otherwise, clients will quickly convince me that nothing can be done.

---

19 Days in The Hole

Former Alcatraz inmate Jim Quillen spent 19 days in solitary confinement, locked in a pitch-dark, sound-proof cell. To survive this torture he invented a game that kept his mind focused on a solvable problem:

"Since total silence and darkness were to be my constant companions for 24 hours of each day of solitary confinement, it was imperative to find a way to keep my mind occupied. I invented a game simply to retain my sanity. I would tear a button from my coveralls, then fling it into the air, turn around in circles several times, and, with my eyes closed, get on the floor on my hands and knees and search for the button. When it was found, I would repeat the routine, over and over until I was exhausted, or my knees were so sore I could not continue" (Quiellen, 2015).

Step 4: Don't Make it Worse

By definition, there's no way to directly fix a crisis, but what can your client do to keep it from getting worse? Usually, this means keeping up the regular habits of sleep, exercise, and diet that are the backbone of this book. It also means avoidance – healthy avoidance – of intoxication, self-harm, heated arguments, and other destructive behaviors.

Together, these steps keep the client's focus on what they *can* do and away from the magnetic pull of what they can't. This preserves a sense of self-efficacy, which is a buffer against the depressing outcome of learned helplessness.

Crisis Survival

A crisis is a terrible situation without a ready solution. There are four basic steps to surviving a crisis:

Step 1. Look for solutions

You may not be able to fully fix the problem, but look for partial solutions.There may also be solutions in the future, but the wait is long, like an upcoming medical appointment to determine whether a new mass is cancerous. If there's truly nothing more you can do in the meanwhile, don't frustrate yourself by trying to fix what can't be fixed.

Step 2. Accept your emotions

Allow your emotions to come and go. Visualization can help. Picture your thoughts and emotions floating down a stream like leaves on the water. Some of those leaves are rotted and ugly, some look like they're on fire, and some look strangely beautiful. Rather than trying to stop the stream, allow it to flow, changing on its own. With this technique you can put a little space between you and your emotions, while still acknowledging their reality. It works better than trying to change them, getting caught up in them, or shutting them down entirely.

Step 3. Improve the moment

You may not be able to change your emotions, but you can improve the moment while you wait for solutions to come. Do something different, something that will distract you from the worry at hand. If you're indoors, try walking in a forest. Outside? Come in, light some candles, and cozy up in a blanket. Try out activities from the "ACCEPTS" worksheet (page 122) or the "Antidepressant Activities" section of this chapter (page 123). Most of them can be done whether you're in a crisis or not.

Step 4. Don't make it worse

When there's nothing you can do to improve a crisis, focus instead on how you can keep it from getting worse. Self-medicating, binge eating, sending angry emails, and letting go of the anchors that keep your mood stable are all examples of behaviors that make a crisis worse. The anchors that help stabilize mood are different for each person, but often include sleep, regular wake times, exercise, social supports, medication, and a healthy diet.

There are many possibilities to explore in those four steps. If something doesn't work for you, then move on to the next strategy. Keep a running list of strategies that work and those that make things worse (see **Sample Crisis Survival Guide**).

The goal here is not to solve the crisis or end the distress. Time fixes many problems that we can't fix ourselves, and it would be nice to be able to fast-forward to that better place. Short of that, improve the moments in that long wait, avoid the frustration of wrestling with problems that can't be solved, and stay away from things that make it worse.

Sample Crisis Survival Guide

Distracting Activities:

- Visit an animal shelter and spend time with dogs or cats

- Go for a walk

- Clean out some clutter

- Plan my next vacation

- Play *Words with Friends*®

- Shop for something inexpensive, and spend a long time looking for it

- Go to the movies

Soothing and Distracting Sensations:

- Go swimming

- Aromatherapy

- Stand on one foot

- Chew on a strong flavor, like ginger, mint, citrus, or pepper

What to Avoid:

- Breaking things

- Ranting on social media

- Staying in bed during the day

- Going to places where I'd be tempted to drink

ACCEPTS: Seven Strategies to Survive a Crisis

When you are stuck with troubles that you can't resolve, these seven steps will help preserve some peace of mind and mental sanity.

Activities. Engage in activities that are easy and engrossing (see "Antidepressant Activities" for ideas).

Contribute to others. Doing things for other people gets you out of your head.

Comparisons. Think of a time when things were worse, or of someone else whose problems are bigger.

Emotions. Change your surroundings to promote positive emotions. Play your favorite music, engage with nature, watch a comedy, cook your favorite meal, or reminisce over positive memories.

Passing by. If you can't get negative thoughts out of your head, visualize them passing by like leaves floating down a stream.

Thoughts. Find a simple, comforting thought and repeat it in your head, such as "This too shall pass," "Roll with it," "I will survive," or a spiritual text, poem, or song.

Sensations that soothe. Soothe your senses by taking a hot bath or shower, getting a massage, stretching, using aromatherapy, or savoring a piece of fruit.

Antidepressant Activities

The following section describes activities with inherent antidepressant qualities, including absorbing activities, exercise, brisk walking, contact with nature, and the mindful use of electronic media.

Absorbing Activity

Depression is not "all in your head," but depression can fill a person's head with painful stuff. Ruminative worries, self-criticism, scorn, dread, and doubt. It's hard to turn these thoughts off, but an absorbing activity can help clients get out of their head. These include activities like riding a bike or playing a game, where it's hard to think about anything else while doing them. The following list describes some other qualities that create absorption. Absorbing activities need not fit all these criteria; just one will do.

1. **Time flies.** When someone is absorbed in the moment, they lose their sense of time, no longer thinking about the future or the past. They don't watch the clock, wondering when it will be over.

2. **Lack of self-consciousness.** The person's focus is on other people, the outside world, or a greater cause, rather than on themselves. They are too absorbed to worry about their inner state, and if someone asks how they're feeling, they might not even know the answer.

3. **Challenging enough.** Absorbing activities give people a sense of competence about what they are doing. If there are obstacles, they can be overcome, and it's not filled with frustrations and failures. On the other hand, the activity is not so easy as to be boring.

4. **Sensory involvement.** Absorbing activities directly engage the senses: sight, sound, smell, movement, or touch. Examples of these activities include cooking, sports, music, knitting, and bird watching.

5. **Clear goals and instant feedback.** It's easier for people to keep focused when they know what they're aiming for and can see where they're going. In painting, every stroke changes the picture; when cleaning, every motion removes a little more dirt. Cooking, sports, web design, and playing musical instruments are other good examples. Tasks that feel directionless and uncertain are unlikely to hold a person's attention very long.

6. **Slightly addictive.** Absorbing activities are slightly addictive in that the more someone does the activity, the more they want to continue doing it. If their family calls them to dinner, they'll probably reply, "Just a minute, I'm in the middle of something," or they might not hear their family at all. If it's a book, it's a real page-turner. If it's a show, it's worthy of binge-watching.

7. **For the love of the game.** When someone engages in an absorbing activity, they enjoy it for its own sake, rather than the outcome. Even if the computer doesn't get fixed, they still liked tinkering with it. Shopping for garden supplies is a small pleasure even if they didn't find the seeds they were looking for. Activities that involve learning, creativity, and skill-building tend to fall into this category.

8. **A higher cause.** Absorbing activities serve a purpose that's greater than our own needs and desires. Whether someone volunteers at an animal shelter, plays games with their kids, or reads a religious or spiritual text, they do it because they value the cause, regardless of how it turns out.

Use the following two worksheets to help clients identify activities they find absorbing.

Absorbing Activities

When you are depressed, it's common for your mind to stir with rumination, worry, and self-doubt. The most effective way to pull yourself out of these depressive thoughts is to do something that fully occupies your mind. That is, to engage in **absorbing activities**. Although depression makes it hard to get absorbed, practice will help. What are things that you used to enjoy, were good at, or found engaging? Look back to times when you weren't depressed and think of activities that you found absorbing. The following list gives you some ideas to get you started.

- ☐ A lively conversation with a friend
- ☐ Playing sports, a board game, or a puzzle
- ☐ Comedy or entertainment
- ☐ Binge-watching a streaming series
- ☐ Researching, such as on the Internet
- ☐ Spiritual or religious activity
- ☐ Music or dance
- ☐ Engaging with pets or animals
- ☐ Gardening, hiking, or spending time near bodies of water
- ☐ Doing an art project, cooking, or knitting
- ☐ Riding a bike, exercise, or walking
- ☐ A warm bath
- ☐ Reading a book that's a page-turner
- ☐ Other:

_____

_____

_____

Antidepressant Activity

Some activities can worsen depression, while others help fight it. What makes the difference? Antidepressant activities tend to be absorbing, engaging, and share at least some of these qualities:

1. Time flies when you engage in the activity.

2. You are not focused on yourself while doing it but, rather, on the activity itself.

3. It is challenging enough to hold your attention, but not so challenging as to be overwhelming.

4. It directly engages your senses (e.g., sight, touch, smell, taste, and hearing).

5. It provides you with clear goals and quick feedback.

6. It is slightly addictive. The more you do it, the more you want to do it.

7. You enjoy the activity for its own sake, rather than the outcome.

8. It serves a purpose greater than your own needs and desires, such as volunteering.

Looking back at your answers from the "Absorbing Activities" worksheet, use the chart on the next page to write down all of the activities that you identified as absorbing. Then, check off which qualities these activities fulfilled for you. From that list, choose a few to plan on your calendar at a specific date and time. Good choices need not have all eight qualities; just one will usually suffice.

Antidepressant Activity Chart

Activity	Time flies	Lack of self-consciousness	Challenging enough	Sensory involvement	Clear goals, instant feedback	Slightly addictive	For the love of the game	A higher cause
Ex. Organizing my bookshelf	X		X	X	X			

Brisk Walking

Light exercise is one of the most effective things that people can do for depression, memory, and sleep. It heals the brain, strengthening the nerves in the mood center so they sprout new connections. After an hour of exercise, *brain-derived neurotrophic factor* (BDNF) pumps through the bloodstream, aiding in brain repair. After a few weeks, there is measurable growth in the mood and memory centers.

The dose of exercise needed to treat depression is so light that it may be more accurate to call it brisk walking. Typically, 30 minutes a day of brisk walking, or 45 minutes every other day, is sufficient. Brisk means slower than a jog, but faster than a walk. It should raise both heart rate (ideally by 10 beats per minute) and breathing rate. Those changes in the heart and lungs are *aerobic*, and other forms of aerobic exercise will work just as well as a brisk walk. Swimming, bicycling, basketball, and dancing are perfectly good alternatives.

When to Do It

Exercise can achieve many goals outside of treating depression, and the optimal time depends on the goal. To deepen sleep, clients should ideally exercise in the late afternoon. For those with bipolar disorder, it is preferable that they exercise at regular times each day because daily routines help stabilize mood. The 45-minute rule is not set in stone either. Clients can break it down into three 15-minute chunks. If you are trying to develop an exercise routine with a client who hasn't been very active lately, start with just 10 minutes a day and build from there.

Goal	Optimal time
Improve wakefulness in the morning	Just after waking
Deepen sleep	Late afternoon
Stabilize bipolar disorder	At the same time each day, give or take 15 minutes
Treat mania	Exercise can improve mania by strengthening the brain and deepening sleep. Try 15-20 minutes in the morning and again in late afternoon. Stick to a regular time and avoid overdoing it.
Starting a new exercise routine	When energy and motivation are optimal. Start with just 10 minutes a day and build from there.

How Well Does it Work?

Over 100 clinical studies have looked at the effects of exercise on mental health and brain functioning. In one study conducted at Duke Medical Center, people who recovered from depression through exercise did just as well as those who took the antidepressant sertraline (Zoloft) (Babyak et al., 2000). Given this, why not just take the Zoloft? The answer became clear when they followed up six months later. By that point, 40% of people on Zoloft had slipped back into depression, while only 8% of exercisers had relapsed. Both treatments got people well, but only exercise helped them stay well. Here are more facts that we know about the efficacy of exercise:

- Treats depression about as well as antidepressants
- Doubles the benefits of antidepressants
- Prevents depression better than antidepressants
- Treats depression when antidepressants have not worked
- Helps anxiety, panic, chronic fatigue, and smoking cessation
- Sharpens memory and concentration better than any mood medication

In addition, walking has so many medical benefits that *Scientific American* ranked it first among lifestyle factors that increase health and longevity. Here are just a few of its medical benefits:

- Prevents dementia
- Strengthens bones
- Slows aging and adds three to seven years to the lifespan
- Lowers the risk of stroke
- Improves heart and lung health
- Relieves arthritis and joint inflammation
- Builds muscles
- Promotes weight loss
- Deepens sleep quality
- Reduces pain by lowering endorphins
- Prevents cancer
- Lowers blood pressure, cholesterol, and lipids
- Prevents diabetes

Walking Off Depression

If your goal is to get better from depression, then walk, don't run. *Brisk walking* for about 30 minutes a day or 45 minutes every other day treats depression with an effect that's as strong as an antidepressant. It also prevents depression even better than medication, and it improves memory and sleep as well.

Brisk walking is more than a walk but less than a jog. Ideally, it raises your heart rate by at least 10 beats per minute and makes you breathe a little faster. In other words, it's aerobic. Perhaps you already have some aerobics built into your day, or tasks that could become aerobic with a little modification, like putting on some dance music while you sweep the floor. The following are some ideas about how to incorporate more aerobic movement into your routine.

Playful Aerobics

- Swim

- Hike in nature

- Put on audio books or music while you go for a walk

- Dance

- Join a kickball or softball league

- Turn business meetings into walking meetings

- Do jumping jacks

- Shoot hoops

- Roughhouse with your kids

- Roughhouse with your dog

- Go roller- or ice-skating

- Wash the car

- Try belly dancing

- Sign up for an adult gymnastics class

- Use a standing desk

- Park far away

- Play tag with your kids

- Go rowing

- Do your shopping and errands by foot

- Choose an active volunteer job, like Habitat for Humanity

- Explore a new area

- Jump rope or hula hoop

- Walk the dog, or someone else's dog, or volunteer at an animal shelter to walk a dog

- Join a martial arts class

- Do some aerobic cleaning (e.g., scrub, vacuum, sweep, mop, or rake)

- Bike to work

Indoor Motion

- Join a YMCA or gym with an indoor walking path

- Walk your favorite shopping mall (many malls sponsor walking groups)

- Stay in your living room with a guided indoor walking video (try www.walkathome.com or search for "happy walk" or "walk at home" on YouTube)

- Play active video games (e.g., Wii tennis, Wii fit, Just Dance)

- Place the treadmill in front of the TV or strap a tablet to your treadmill. You can only watch that show if you're on it.

What aerobic activities are you already doing each week? How much time do you spend on each of them?

_____

_____

_____

What are some areas where you could weave exercise into your day?

_____

_____

_____

If your current level of aerobics is close to zero, don't jump into 30 minutes a day. Instead, start with 10 minutes a day. That alone can make a difference. It's estimated that one in 10 cases of depression would be prevented by this minimal level of motion (Harvey et al., 2018). Once you've been able to stay consistent with 10 minutes a day for a week, move up to 20 minutes. After a week of success there, raise the dose to 30 minutes a day. Should you raise it further beyond that? Probably not. Only one in 12 people benefit from higher doses of aerobics. For the rest of us, it's overkill.

"I have to exercise in the morning before my brain figures out what I'm doing."

– Marsha Doble

A Walk in the Woods

Engaging with nature helps depression and calms the brain's worry circuits. In one study, a 90-minute walk in the woods reduced ruminative worry better than a similar stroll in the city. It also lowered activity in the *subgenual prefrontal cortex,* an area of the brain involved in worry, avoidance, and rumination (Bratman et al., 2015). That is no small feat. As we saw in Chapter 2, *depressive rumination* is a repetitive cycle of negative thoughts that's very hard to break.

Spending time in nature also improves concentration and decreases symptoms of ADHD. On the medical side, it is beneficial for diabetes, chronic pain, blood pressure, and the immune system. Some of these effects are measurable after only 20 minutes in the forest, and some continue for several weeks after leaving the woods. Walking beside bodies of water – oceans, rivers, or lakes – also works, as does walking with our four-legged friends. Whether tending a garden or petting an animal, contact with nature is good for the mind and body.

In Japan and Korea, forest therapy is even covered by insurance, where it's called *Shinrin-yoku,* or "forest bathing." This type of therapy is undertaken with a guide, who helps people engage with the sensory experience of the forest. They walk through it slowly, or just sit and observe, paying attention to the finest details. They touch, explore, and appreciate nature's surprises for sessions lasting one to four hours.

No one knows exactly how forest therapy works. Part of it is visual. Forest scenes alone have health benefits. After a surgery, people heal faster when their rooms overlook a forest than when their windows face an urban wall. The air may also have something to do with it. A humid forest is rich in negative air ions, which have benefits in depression. Ocean air and waterfalls are also good sources of these ions. Chemistry is another possibility. Plants emit antimicrobial compounds called phytoncides that improve natural immunity.

From gardening to agriculture, people who work the soil outdoors for at least seven hours a week have half the rate of depression as those who stay inside. Though cause-and-effect hasn't been fully parsed out in that research, we do know that the risk of depression goes down with more time spent in nature (Asai et al., 2018).

In order to connect with nature, clients can search online for public forests, rivers, nature trails, and lakes near them. They can also find local resources at www.traillink.com.

Guided Forest Therapy

Forest therapy is a growing field with its own standards and certifications. Professional guides can be found at www.natureandforesttherapy.org. The following resorts and spas also offer forest therapy, though this is usually a pricier option.

- Arizona: L'Auberge de Sedona (lauberge.com)
- California: Brewery Gulch Inn (brewerygulchinn.com), Gaige House (thegaigehouse.com), Ojai Valley Inn (ojaivalleyinn.com)
- Canada: Ruby Lake Resort (rubylakeresort.com), Trout Point Lodge (troutpoint.com)
- Connecticut: Mayflower Grace (gracehotels.com/mayflower)
- Missouri: Big Cedar Lodge (bigcedar.com)
- New York: Mohonk Mountain House (mohonk.com), Shimmering Light (shimmeringlight.info)
- North Carolina: Skyterra Wellness Retreat (skyterrawellness.com)
- Oregon: Salishan Resort (salishan.com)
- Pennsylvania: The Lodge at Woodloch (thelodgeatwoodloch.com)
- Tennessee: Blackberry Farm (blackberryfarm.com)
- Vermont: Stowe Mountain Lodge (destinationhotels.com/stowe-mountain-lodge)
- Virginia: Earthwalk Ways (earthwalkways.com)

Bringing the Forest Indoors

Indoor plants also improve health and concentration, though not as much as the forest. Wood decor also helps, when the ratio is right. Stress levels go down when walls are covered with 30-40% wood, but too much wood has the opposite effect. That ideal balance resembles the density of wood in a typical forest. Pictures or murals of the woods can achieve these visual benefits as well. Air ionizers and salt lamps mimic some of the qualities of forest air (see "Antidepressant Air Ions" in Chapter 4).

A Tale of Two Transports

Walking in the woods may improve depression, but a different mode of travel can make it worse: the automobile. The risk of depression starts to rise when the commute to work takes longer than 30 minutes one-way. There's a world of difference between the path and the parkway. Here are some of these differences:

	Walking in the Woods	**Driving to Work**
Motion	Walking.	Sedentary.
Threat level	Low. Unless it's an unsafe area, the forest is relatively free of things that trigger worry or threat.	High. Life-threatening accidents, aggressive drivers, and job-risking delays are common.
Mental space	Captivated by nature's ever-changing features, as well as the need to balance our feet on the shifting terrain.	Hours of boredom punctuated by moments of terror. Most sights fly by too quickly to capture attention in a mindful way, but occasional life-or-death matters raise our alertness.
Control	We control our movement and pace.	Traffic patterns set the pace.
Timing	Usually there's no rush to be somewhere.	Time is a pressure cooker.
Social	If strangers pass by, they're generally friendly and greet us face to face.	Eye contact and greetings are rare. Rude cut-offs and tailgaters are the norm.
Surroundings	Nature.	Concrete, steel, and billboards.
Sunlight	Overhead.	Indirect, unless you're in a convertible.
Air	Rich in antidepressant air ions and healthy phytoncides.	Full of unhealthy emissions or, if the vents are closed, air-conditioning units that deplete air ions.

In order to help clients integrate more "path" and less "parkway" into their daily routine, ask them if there are ways they can make their work commute more like a walk in the forest. People who walk, bike, or take the train to work have lower levels of commuting stress than those who drive or take the bus or subway (St-Louis et al., 2014). If they can't change their mode of travel, clients can consider taking scenic routes, leaving early so they're not rushed, avoiding traffic, using an aromatherapy car diffuser, stretching, getting absorbed in music or audio books, opening the sunroof, and slowing down to let a stranger merge, with a smile and a wave.

Mindful Media

Social media, podcasts, Netflix binges, newsfeeds, and cable TV are common ways to escape depression, but do these outlets make things worse in the long term? Yes and no. People definitely use more electronic media when they're depressed, and whether those diversions help or harm depends on how they're used. Here are some ways to make these devices less depressing.

1. **Limit screen time.** Electronic media can be a time warp. If there's little time left over for relationships, work, exercise, creative pursuits, and outdoor activity, it's a problem. Like all simple pleasures, screen time is best in moderation.

2. **Use it as a reward.** Clients can use media as a reward for times when they take action, complete a tedious task, or engage in the many forms of *approach* discussed earlier ("Approach Action" worksheet, page 111).

3. **Watch with intention.** Depression feeds on passivity, and TV is a relatively passive experience. To shake that up, clients can actively search out the programs they want to watch and schedule them on their calendar.

4. **Get absorbed.** Just like a good book, a good TV program is one that fully absorbs our attention. We forget about ourselves for a while and get caught up in the characters. Movies have always had this appeal, but TV rarely did until the advent of high-quality series on ad-free networks, like HBO, Showtime, Netflix, and Amazon. While earlier shows were written to make sure people hung on through the advertising breaks, these shows are designed to get people fully absorbed, providing needed rest from depressive rumination. However, there could be too much of a good thing. Binge watching is associated with anxiety and depression (Sung et al., 2015).

5. **Move around and laugh a little.** Electronics are a stationary pursuit, which is another reason they can increase depression. Have clients try stretching while they watch TV or put their tablet on a treadmill. Comedy can also help. Stress hormones fall when people laugh, improving mood and sleep. It even burns calories (10-15 minutes of laughter = 50 calories).

Depending on how it's used, electronic media can also be depressogenic. The following are some qualities of electronic media that have been linked to depression.

1. **Social comparisons.** The brain is built to make social comparisons, and for the depressed brain those comparisons tend to come up negative. People have more depression when they compare themselves to others through social media.

2. **An unruly social media circle.** Social media can be a way to find and keep up with supportive friends. On the other hand, unwanted contacts, arguments, and particularly cyberbullying have all been linked to depression (Rosenthal et al., 2016).

3. **Advertisements.** Advertising raises the odds of depression. There are at least two reasons for this. Marketers stir up anxiety so they can offer their product as the solution to all that angst. Their aim is to convince viewers that they're not good enough, safe enough, or attractive enough unless they have that special product (Primack et al., 2009). Ads are also annoying. They interrupt the program, which keeps people from getting fully absorbed in what they're watching. Encourage clients to press mute and walk around during the ads. They probably wouldn't invite a door-to-door salesperson into their home, so why let in the virtual version.

4. **Gratuitous violence.** The brain's emotional center – the amygdala – is more sensitive to images than words. Graphic depictions of violence are not just disturbing; they can even cause PTSD. After 9/11, people who repeatedly watched footage of the tragedy had more symptoms of PTSD, even when they had no personal connection to the losses in New York, D.C., or Pennsylvania (Otto et al., 2007).

5. **Daily news.** Staying informed is an essential part of being a citizen, but consuming too much news increases anxiety and depression (Potts & Sanchez, 1994). This is particularly true of programs that play on fear and anger. Clients should watch enough news to stay informed, but not so much that they're watching the same story over and over again. Better yet, they can catch up on the news by reading or listening, preferably through a podcast or radio station that's relatively free of advertising and sensationalism. Spoken media is less likely to agitate the amygdala.

6. **Reality TV.** Reality shows play on primitive fears, like being shamed, rejected, exposed, or just not good enough. By putting everyday people on the screen, they engage the audience, encouraging them to compare themselves to these newly-minted stars. Social comparisons like that fuel depression in the same way that social media does. As an alternative, clients can try classic movies or fantasy films. Watching someone who lives in the 1940s or on a futuristic starship is less likely to trigger comparisons with our own lives and more likely to foster escape (Barcaccia et al., 2018).

Timing: Daily Rituals to Stabilize Mood

What would you do if your watch ran slow? You'd probably be late a lot, and your sleep schedule would be off. If it ran slow by an hour every day, those hours would build up, and after 12 days, you'd be up all night and asleep all day. Your friends might think you were depressed or losing your mind, but there's really only one thing wrong: You have a broken clock.

In many ways, that's what mood disorders are, particularly the bipolar type. From genetics to neurohormones, mood disorders have their roots in disruptions of the biological clock and the circadian rhythms it regulates. Those include the rhythms of sleep, appetite, energy, and motivation. That's why it takes so much effort to socialize, get out of bed, or do the dishes when depressed. It's as if the body just doesn't know that it's time to do those things.

Actually, everyone's clock is a little off, mood disordered or not. The average person's clock runs 15 minutes slow, but nature has devised a solution to correct that. Special sensors in the eye called *melanopsin* respond to the rise and fall of the sun, which resets the biological clock every 24 hours. That's probably what your client would need to do with that broken watch as well: reset it every morning so it doesn't stray too far.

What works in nature works for mood disorders as well. Regular routines in the morning and evening stabilize mood and sleep, but what about the rest of the day? Some activities have a more potent effect on the biological clock than others, and doing them at regular times is important for clients with a slightly broken clock. **Social rhythm therapy** is one strategy that helps clients entrain their biological clock through regularly-timed activity. The bulk of the research on social rhythm therapy has been undertaken in bipolar disorder.

The way to fix a broken biological clock is to reset it throughout the day. As we discussed in Chapter 3, *zeitgebers* (or "time-givers") are those events that reset the biological clock. Morning sunlight and evening darkness are the most important zeitgebers. These are the bookends of the day and are the best times to intervene when the circadian rhythm needs realignment. **Outside of morning light and evening darkness, the four most important zeitgebers are:**

- Goal-directed activities (like work, school, or chores)
- Social interactions (with people or pets)
- Meals (particularly dinner)
- Exercise

Those time-givers have one thing in common: They all cause hormones to rise or fall, and it's those hormones that run the biological clock. On the pages that follow are several worksheets that you can use with clients to help them identify their own personal *zeitgebers*. By identifying key activities that set their biological clock, their mood will gradually improve as they build these activities into their daily life at regular times. Just how precise should that regularity be? Give or take 15 minutes, according to research on social rhythm therapy.

Social Rhythm Therapy

What does it help?

Bipolar disorder.

How long does it take to work?

Clients should see results gradually over four to eight weeks, and even more benefit after three to six months.

The research

Social rhythm therapy has been found to lower the risk of new mood episodes in bipolar I disorder by 66% over a two-year period (Frank et al., 2005). It has also been found to treat bipolar II depression as well as quetiapine (Seroquel), although the medication took effect sooner (Swartz et al., 2018). In fact, it is the only psychotherapy that has been studied on its own – without medication – in the treatment of bipolar II disorder. However, when it comes to bipolar I disorder, therapy without a mood stabilizer is not recommended because of the risks that mania carries.

How does it work?

Regular routines stabilize the biological clock, which is tightly linked to mood disorders.

Social Rhythm Therapy

Social rhythm therapy is a treatment that stabilizes mood by restoring the daily rhythms of the biological clock. We can actually all use a little help from social rhythm therapy. The average person's biological clock runs a little behind, by about 15 minutes a day. However, people with mood disorders are hit especially hard by this disconnect because their clocks tend to lag even farther behind. This problem is more pronounced in bipolar disorder, but non-bipolar depression is close behind.

The way to fix a broken biological clock is to reset it throughout the day. The German's have a word for events that set the biological clock – *zeitgebers* – which roughly translates to "time-givers." Morning sunlight and evening darkness are the most important zeitgebers. Other strong zeitgebers include goal-directed activities, socializing, meals (especially dinner), and exercise. Use this worksheet to identify some routines to keep your clock running smoothly.

Goal-Directed Activity

Goal-directed activities – like work, school, and chores – alter brain chemistry, raising epinephrine and dopamine, and shifting the gears of the biological clock. It's the time that you first take on these activities each day that matters. Aim to start them at a regular time, give or take 15 minutes. The exact activity may vary from day to day, as long as it's active, goal-oriented, or productive in quality. Shopping, chores, work, reading, paying bills, running errands, doing crafts, planning trips, and taking online classes all count. What are some goal-directed routines you can use to wind up your biological clock each day?

Goal-directed activities	Start time

Social Interactions

Social interactions can also set the clock, particularly if they are active and engaging. Talking to your kids in the car or planning a project with colleagues count as active social interactions, but sitting with strangers at a bus station probably doesn't. The reason: Active involvement with other people alters the neurohormones that set the biological clock. Can you recall the rush of attraction on a first date or the anger of a marital fight? Did you feel those interactions on a physical level, with a racing heart or nervous stomach? That was those neurohormones circulating in your body.

When social interactions get intense, it can feel uncomfortable, as if your nerves are overstimulated. Intense interactions can disrupt the clock, particularly if they happen in the evening and interfere with sleep. The following scale lets you rate the intensity of your social interactions from 0-3.

	Rating	Effects	Examples
0	**Alone**	N/A	N/A
1	**Neutral.** Others are present but not involved.	Few emotional or physical effects	Making a deposit with a bank teller, waiting for a bus with strangers, saying hello to a neighbor
2	**Moderate.** Others are actively involved.	These interactions keep you engaged and involved, alert but not over-stimulated. It's easy to move on from these interactions without endlessly replaying them in your mind.	Making plans with your family, discussing a project at work, light conversation with a friend
3	**Intense.** Others are very stimulating.	These interactions make you excited, anxious, angry, or over-stimulated. They may cause physical sensations, like racing heart, tremor, or muscle tension. The effects linger so that it's hard to sleep or turn your mind off after them.	Major events or celebrations, which may be positive (a first date, wedding, reunion, or job interview) or negative (a funeral, argument, or feeling bullied or embarrassed)

To set your biological clock, think of some moderate-intensity ("level 2") interactions that you can build in at regular times in your day. As with goal-directed activities, these routines don't have to involve the same people every day.

For example, on weekdays, a morning work meeting could fill this role, and, on weekends, walking the dog could fill the role. That's right, pets count! When dog owners spend time with their canine, it activates the same areas of the brain that light up when they're talking with their best friend.

Moderately engaging social interaction	Start time

Sleep, Meals, Exercise, and More

Goal-directed and social activities are not the only things that shift neurohormones. Just about anything that affects you physically can serve as a zeitgeber. For many people, the timing of meals and exercise has this effect. As you learned in Chapter 4, the time you get out of bed plays a big role too. Are there other routines that give a sense of structure to your day and help keep your energy and sleep on a stable course? List them here.

_____

_____

_____

_____

Putting it All Together

Once you've thought of some routines to start incorporating into your schedule, use the following "Social Rhythm Chart" to keep track of them and see how they affect your mood.

Social Rhythm Chart

Instructions

The following chart will help you keep track of the key routines that set your biological clock and balance your moods. In the first column, write down the routines you identified in the "Social Rhythm Therapy" worksheet. Remember, important routines to think about are goal-directed activities, social interactions, exercise, and meal times. The bookends of the day (morning and evening) are already included in the chart, as these are essential parts of your routine. Officially, the day starts when you get out of bed and stand up. Standing activates nerve cells that keep your blood pumping in the upright position, and those nerve cells help set the biological clock.

Notice that the chart doesn't include the time you fall asleep. That one is harder to control than the time you get up, and worrying about it too much causes frustration and insomnia. Instead, create a wind-down routine and do it at regular times in the evening (see Chapter 6).

For each routine, identify an ideal time that you'd like to start it. Choose a time that's likely to have a good effect on your mood and energy, as well as one that's practical. You can adjust the "ideal time" as you try to figure out what works best. You can also use generic categories in the first column, like "goal-directed activity," instead of identifying a specific activity. The specific activity may change from day to day but – ideally – the timing will not.

Each day, record the actual time that you started the routine. Aim for regular times (give or take 15 minutes). Next, rate how involved other people or animals were during the routine using the 0-3 scale previously described on page 137. Finally, at the bottom of the chart, rate your overall mood or energy level for each day using the following -5 to +5 scale:

Mood/ Energy	Level	Distressing?	Causes problems?	Able to pull out of it?	Other people notice?
Depressed, unmotivated, or low energy	-5	Very	Major	No	Yes
	-4	Yes	Major	Sometimes	Yes
	-3	Yes	Minor	Sometimes	Yes
	-2	Somewhat	Minor	Yes	Sometimes
	-1	No	No	Yes	No
	0				
Hypo/manic, energized, or irritable	1	No	No	Yes	No
	2	Somewhat	Minor	Yes	Sometimes
	3	Yes	Minor	Sometimes	Yes
	4	Yes	Major	Sometimes	Yes
	5	Very	Major	No	Yes

With continued use, this chart will help you see how changes in your daily routine affect your mood. If your mood gets worse, look back over the previous one to two weeks to see if there was a change in the timing of your routines or the intensity of your social interactions. For example, a drop in meaningful social interactions can trigger depression, while a sudden increase can trigger hypo/mania or mixed states. If things are improving, look back to see which routines helped make that difference.

Social Rhythm Chart

Week of: _____		Sunday		Monday		Tuesday		Wednesday		Thursday		Friday		Saturday	
Routine	**Ideal Time**	Actual Time	people	Actual Time	people	Actual Time	people	Actual Time	people	Actual Time	people	Actual Time	people	Actual Time	people
Get out of bed and stand up															
Evening wind-down															
Mood/energy -5 to +5															

Social Rhythm Disruptions: Planning Ahead

Holidays, Trips, and Major Events

Big events are stressful for everyone, even when they are positive. For people with bipolar disorder, they can trigger new episodes by disrupting daily routines. To reduce that risk, maintain regular timing with the routines you've identified on the "Social Rhythm Chart." Especially important are daily wake times, evening wind-down, and exposure to light and darkness at the bookends of the day.

Plan ahead with your travelling companions. What major activities do you anticipate? If there are exciting activities at night, can you opt out of them or take extra steps to protect your sleep? If any of your daily routines will get lost in the travel, can you substitute a similar one at the same time?

Jet Lag

Jet lag is a powerful disruptor of the biological clock. Flying across more than two time zones is one of the top risk factors for new episodes in bipolar disorder. Traveling by land and sea doesn't cause as much of a problem because they allow time for the biological clock to adjust.

You can minimize these problems by slowly adjusting your sleep/wake times, and your exposure to light and darkness, before boarding the plane. By shifting those times over a few days rather than a few hours, your body will think it's going on a road trip instead of an airplane.

Jet Lag Rooster is a free, online program that creates a preventative plan before and after you travel (www.jetlagrooster.com). Developed by sleep scientists, it asks for your flight information and tells you how to adjust your sleep and when to seek light or darkness. A dawn simulator (Chapter 4) or blue light blocking glasses (Chapter 6) can be used at those times.

You can use this jet-lag plan to shift your daily routines. If the plan suggests moving your bedtime up an hour, move all your routines up an hour on that day. If it asks you to wake up an hour earlier, shift those routines back an hour.

Intense Activity

Intense activities can feel good or bad, and they can be exciting or overstimulating. Although these types of interactions can include other people (e.g., first date, job interview, celebrations, heated arguments), they can involve solo pursuits as well, such as taking on new projects, online shopping, playing video games, watching sports or political commentary, or anything that makes you want to keep going, often at the cost of sleep.

Hormones surge during intense activities, and that can disrupt mood if the events happen too suddenly, randomly, or too late in the day. You don't need to avoid intense activities to keep your mood stable; you just need to try to keep them from disturbing sleep and, if possible, move them to the morning.

Intense interactions with other people are harder to control, so you may need to enroll the help of those close to you in the effort. You can invite your close friends or relatives to read the worksheets in this section so they understand that there's a valid medical reason behind your request. In addition, you can use the following chart to help you enlist their support and develop a workable plan together. That will likely involve creativity and compromise.

Destabilizing Interaction	Effects	Management Plan
Ex. Arguments in the evening	Can't sleep even if we resolve the argument, more reactive and irritable the next day.	We can set aside time before 3:00 p.m. for heated discussions. I'll promise to pick up where we left off. I won't use this plan to avoid addressing issues.

Evening

Morning and evening are critical times for the biological clock. Routines at these bookends of the day help restore the circadian rhythms that break down in bipolar disorder, depression, and insomnia. An evening routine has two goals:

1. Induce slower brainwaves through meditative activity
2. Raise melatonin, the hormone involved in sleep, by lowering blue light

In this chapter, I'll discuss environmental cues that clients can use to set the stage for sleep, including light, temperature, sound, and scent.

Evening Wind-Down

Sleep doesn't begin when we doze off. It takes time to shift into the slower brainwaves of sleep. In Chapter 4, we learned how sunrise improves wakefulness by gradually lifting the brain out of deep sleep, and the same idea applies to the descent into sleep. People sleep deeper when they gradually shift from the fast brainwaves of an energizing activity to the slower settings of a more meditative mode. An evening wind-down is a 30-60 minute routine that allows the brain to shift into this more restful state.

These wind-down activities are particularly important for night owls, who are naturally more active in the evening and less-so in the morning. This *evening chronotype* is a risk factor for depression, bipolar disorder, and substance abuse. For these clients, the reward system is imbalanced. Dopamine is depleted in the morning and surges at night when they should be slowing down for sleep. An evening wind-down can help these clients calm their activated minds.

Evening activities shouldn't be rewarding or addictive. Instead, it should wind-down: The more people do them, the less they want to do them. Some of these activities need to be personalized, while others are more universal. For example, reading may put some to sleep but activate others, whereas mindfulness meditation is more universally effective in promoting sleep. Use the **Evening Wind-Down** worksheet to help clients brainstorm activities to incorporate into their bedtime routine.

Evening Wind-Down

Developing a wind-down routine in the evening helps stabilize mood and deepen sleep. To help you wind down at night, think of activities that are passive, meditative, relaxing, or just boring. These activities shouldn't compel you to stay up late doing more and more. They often have no goal other than to lull you into sleep. Examples include:

- Mindfulness meditation
- Journaling
- Visualizing pleasant scenes or abstract shapes
- Stretching

- Deep or rhythmic breathing
- Reading a dull book
- Doing a repetitive, boring chore
- Preparing clothes or food for the next day

What's right for some is wrong for others. For example, people who enjoy getting things neat and straight might find that folding clothes winds them up, while for others it's a bore. What are some activities that could help you wind down at night?

_____

_____

_____

In contrast, you want to avoid energizing activities at night. Move those things to the morning where they will help you wake up faster. The following are some examples of energizing activities:

- Problem solving
- Worrying
- Exciting projects
- Intense conversations
- Shopping
- Entertainment

Blue Light

There's something in the evening air that worsens sleep, depression, and bipolar disorder. It's classified by the World Health Organization as a possible carcinogen, and it's been linked to weight gain, diabetes, heart disease, and cancers of the breast and prostate (Lunn et al., 2017). It's hard to get away from, but it's easy to filter out. It's blue light.

Blue spectrum light regulates the body's internal clock. Electronic devices, television screens, and energy-efficient bulbs are all strong emitters of this wavelength. Blue light doesn't always look blue. When mixed with other colors, it appears white, like the glow of a florescent bulb. Small screens may seem innocent, but reading a smartphone at close range gives the same dose of blue light as watching a large TV screen from across the room.

In pre-electric days, blue light faded at night, leaving only the yellow glow of stars and candles. Melatonin rose as the sun set, and fell in the morning as the sky turned bright blue. This routine was disrupted once a month by a full blue moon. Ancient beliefs that the lunar cycle caused mental health problems were so strong that the word "lunatic" became a synonym for mania. A lot of old medical beliefs were faulty, but not this one. There is an uptick in visits to the psychiatric emergency room on nights of a full moon (Erren & Lewis, 2019).

Clients don't have to disconnect the power at night to fix this problem. Blue light blocking glasses filter out the blue spectrum. Wearing them before bed improves sleep, mood, and physical health. Unlike sunglasses, blue light blocking glasses don't darken the view, but they do infuse it with a warm, yellow glow. People can still read, watch TV, and do their usual activities with them on (though, for safety reasons, they shouldn't be used while driving or operating dangerous machinery). Lately, everyone from sports figures to Hollywood celebrities is donning these amber-tinted glasses at night, though it's people with mood disorders who need them most. Indeed, the most profound benefits of blocking blue light at night are seen in bipolar disorder. Small studies suggest that it helps unipolar depression as well, though the data is inconsistent.

When to Wear Them

In order to get the best effects for sleep, clients should put these glasses on about two to three hours before bed. Although two to three hours is ideal, one hour or even 30 minutes may work and is likely to lead to better long-term adherence. Clients will get the best results by wearing them at a regular time, particularly if they have bipolar disorder.

During active mania or mixed states, clients can put them on earlier (around 6:00 p.m.) as in the dark therapy protocol (page 149). However, the glasses shouldn't be worn before 6:00 p.m., as that can flip the circadian rhythm the wrong way. That's a warning worth emphasizing, as some clients feel less anxious with the glasses and attempt to wear them during the day.

The glasses can be removed when the client is ready for bed, but the bedroom should be pitch dark. It's surprising how important that last part is. In one study, people who slept in dimly lit rooms had double the risk of depression over a two-year period compared to those who slept in complete darkness. The risk of depression rose with the intensity of light, but even five lux (equivalent to a night light) was enough to raise it (Obayashi et al., 2018).

Carefully controlled experiments with animals have arrived at the same conclusion. The health risks of blue-spectrum nocturnal light are so significant that controlled studies in humans are now considered unethical.

Choosing a Pair

Strong blue light blockers (at least 90%) work best, but the market is crowded with products that don't rise to that standard. Uvex makes inexpensive glasses that work. The following two models were endorsed by mood researchers and *Consumer Reports*:

- Uvex S0360X Ultraspec 2000 in SCT Orange Lens ($7 at Amazon). This model fits over regular glasses.
- Uvex 3S1933X Skyper in SCT Orange lens ($7-11 at Amazon)

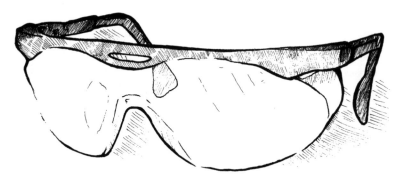

Uvex Skyper Blue Light Blocking Glasses®

More stylish models with good blockage are available at lowbluelights.com for around $50. Opticians sell prescription versions with various levels of blue light blockage, but it's not clear if they block in the 90% range. Clients can test their lenses by looking at a rainbow image online. The blue portion should look gray or brown; if it looks blue, consider a different pair.

Blocking Blue Light During Sleep

It's just as important to block out blue light while sleeping as it is before bed. The eyelids are translucent, and even low levels of light filter through and affect the brain. Blue light blocking glasses are uncomfortable to sleep with, so it's best to create a pitch-dark room for sleep. Popular ways to light-proof a bedroom include:

- Using blackout curtains
- Pressing aluminum foil against the windowpanes and attaching it with painter's tape
- Placing black electrical tape over any LED lights on electronic devices
- Purchasing a draft snake or using a rolled-up towel to cover the bottom of the door
- Sleeping in the basement
- Wearing a sleep mask (Note: Although this will work, it might prevent the mood-lifting benefits of a dawn simulator, which will be necessary if blackout curtains are blocking out the morning sun.)

The Science of Blue Light

The eye has a special receptor called *melanopsin* that only responds to blue light. When blue light fades in the evening, this receptor raises melatonin, the hormone that regulates sleep. Melatonin also improves metabolism and aids repair of damaged cells, which is why blue light pollution is linked to so many physical health problems.

Reducing Blue Light Exposure: Troubleshooting

"I can't sleep in the dark."

Low-blue lightbulbs are safe for the brain and won't interfere with melatonin. They give off an amber hue and are available as nightlights and regular bulbs. A good model is available at lowbluelights.com for under $10. Alternatively, search your favorite online retailer for "amber night light" or "blue-free night light." The following are some effective models:

- Maxxima MLN-16 Amber LED Night Light

- SCS Nite-Nite Light Bulb

- SCS Lighting Sleep-Ready Light

"I can't sleep without the TV on."

A lot of people use TV to drown out distractions or worry at night. There's nothing wrong with that, except the blue light. Try podcasts, radio, or, even better, music, which has good evidence to improve sleep and mood when used at night (see page 151).

"The glasses aren't comfortable."

It's a good idea to start with the $10 glasses, but if they work well you may want to upgrade to a more comfortable pair at lowbluelights.com or somnilight.com (around $50).

"I don't like to wear glasses."

The glasses themselves are not necessary. Rather, all that's needed is to eliminate blue light. You could read in a very dark room with a low-blue bulb or a low-blue reading light. Bulbs that achieve this effect are listed above. Low-blue lamps are available at somnilight.com and lowbluelights.com, or you can use the night mode on the PER2LED dawn simulator. Electronic devices will still pose a problem, but there are screen covers at lowbluelights.com that can solve that.

"I don't want people to see me in them."

These glasses help mood, but they are not just for people with mood disorders. Many professional sports teams wear them for their performance-enhancing effects. After all, they play better when they sleep better, and unlike steroids, there are no prohibitions against them. So many celebrities have taken them up that one journalist quipped about "celebrities trying to look cool by wearing blue-blocking lenses."

"Can I use a similar pair of amber glasses?"

Probably not. Most blue light-blocking glasses do not block enough light to improve sleep and mental health. Others were designed for entirely different purposes, like night driving, computer safety, or video gaming.

"Can I still use electronics at night if I wear blue blockers?"

That depends on how energizing they are. If you *really* want to use them, that may mean they are too engaging and better saved for morning. Generally, it's best to keep electronics out of the bedroom, and definitely don't leave the TV running while you sleep. It will saturate the room with blue light. In contrast, a pitch-dark room deepens sleep, reduces depression, and improves weight loss. If sound is comforting while you fall asleep, try listening to mindfulness apps, sleep-inducing music, or a mellow audio program, like a podcast, old-timey radio show, or book on tape.

"Can't I just adjust the settings on my devices?"

Most electronic devices have settings to reduce blue light in the evening (TV sets are an exception). There's *Night Mode* on iPhone, *Blue Shade* on the Kindle, and *Twilight* or *Blue Light Filter* apps on Android. For computers, there are free apps that do a good job, such as *F.Lux* for Windows (justgetflux.com) and *Candlelight* by Oliver Denman for Mac.

However, these settings do not filter out enough blue light or take care of the many other sources of this wavelength. To test them, turn the settings on and pull up an image with something blue, like a rainbow. Then, look at the screen through a strong pair of blue light blocking glasses. Do the blue stripes in the rainbow change when you put the glasses on? If they do, then the app is not blocking enough blue.

A good way to use these apps is to set them to turn on around 6:00–7:00 p.m. Start to dim the lights in your home around that time too, particularly the bright energy-efficient bulbs. Smart bulbs, such as Phillips Hue, can be programmed to dim and shift toward a warmer spectrum in the evening. Then, around 8:00–9:00 p.m., put on the blue light blocking glasses. This strategy is not as beautiful as the sunset over the Blue Ridge Mountains, but it will do.

"Can't I just take melatonin?"

That's been tried, but it's not the same. Artificial melatonin does not improve mood and only adds, on average, 10 minutes to the total sleep time. Melatonin is just the end result of a complex process that's set in motion when the brain enters a dark room.

"I tried the glasses, but they didn't make me tired."

The glasses are better at deepening sleep than helping people fall asleep. You can still get the health benefits from the glasses even if they don't improve your sleep. For example, some studies have found that the glasses improved mental health even when people slept less while wearing them.

"Can I wear them while driving?"

No. You won't be able to see clearly enough to drive safely with them. Remember, yellow and blue make green, so green stop lights look yellow when the blue is stripped away – and that's just the start of the problems.

"I feel calmer when I wear the glasses. Can I wear them during the day?"

These amber glasses have a calming effect, but wearing them before 6:00 p.m. can cause depression. Physiologically, it would be like being in a pitch-dark room during the day. That's not a big deal for a few minutes, but too much of that can flip your biological clock in the wrong direction.

Dark Therapy

Just as morning light helps depressive symptoms, evening darkness improves mania and mixed states. Light and darkness set the body's internal clock, and moods are better when that clock is running well. Timing is key here. Dark mornings and bright nights can both destabilize mood.

A Famous Case

Mr. J went in and out of mania and depression for many years. His condition was so untreatable that he went to the National Institutes of Health for help in the 1990s. They treated him with a routine of total darkness for 14 hours every night (from 6:00 p.m. to 8:00 a.m.). With this *dark therapy*, he improved so rapidly that they eased the schedule from 14 hours of darkness to 10 hours each night (10:00 p.m. to 8:00 a.m.) (Wehr et al., 1998). He stayed well with that regimen, and so dark therapy was born.

Dark Therapy the Easy Way

Traditional dark therapy requires total darkness. Even a distant street lamp or a brief flick of the bathroom lights can interfere with it. An easier approach is to wear amber glasses in the evening. Doing so creates a virtual darkness by blocking out blue spectrum light. This easy method works as well as the traditional way, as long as the client sleeps in a pitch-dark room. Indeed, dark therapy with amber glasses improved mania within one week in a randomized-controlled trial of hospitalized bipolar patients (Henriksen et al., 2016).

The glasses had a large effect in that study, about as large as what we see with medications. The method was simple: Participants either wore the glasses or stayed in a pitch-dark room from 6:00 p.m. to 8:00 a.m. Although the glasses didn't make them sleep more (they actually slept less!), their sleep became more regular with this therapy.

Clients who have severe symptoms of bipolar mania or mixed states should start with a full 14 hours of darkness a day (6:00 p.m. to 8:00 a.m.) and transition to 10 hours (10:00 p.m. to 8:00 a.m.) as they start to recover. When transitioning, they should adjust by one hour every two nights (e.g., darkness at 7:00 p.m. for two nights, then 8:00 p.m. for two nights, until they reach 10:00 p.m.). If reducing the dark time makes their symptoms worse, just backtrack and increase their dark exposure by an hour. For milder symptoms, clients can start with 10 hours of darkness by wearing the glasses two hours before bed and then sleeping in a pitch-dark room for eight hours.

It's best to keep the lights down low while wearing blue light blocking glasses. It is also important that clients do not use dark therapy during the day. Remember: The idea is to set their biological clock, and daytime light helps with that. Although blue-blockers can cause vivid dreams and headaches, they are reasonable and safe to use in a therapy practice. I've included a helpful handout on the following page.

Dark Therapy in Six Steps

1. **Evening.** At 6:00 p.m., put on blue light blocking glasses. Wear them until you're ready for bed, and keep the lights down as low as you're comfortable with. Don't take the glasses off unless you're in a pitch-dark room. Pitch-dark means you can't see your hand in front of your face.

2. **Sleep.** Get your bedroom pitch-dark using the techniques on page 146. When you're ready for bed, lay down in the pitch-dark room and take the glasses off.

3. **Overnight.** If you get up at night and turn the lights on, make sure to wear the glasses. Otherwise, remain in your pitch-dark bedroom throughout the night, whether asleep or not.

4. **Morning.** At 8:00 a.m., turn on the lights, or use a dawn simulator to wake up. Don't wear the glasses during the day.

5. **As you improve.** Once your symptoms improve, you can put the glasses on later in the evening. Move the start time up by one hour every two days until you're wearing them two hours before bed.

6. **Prevention.** Once recovered, keep wearing the glasses two hours before bed and sleep in a pitch-dark room. Doing so will help prevent bipolar episodes, as well as other health problems, like cancer, weight gain, and diabetes. The glasses also deepen sleep quality, which improves concentration the next day.

Troubleshooting: If you can't get the room pitch-dark, use a sleep mask. If you can't tolerate complete darkness, use a low-blue nightlight. If you're used to having the TV on in the bedroom, try music or podcasts instead. (A good sleep-inducing soundtrack is *Weightless* by Marconi Union.) Don't expect this therapy to make you sleep. Dark therapy gives your brain many of the healing properties of sleep even if you're wide awake all night.

Bottom Line: During dark therapy, you'll need to be in virtual darkness (with blue light blocking glasses) or pitch darkness for the entire evening.

Evening Playlist

Music can energize or calm the brain. Repetitive music has been used for centuries to induce trances and, more recently, its sleep-inducing effects have been explored. Relaxing music helps people fall asleep faster and improves sleep quality, according to the results of 20 controlled studies. Statistically speaking, these effects are in the moderate range, which is actually greater than the effects seen with sleep medication. In direct comparisons, music has outperformed progressive muscle relaxation, acupuncture, and audiobooks (Feng et al., 2018).

How does music do this? There are at least two possible mechanisms. Relaxing music reduces the fight-or-flight response, in turn lowering blood pressure, heart rate, and stress hormones like cortisol. It can also distract from negative, anxious thoughts, which is a quality that's particularly useful in clients with depression. Indeed, a steady routine of evening music can improve both sleep and depression (Chan et al., 2010).

How to Use Music for Sleep

Music can be integrated into an evening wind-down routine. Ideally, clients will start their sleep playlist 30-60 minutes before bed and listen while they fall asleep. They can program their music player to cut off in the late evening or keep playing; both methods have been successful in the research. Unlike sleep medicines, the benefits of music don't wear off with time. In fact, it has a slow build, so clients should give music a try for three to four weeks before deciding if it's helpful (Wang et al., 2014).

Which Songs Work?

The exact songs need to be personalized, but qualities that make for a good snoozer include:

- Instrumental music with a regular rhythm
- Bass tones
- Tranquil melodies
- Familiar tunes
- Slow tempos (e.g., 60-80 BPM; You can check tempos of specific songs at songbpm.com)

The Top 10 Sleep Tracks

In 2011, the instrumental group Marconi Union collaborated with the British Academy of Sound Therapy to create a track for sleep and relaxation. Using biofeedback, they adjusted the tones until they arrived at an eight-minute piece called *Weightless*. When sleep researchers tested the effectiveness of this soundtrack against other relaxing songs, *Weightless* rose to the top for its ability to induce sleep and relaxation. In particular, it lowered anxiety by a remarkable 65% and decreased other physical markers of stress, such as heart rate and blood pressure, as well (Curtin, 2017). The relaxing effects of this song were so dramatic that researchers had to caution against driving while listening to it. Other songs that were tested, in order of success, were:

1. *Weightless*, by Marconi Union
2. *Electra*, by Airstream
3. *Mellomaniac* (Chill Out Mix), by DJ Shah
4. *Watermark*, by Enya
5. *Strawberry Swing*, by Coldplay
6. *Please Don't Go*, by Barcelona
7. *Pure Shores*, by All Saints
8. *Someone Like You*, by Adele
9. *Canzonetta Sull'aria*, by Mozart
10. *We Can Fly*, by Rue du Soleil

All 10 songs are available on a public Spotify playlist: *Relaxing Songs* by Melanie Curtin. *Weightless* is also available free on YouTube, on CD, or through most streaming services. There is even a 10-hour version to last through the night, or clients can play the eight-minute track on repeat.

In addition to the top 10 playlist, clients can search online for terms like "relaxing playlists" or "sleep playlists" to personalize their evening playlist further. Research on music and sleep has favored the following genres in particular:

- Celtic harp
- Gregorian chants
- Electronic music
- New age music
- Classical music, including Indian and Chinese classical

Specific pieces:

- Beethoven, *Moonlight Sonata* and *Symphony No. 9 Movement 3*
- Satie, *Gymnopédie No. 1*
- Bach, *Air Suite No. 3 in D Major BWV 1068*
- Brahms, *Clarinet Quintet in B Minor*
- Debussy, *Clair De Lune*
- Pachelbel, *Canon in D*
- Mozart, *Serenade No. 10*
- Barber, *Adagio for Strings*
- Jules Massenet, *Méditation from Thaïs*
- Kitaro, *Lord of Wind*
- Yu-Xiao Guang, *Everlasting Road*

Binaural beats are another option. These electronic sounds are designed to induce different types of brainwaves. For sleep, research supports the role of 5 to 7 Hz *theta wave* binaural beats, which are associated with a state of deep relaxation. If clients don't like the electronic textures of binaural beats, they can try searching for "binaural beats nature." Nature sounds like rain, wind, or the ocean can also help insomnia, as can white noise. Clients can use the following worksheet to experiment with different evening sounds and see what works best for them.

Nighttime Music & Sounds

Relaxing music before bed improves sleep. It can be used both before and during sleep. Use the following worksheet to find out what types of music or sounds work best for you, and keep in mind there are always people who sleep better in silence.

Make a playlist of songs that could improve your sleep. Try natural sounds, white noise, and theta wave binaural beats as well. How does each method affect your sleep?

_____

_____

_____

If you have anxiety, racing thoughts, or wired energy at night, how does listening to an evening playlist affect those symptoms?

_____

_____

_____

How does listening to an evening playlist compare to silence?

_____

_____

_____

Evening Air

More than any other sensory system, the olfactory nerves in the nose have a direct connection to the brain. Aromatherapy influences neurotransmitters in ways that induce relaxation and sleep. The best-studied scents for sleep are lavender, bergamot, chamomile, and cypress. Other scents are sometimes mixed into those evening oils, including geranium, mandarin, sweet marjoram, clary sage, ylang, eucalyptus, frankincense, rose, orange, jasmine, and rosemary (Hwang & Shin, 2015). Clients can use them before bed or throughout the night with an oil diffuser.

Hot Baths, Cold Rooms

Temperature is just as important as light in regulating the biological clock. A drop in temperature in the evening prompts the body to enter sleep. Clients with depression are less likely to respond to that prompt because depression elevates body temperature and prevents it from rising and falling with the circadian rhythm. Add to that the unchanging indoor climates that modern life has created through the wonders of HVAC, and we have a set up for insomnia. There are two ways to accentuate that prompt. Clients can take a hot bath one to two hours before bed, and sleep in a colder room. Both methods improve sleep.

A Hot Bath

A hot bath one to two hours before bed causes body temperature to fall overnight, setting in motion biological changes that ultimately deepen sleep. Clients should soak for 10-30 minutes, with the water covering their body from the neck down. The temperature should be as hot as they can comfortably touch, but not so hot that it's painful (104°F). Lower temperatures are relaxing but do not have a significant effect on sleep (Dorsey et al., 1999; Liao, 2002). To protect their skin, clients shouldn't stay in the bath for longer than 30 minutes and they should never let the temperature rise above 104°F. To accentuate the warming effect, clients can also drink a hot beverage before or during the bath, such as a relaxing, caffeine-free herbal tea (e.g., chamomile, valerian, or lavender).

Hot baths are not for everyone, and there are a few warnings to bear in mind, most importantly fainting or falls because blood pressure can drop when standing up from the tub. Clients with risk factors noted below should consult with their physician first. If a hot bath is not safe or feasible, a foot bath (soaking both feet in hot water for 20-30 minutes), hot shower, or infrared heating blanket might help.

If the hot bath works, the client will fall asleep easier and sleep deeper with fewer awakenings. Over time, it may improve depression as well. A hot bath may treat depression by reducing inflammation and reviving the brain's reward center. In particular, the results of an intriguing controlled study tested whether a hot bath twice a week could treat depression better than a fake version of light therapy, which was used as the placebo. After two months, the baths worked, and the effect was about as strong as what we see with antidepressants (Naumann et al., 2017).

A Hot Bath: The Risks

- **Falls and blood pressure drops.** Clients should consult with their physician if they have any of these risk factors: age over 65, dizziness, taking medicines that lower blood pressure, diabetes, or medical problems affecting the heart, lung, or kidneys.

- **Accidental drowning:** Clients should avoid alcohol, sleep medications, and sedatives both during and before taking a bath.

- **Skin burns, infection, and breakdown.** Hot baths should be avoided if there are any cuts to the skin, active skin disease, neuropathy or numbness, or any infection. They shouldn't stay in the bath for longer than 30 minutes or let the temperature rise above 104°F.

- **Fertility.** Pregnant women should avoid hot baths. Men attempting to conceive should also avoid them as they may temporarily lower the sperm count.

- **Children.** A hot bath is not appropriate for children, who should avoid water temperatures above 100°F.

A Hot Bath: Practical Tips

- Ideal water temperature: 104°F

- Use lower temperatures in that range for elderly clients.

- Clients can measure the water temperature with a "bath" or "pool" thermometer ($5-10).

- The bath should cause an increase in body temperature: 1-3°F. This part is optional, but curious bathers can use an oral or ear thermometer to measure their body temperature before and at the end of the bath. Clients who prefer to warm themselves through other methods, like a heating pad or sauna, can check their temperature to make sure it rises 1-3°F during the process.

- To prevent falls, it's best for clients to rise slowly and hold onto something firm while getting out of the tub. If clients experience any dizziness, they should sit for a minute or two before standing. A chair next to the tub can help.

- After the bath, clients should drink a small glass of water (2-4 ounces) to ensure hydration.

- Hot baths may be uncomfortable but should not be painful. Clients will likely break a sweat.

A Cold Room

Sleep doctors recommend lowering the room temperature to 60-65°F overnight and bundling up with blankets. That may be too cold for some, and there are always people who sleep better in a warm room, so this needs to be individualized. Clients can set a programmable thermostat to lower the temperature in the evening and get as close to the recommended temperature as they are comfortable. A rise in temperature helps wake people up, so clients should set it to rise in the 30-60 minutes before their alarm goes off. A fan is a good economical option on hot summer days, as it can effectively lower the temperature through the "wind chill factor."

Can a Mattress Deepen Sleep?

A new mattress made out of fishing line is catching on in Japan. Called the high rebound mattress, it proposes to deepen sleep by lowering core body temperature through the night. Compared to a memory foam mattress, sleeping on the high rebound mattress made by Airweave deepened sleep by 25%. The high rebound mattress can be placed on top of a regular mattress and – despite its odd material – provides a comfortable rest (Chiba et al., 2018).

7

Sleep

Treating Insomnia

There are two types of clients who have trouble sleeping: those with *primary insomnia* (who have insomnia but no other mental health issues) and those with *secondary insomnia* (in which the sleep problems are intertwined with another psychiatric disorder, such as depression or bipolar disorder). Both groups will benefit from the two-staged sleep therapy presented in this chapter. However, for people with mood disorders, there is even more good news. This insomnia package has significant benefits for depression and bipolar disorder as well.

Guiding Principles

Insomnia is a normal part of life, and that's a guiding principle of this therapy. Now and then, we can't sleep. Sometimes, it goes on for a few days, but eventually our system self-corrects and we fall back into a normal rhythm. That is, unless something gets in the way of that self-correction. Oversleeping, caffeine, and worrying about sleep are natural reactions to insomnia, but they tend to prolong the problem.

The first step in treating insomnia is to break those habits that get in the way of restoring sleep. Those habits developed for good reasons, so expect some questioning from the client when you introduce the techniques in this chapter, such as *"I have to sleep in on weekends to catch up; otherwise, there's no way I could function at work"* or *"The TV helps me sleep. If I don't leave it on in the bedroom, then my mind races with anxiety."*

The psychology of insomnia bears some resemblance to phobias. Just as a phobic client has an intricate routine to avoid bridges or snakes, so too does an insomniac. Only here, the insomniac's phobia involves not sleeping and fears about how that will impact their health, wellbeing, or functioning the next day. Listen with empathy as you guide the client to test out the changes in this therapy. The most important change is to rise from the bed at the same time and avoid daytime naps.

Sleep and Mood Disorders

Depression and hypo/mania pit people in a struggle with their own mind. They can't control their own thoughts, which can flood with worries, rumination, and self-reproach, particularly when they're lying in a dark room waiting for sleep. For these clients, sleep is an escape, a way to turn their mind off. However, that anxious desire for sleep only worsens the problem because anxiety makes it hard to settle down.

For clients with depression, sleep problems can manifest in a variety of ways. They can have trouble falling asleep (*initial insomnia*), staying asleep (*middle insomnia*), early morning awakening (*terminal insomnia*), and oversleeping (*hypersomnia*). Ideally, treating the depression would resolve these problems, but insomnia is habitual and can linger long after depression is gone. That ongoing insomnia makes mood problems more likely to return, and it also increases the risk of suicide (Lin et al., 2018).

In contrast, clients with hypo/mania have a "decreased need for sleep," though that's not necessarily how it looks in real life. During hypo/mania, clients remain active despite sleeping very little. That's what "decreased need for sleep" looks like, but it's not how it feels, because most clients feel they need the sleep. They have a sense that their mood would improve if they got more sleep. In addition, when hypo/mania is mixed with anxiety or depression, the level of distress that clients experience is off the charts. The ruminative thoughts in their head are jet-fueled, racing through their mind in all directions. Therefore, they often crave sleep to escape the noise in their head. The bottom line is that most clients with hypo/mania say they need more sleep even if they do keep going without it.

Another reason that people with mood disorders have trouble sleeping is that they tend to be night owls, which means that their biological clock runs a little slow. Oversleeping on weekends is a common way to compensate, but that can delay the clock even further. When that pattern goes on too long, it creates a chronic, low-grade version of jet lag called *social jet lag*.

Other Causes of Insomnia

Insomnia can also develop as part of the normal aging process. Each new decade of life brings with it new patterns of sleep. With age, we tend to fall asleep earlier and wake up more often throughout the night. Older individuals also need less sleep. These are normal changes but can turn into a treacherous struggle if clients develop habits that make the problem worse.

Whether it's aging, mood disorders, trauma, anxious tendencies, a slow biological clock, or some combination of these, sleep issues usually develop out of a real problem that fails to self-correct. The first step is to undo the changes that are getting in the way of that self-correction. Sometimes that's called *sleep hygiene*, but here we'll call it *first aid*.

First Aid for Insomnia

When insomnia goes on too long, people start to worry about their sleep. That anxiety activates the fight-or-flight system, which makes people even more alert and awake. The bedroom becomes a place of struggle rather than rest, which worsens the problem further. First aid for insomnia aims to reverse those trends before those anxious habits become ingrained. The primary steps involve:

1. Waking up at a regular time
2. Avoiding daytime naps
3. Only using the bed for sleep (and intimacy)
4. Only going to bed when sleepy
5. Avoiding caffeine, alcohol, and light in the evening
6. Engaging in an evening wind-down routine

What if the client is taking sleep medicine? These steps can still work and can also be used while clients are tapering down their sleep medicine. The issue in these cases is usually that the sleep medicine is not working and the client needs something stronger. That's what this program is – a stronger treatment – which is why the American Academy of Sleep Medicine recommends it above sleep medications.

The following handout, **First Aid for Insomnia**, explains the six steps in greater detail. Many sleep issues improve with these basic steps. If these steps don't work, then it may be that the insomnia has become habitual, in which case the advanced moves discussed later in this chapter will be necessary.

First Aid for Insomnia

1. Wake up at a regular time.

Sleep is a 24-hour cycle, and the time that you fall asleep is just one point in that cycle. It's also the hardest point to control. Instead of struggling with the evening side, pour your efforts into the morning by rising out of bed at a regular time. The rest of the cycle is anchored to the morning, and irregular wake times make it harder to fall asleep when you need to. Insomnia doesn't make it easy to wake up in the morning, but stick to this rule even if it means you'll be sleep deprived that day. Follow the tips in Chapter 4 to help you get out of bed. Sleep deprivation is actually the best antidote to insomnia. It increases *sleep drive,* a biological force that helps people fall asleep.

2. Avoid daytime naps.

Napping drains the fuel that the body needs to fall asleep. That fuel is called *sleep drive,* and it builds up the longer you stay awake. If you still can't sleep after sticking to a regular wake-up schedule and avoiding daytime naps, you may wonder why that fuel isn't kicking in. There's another force that can override it: anxiety.

Anxiety trumps sleep drive, and for a good reason. It's not safe to fall asleep if danger is near. Unfortunately, the body can't tell the difference between anxiety about a predator and anxiety about sleep.

What if you're calm and worry-free but still can't sleep? It may be that your circadian rhythm is off. That rhythm, which is regulated by the time you wake up and the cycle of sunrise and sunset, has to be in place for sleep drive to take effect. The circadian rhythm breaks down when you wake at irregular times, have too much activity or light in the evening, or have an active mood problem like depression or hypo/mania.

3. Only use the bed for sleep.

The goal of this step is to train your body to associate the bed with sleep. That means no electronics, eating, worrying, or reading in bed. Sex and intimacy are allowed. Stay out of the bedroom, and definitely out of the bed, unless it is evening and you are falling asleep. Worry is one bedroom activity that's particularly hard to control. A dark bedroom is necessary for sleep, but the empty space invites worries, including the "what if I don't fall asleep" worry. It's tempting to turn to television or electronics to distract from the worry, but that will only prolong the insomnia. Two solutions:

- *Change your space.* If you're unable to sleep after about 20 minutes (just approximate – don't watch the clock!), then move to another room and sit in the dark until you feel tired. Then try again. If sitting in the dark is difficult, use a low-level yellow light and wear blue light blocking glasses.

- *Schedule time for worry.* Set aside a regular time in the afternoon to do all the worrying, problem solving, and planning you need to. Worry *on purpose* for 20 minutes, and do it in a room other than your bedroom. Think about everything you need to do and all that could go wrong. Write the worries down. If you run out of worries, go over the same ones again, but don't stop until the 20 minutes are up. By inviting worry in, this paradoxical technique gradually reduces anxiety and trains the brain to worry at an earlier hour.

4. Only go to bed when sleepy.

Trust your body to sleep when it needs to. As long as you don't nap in the day or fall asleep so early that you're up most of the night, this principle will not steer you wrong. When insomnia goes on too long, people lose trust in their body's natural sleep mechanisms. They try to take control of the sleep gears, but those were not designed for manual operation. The result is frustration and further breakdown of the gears.

There's a good reason that the sleep gears weren't designed for stick-shift mode. When you drive a stick shift, you have to be awake to operate the gears. Otherwise, the car would crash. That's the paradox of insomnia. Falling asleep is about as complicated as landing an airplane. There is no way that your body would let you operate such delicate controls unless you were wide awake, which means you'd never fall asleep.

Instead, you'll need to restore trust in your built-in sleep mechanisms in order to fall asleep. There are two:

- *Sleep drive:* The more sleep deprived you are, the more your sleep drive increases. Stay up too long, like two to three days, and eventually you'll crash. Guaranteed.

- *Circadian rhythm:* This is the 24-hour cycle that regulates sleep and other basic functions, like appetite and temperature. The circadian rhythm is regulated by morning light, evening darkness, the time you get out of bed, and other daily activities.

These mechanisms aren't perfect, but they're all we have. Allow your body to make mistakes, like staying awake at night when it ought to know better. Your sleep gears may be a bit rusty if you've had a tight grip on the steering wheel for a long time. This sleep program will put the right conditions in place so your natural sleep mechanisms can take over at the wheel. Give them time to relearn the road.

5. Avoid caffeine, alcohol, and light in the evening.

Caffeine. For most people, 2:00 p.m. is a good cut-off time for caffeine, but an earlier cut-off may be needed for highly caffeinated drinks or people who metabolize caffeine slowly. Chocolate is also a strong source of caffeine, particularly dark chocolate.

Alcohol. Alcohol is a tempting sedative, but its effects on sleep can be disastrous. For one thing, it's not just a sedative. It has stimulant properties as well. Alcohol also disturbs sleep waves, which means the sleep it brings is not as restorative. It often makes people wake up in the middle of the night, with worse insomnia than they started with. Even when it does work well, the solution is short-lived because tolerance quickly develops, causing an addictive cycle with worse insomnia.

Light. Use dim, yellow light in the evening and avoid electronics for one to three hours before bed (or wear blue light blocking glasses). Sleep in a pitch-dark room, or use an eye mask while in bed. Even small amounts of light (5-10 lux, the equivalent a nightlight) can interfere with melatonin, which is the hormone that enables sleep.

6. Set the stage for sleep.

Start a wind-down routine at the same time each evening. Relaxing activity before bed deepens sleep, while problem solving and engaging activity lightens it. A drop in temperature before bed helps activate sleep hormones. Program the thermostat to go down to the 60-65°F range at night. In the morning, have it rise to a warmer temperature to trigger wakefulness.

When will I see results?

These six steps should work within three to four weeks. After that, you may have occasional nights of insomnia, but sticking to this plan will keep it from spiraling into a full-blown problem. If you don't see results, move on to the advanced steps for insomnia in the following section.

Troubleshooting

"I've heard that insomnia is bad for your health, so isn't it dangerous to allow sleep deprivation?"

Healthy sleep is not just about quantity. Timing and quality are just as important. Irregular circadian rhythms, like oversleeping in the morning or napping during the day, are also bad for your health. They can even be a medical problem in their own right, called *social jet lag*. Brief sleep deprivation, like the type we're using to reset your sleep, actually has a few medical benefits. It treats depression, reduces inflammation, and protects brain cells by raising levels of *brain-derived neurotrophic factor* (BDNF) (Schmitt et al., 2016).

"I can't function if I don't sleep, so I have to sleep in or take naps to catch up."

Sleeping in and taking naps are temporary cures for a chronic problem. They also perpetuate that problem. If they were working for you, you probably wouldn't need this therapy. But if you really have insomnia, you are probably sleep deprived more days than not. This therapy requires you to keep that sleep deprivation at a steady level, and to ignore the urge for temporary relief through a daytime nap. It's similar to managing a skin problem, where the doctor asks you not to scratch the itch. Keep your eyes on the long-term gains, which are greater than the short-lived relief of a nap.

"Napping is part of my daily routine and helps me function."

Napping can be healthy, particularly after age 60. Sleep can improve in that age group when it's divided into two shifts. The first shift involves a brief afternoon nap (45 minutes to two hours long), followed by a longer round of sleep in the evening. However, if you have insomnia it's a different story, even if you are over age 60. Napping needs to stop. Once you've recovered from insomnia, you can reintroduce the napping ritual. If your sleep stays stable, continue with regular naps; otherwise, it's best to give them up.

"My issue is not oversleeping. I wake up too early and can't fall back asleep."

Use the 20-minute rule if you wake up too early. If you're unable to fall asleep after 20 minutes, get up and sit in the dark, or if you have the lights on, wear blue-light filtering glasses. Don't turn on the lights or start your day just yet. Stay in the dark until your wake-up time. That will keep your circadian rhythm from drifting too much.

Advanced Steps for Insomnia

First aid works well in the early stages of insomnia, but it may not be enough if the problem has gone on too long. For these clients, the insomnia has developed a life of its own, propelled by a vicious cycle. They need a stronger force to counter it: **cognitive behavioral therapy for insomnia (CBT-I).**

In 2013, the *New York Times* called CBT-I the most "significant [advance] in the treatment of depression since the introduction of Prozac." Why? Because a large controlled study found that it doubled the rate of recovery from depression. That result has been confirmed in half a dozen studies. CBT-I treats depression, helps antidepressants work better, and lowers the rate of mood swings in bipolar disorder by a factor of eight (Harvey et al., 2015). It's also the most effective treatment we have for insomnia. Both the American Academy of Sleep Medicine and the American College of Physicians recommend it as a first-line treatment, before sleep medication. When clients meet that fact with disbelief, I'll remind them of a few other areas of health where medication falls short:

- Physical therapy improves walking more than medication
- Weight lifting builds muscle better than anabolic steroids
- Calorie reduction leads to more weight loss than a diet pill

CBT-I harnesses the biological forces that drive sleep, and those forces are more complex and powerful than a sleeping pill.

On average, sleep medications help people fall asleep about 20 minutes faster than a sugar pill and do little to improve the quality of that sleep. (Huedo-Medina et al., 2012). So why do their adherents give them such high marks? One possible reason is that sleeping pills are also amnestic, so they make people forget how poorly they slept.

There are good reasons why sleep medicines have such meager effects. It is difficult for a pill to accomplish all the wondrous things that happen during sleep. Brainwaves cycle from slow to fast, muscles go lax so we don't act out our dreams, body temperature drops, and the things we learned during the day somehow get solidified.

Our internal sleep mechanisms do all that and do it safely. The heart keeps pumping and the lungs keep breathing. Sleep medicines have many safety problems that CBT-I does not, including falls, accidental injuries, memory problems, and addiction. They can also suppress breathing, particularly when combined with other sedatives, like alcohol or opioid pain medicines.

While sleep medicines do work faster than CBT-I, which can take a few weeks to yield results, the benefits of CBT-I tend to last longer than those of sedatives. If clients are already taking a sleep medicine, they can continue it during this program, whether they take it as needed, nightly, or are slowly tapering it off.

	Sleep Therapy	Sleep Medicine
Benefits	Slow but strong	Fast but fairly weak
Long lasting?	Yes	Usually not
Safe?	Yes	No
Natural?	Yes	No
Treats depression?	Yes	No

What About a Sleep Study?

Surprisingly, an overnight sleep study (or *polysomnography*) reveals little about insomnia. These tests are used for sleep apnea (not breathing at night), narcolepsy (sudden attacks of sleep during the day), and parasomnias (abnormal behaviors or movements during sleep such as sleep walking). Sleep apnea is more common in people with post-traumatic stress disorder, obesity, thick necks, loud snoring, and high blood pressure.

For people with pure insomnia, a sleep study will tell them what they already know: They are not sleeping well (and are probably sleeping worse in a sleep lab).

Cognitive Behavioral Therapy for Insomnia (CBT-I)

CBT-I is significantly more effective than first aid for insomnia, although it starts from the same principles. The therapy has three components: education, cognitive work around anxiety, and a behavioral phase called *bed restriction*.

1. **Education:** CBT-I is difficult work, and clients need to understand the rationale behind it. When introducing this technique to your clients, it is important to fully discuss the research outlined in the previous section on "Advanced Steps for Insomnia."

2. **Cognitive work:** The cognitive portion of this treatment addresses the client's fears around insomnia. As a therapist, help them unravel those fears with questions like, "What's the worst thing that could happen if you don't sleep?" As clients line those feared scenarios up, they will often realize that their worst fears are already happening. They are tired, irritable, and can't concentrate at work. Once clients realize this, they'll be less resistant to the next step, which asks them to limit their time in bed.

3. **Bed restriction:** Insomniacs fear sleep deprivation and dance around it like a cat on a hot tin roof. Their lives are filled with random patches of anxious struggle, fitful sleep, desperate naps, and scattered states of sleep deprivation. In this therapy, you'll be asking them to replace those random bouts of sleep deprivation with a structured program called *bed restriction*.

   Bed restriction asks clients to limit their time in bed based on how much they are sleeping at night. Basically, they take the average amount of sleep they get each night and add 1/2 hour. If they are only sleeping 6 hours on average they are only allowed to be in bed for 6 1/2 hours. This causes sleep drive to build up so the client falls asleep easier. As their sleep improves, the amount of time they are allowed in bed increases flexibly. The full details are described in the worksheets at the end of this chapter.

   The rationale behind bed restriction is that it increases sleep drive, which is one of the forces that powers sleep. "*But wait,*" the client says, "*I've already got plenty of sleep deprivation, and it hasn't helped the problem.*" That is because their sleep deprivation occurs in random bouts, much like a client with social phobia gets random, unwanted exposures to social situations. In that case, a program of structured exposures is needed. Likewise, a structured system of sleep deprivation is necessary to restore *sleep drive* in someone with insomnia.

   The aim of bed restriction is to concentrate all that sleep deprivation in one place: the evening. No more scattering it around, spending it here and there on naps and oversleeping.

The worksheets for CBT-I require a bit of work, graphing their sleep patterns and calculating their average time asleep. What if clients can't put up with all those details? No worries. You can still do the therapy by approximating the times for bed restriction.

To do that, first ask them to estimate how many hours of sleep they get each day. Look for an average, understanding that some days are more and some are less. Then, add 30 minutes to that number. That's how long they are allowed in bed for the next week. Ask the client when they need to wake up, and use that to set a time for them to get in and out of bed so they are only in it for the allowed hours. At their next session, get another estimate of how much sleep they got on average over the past week, and go through the same process to set a new schedule with a time to get in bed and a time to get out.

Things may get worse before they get better during bed restriction, particularly in the first week. After that, sleep consolidates, and clients spend more of their time in bed asleep. In medical terms, their sleep has become more efficient.

Although daunting, there is a hidden benefit to systematic bed restriction. It brings a needed dose of predictability to the uncertain world of insomnia. The regimented program allows clients to give up the struggle. The following pages contain handouts, worksheets, and sleep logs that clients can use to implement the steps of CBT-I and track their progress throughout this treatment.

The Steps of CBT-I

Step 1: Continue First Aid for Insomnia

During CBT-I, you'll continue to follow all but one of the basic steps outlined in the "First Aid for Insomnia" handout. To recap, those steps are:

1. Wake up at a regular time

2. Avoid daytime naps

3. Only use the bed for sleep (and intimacy)

4. ~~Only go to bed when sleepy~~*

5. Avoid caffeine, alcohol, and light in the evening

6. Set the stage for sleep

*In CBT-I, only rule #4 is going to change. Instead of waiting until you're tired to go to bed, you'll develop a set time to get in and out of bed. To figure out those times, you'll first need to take a few sleep measurements.

Step 2: Measure Your Sleep

In the first week of this therapy, you'll measure two aspects of sleep: (1) the average time you spend asleep each day and (2) the average time you spend awake *in bed* each day. While you gather that information, sleep according to your usual habits and follow the basic first aid rules as best you can. Each night record:

1. The time you got in bed at night and the time you got out of bed in the morning.

2. The total hours you spent asleep (use your best guess; don't watch the clock).

3. The total hours you were awake in bed.

4. If using a sleep medicine, the milligrams (mg) you took.

The **Sleep Log** for week one (page 169) will help you gather this information. At the end of the week, add the hours you spent asleep for all seven days and divide by seven. That is your *average daily sleep.*

Step 3: Restore Your Sleep Drive by Limiting Time in Bed

In the second week, you'll limit the time you spend in bed. The mild sleep deprivation this creates will intensify your sleep drive. It will be difficult at first, but as that drive grows, sleep will come more naturally.

First, take your *average daily sleep* from step 2 and add 1/2 hour. That number is the total amount of time you are allowed in bed each night. (The extra 1/2 hour is a buffer to give you time to fall asleep.) Whether you are asleep or awake, you can only lie in bed for that amount of time. If that sounds harsh, there is a cushion. You don't need to limit your time in bed by less than 5 hours. If you have bipolar disorder, you shouldn't limit it below 6½ hours. Bed deprivation beyond that is not necessary for this therapy to work. So, if you clocked in at 4 hours allowed in bed, feel free to move it up based on these guidelines.

You can schedule your time in bed for any period in the night, but it's best to keep it at a regular time. Most people base it on their wake-up time. For example, if they need to get up at 8:00 a.m. and are only allowed 6 hours in bed, they'll get into bed at 2:00 a.m. and out at 8:00 a.m. Alternatively, you can schedule it based on the time you're most likely to fall asleep. Suppose you fall asleep best around 10:00-11:00 p.m. When you stay up beyond that, you tend to be up all night. If you are only allowed 6 hours in bed, you could get in bed at 10:00 p.m. and set an alarm to get up at 4:00 a.m.

What should you do when you're not in bed and it's still evening? Stick with the evening routines in Chapter 6. Keep the lights low or wear blue light blockers, but don't get too relaxed. You don't want to accidentally fall asleep.

During this week of bed restriction, continue to record the time you spend awake and asleep in bed using the **Sleep Log** for week two (page 171).

Step 4: Daily Fine-Tuning

As you get into the third week of this therapy, you can start making nightly adjustments to the time allowed in bed with measure a called *sleep efficiency*. Sleep efficiency is the percent of time you spend asleep in bed. If you spend half your time in bed trying to fall asleep, your efficiency is 50%. An ideal number is at least 85%, meaning that you actually slept for at least 85% of the time you were in bed. Use the **Measure Your Sleep Efficiency** worksheet to help measure this.

Measure Your Sleep Efficiency

Efficient sleep means that you are asleep for most of the time that you're in bed at night. You can measure your sleep efficiency with a simple method.

First, add up the time you are in bed during a 24-hour period. Include times when you shouldn't have been in bed, like reading during the day or napping. Include times awake and asleep. Do not include times of intimate or sexual activity.

Time in bed: _____

How much time did you spend asleep in that 24-hour cycle? _____

Sleep efficiency = (Time asleep) / (Time in bed) * 100 _____

Example:

Vicky awoke at 9:00 a.m. and got out of bed. She tried to nap for **1 hour** in the afternoon but couldn't. In the evening, she laid awake **1½ hours** before falling asleep. She slept for **6 hours**, and then awoke earlier than expected. She stayed in bed for another **½ hour** and then got up.

Time in bed = 1 hour + 1½ hours + 6 hours + ½ hour = 9 hours

Time asleep = 6 hours

Sleep efficiency = 6 / 9 * 100 = 67%

Using Sleep Efficiency to Adjust Time in Bed

Maintaining healthy sleep is a lot like keeping a car on the road. If the car veers right, you turn a little to the left. If it strays to the left, you nudge the steering wheel to the right. In the first two weeks of this therapy, your sleep was off the road. You needed a strong pull to get you back on, which that first week of bed restriction was designed to accomplish. If your sleep didn't budge with that first week of bed restriction, try another week until you see an increase in your average time asleep.

Once you're on the road, you'll use your sleep efficiency to make small adjustments to the time you're allowed in bed, just as you nudge the steering wheel left and right to drive. When sleep worsens, tighten the reins and restrict time in bed a little more. When it improves, loosen the reins and allow more time.

Begin with the time you were allowed in bed from the night before. Then, calculate your sleep efficiency for that night. Use this guide to figure out if you need to tighten or loosen the amount of time in bed:

- Sleep efficiency less than 80%: Subtract 15 minutes from the time allowed in bed

- Sleep efficiency 80-85%: Continue with the same time allowed in bed

- Sleep efficiency greater than 85%: Add 15 minutes to the time allowed in bed

> **Example:**
>
> Vicky was sleeping well, so her sleep program advised her to allow a generous 8 hours in bed. On most nights she got 6½ to 7 hours of sleep, resulting in a sleep efficiency between 80-85% (6.5/8 * 100 = 81%). This let her keep to the 8-hour limit. Then, she had a rough night. Her sleep efficiency dropped to 67%. She lowered her time in bed by 15 minutes, from 8 hours to 7 hours and 45 minutes (or 7.75 hours).
>
> The next two nights, she slept about 6 hours and 15 minutes, which brought her sleep efficiency to 81% (6.25/7.75 * 100 = 81%). Based on the guidelines for 80-85%, she kept her time in bed the same at 7 hours and 45 minutes. After a few days, she started sleeping 7 hours, which brought her sleep efficiency to 90% (7/7.75 * 100 = 90%). She then added 15 minutes to her time allowed in bed, returning it to 8 hours.

If you have bipolar disorder, you can use sleep efficiency with one modification: Don't restrict your time in bed to less than 6½ hours. That's a safety measure to keep away mania and mixed states.

Once your sleep is improved and you're making those daily adjustments, you'll no longer need to keep the visual sleep log and instead can track your sleep efficiency with the "Sleep Log" for week three and beyond (page 172).

Further Reading

There is a free app to guide you through these techniques. Search for "CBT-I Coach" in your app store or look online at mobile.va.gov/app/cbt-i-coach. A good book is *Overcoming Insomnia: A Cognitive-Behavioral Therapy Approach* by Jack Edinger and Colleen Carney.

Client Worksheet

Sleep Log: Week One

Date	Med?	Hours awake in bed (fill in boxes)									Time in and out of bed		Hours asleep (fill in boxes)																							
		4.5	4	3.5	3	2.5	2	1.5	1	0.5	IN	OUT	0.5	1	1.5	2	2.5	3	3.5	4	4.5	5	5.5	6	6.5	7	7.5	8	8.5	9	9.5	10	10.5	11	11.5	12

Add all hours asleep for past 7 days: ▼ Divide this by 7: ▼ Add 0.5 to this: ▼ Spend only this much time in bed each night for the next week.

Adjustments: If your final number is less than 5, you can raise it to 5 hours. If you have bipolar disorder and it's less than 6.5, raise it to 6.5 hours.

Examples

1. Can't fall asleep

You go to bed at 10:00 p.m., toss and turn for 3.5 hours, and then fall asleep around 1:30 a.m. You sleep through the night and wake up at 9:00 a.m., which gives a total of 7.5 hours of sleep. Your sleep chart would look like this:

Date	Med?	Hours awake in bed (fill in boxes)									Time in and out of bed		Hours asleep (fill in boxes)																						
		4.5	4	3.5	3	2.5	2	1.5	1	0.5	IN	OUT	0.5	1	1.5	2	2.5	3	3.5	4	4.5	5	5.5	6	6.5	7	7.5	8	8.5	9	9.5	10	10.5	11	11.5	12
9/16	No			▓	▓	▓	▓	▓	▓	▓	10pm	9am	▓	▓	▓	▓	▓	▓	▓	▓	▓	▓	▓	▓	▓	▓	▓									

2. Waking up during the night

On this night, you go to bed at 10:00 p.m. and fall asleep within 15 minutes. You wake up two times during the night, each time losing about 30 minutes of sleep to go to the bathroom and fall asleep again. Then, you awake a third time at 5:00 a.m. This time, you are unable to fall asleep, and lie in bed for 3.5 hours before getting up to start your day at 8:30 a.m. Your total sleep is around 6 hours, and you spent 4.5 hours awake in bed (or in the bathroom). Here is your sleep chart for this night:

Date	Med?	Hours awake in bed (fill in boxes)									Time in and out of bed		Hours asleep (fill in boxes)																						
		4.5	4	3.5	3	2.5	2	1.5	1	0.5	IN	OUT	0.5	1	1.5	2	2.5	3	3.5	4	4.5	5	5.5	6	6.5	7	7.5	8	8.5	9	9.5	10	10.5	11	11.5	12
9/16	No		▓	▓	▓	▓	▓	▓	▓	▓	10pm	8:30am	▓	▓	▓	▓	▓	▓	▓	▓	▓	▓	▓	▓												

3. Taking daytime naps

Although daytime naps should be avoided during this therapy, still chart them if they occur. You can use a separate color for that. Imagine you are so tired that you fall asleep on the sofa from 4:00 p.m. to 6:00 p.m. Later that night, you have insomnia and lie in bed from 11:00 p.m. to 1:00 a.m. You then take 5 mg of zolpidem (Ambien), which quickly puts you to sleep, and you wake up at 7:00 a.m. You would add the nap time to your total time asleep that day like this:

Date	Med?	Hours awake in bed (fill in boxes)									Time in and out of bed		Hours asleep (fill in boxes)																						
		4.5	4	3.5	3	2.5	2	1.5	1	0.5	IN	OUT	0.5	1	1.5	2	2.5	3	3.5	4	4.5	5	5.5	6	6.5	7	7.5	8	8.5	9	9.5	10	10.5	11	11.5	12
9/16	5mg						▓	▓	▓	▓	11pm	7am	▓	▓	■nap■	▓	▓	▓	▓	▓	▓	▓	▓	▓	▓	▓	▓									

Client Worksheet

Sleep Log: Week Two

What time are you most likely to fall asleep at night? _____. What time do you need to get up each morning? _____.

Devise a schedule using those two times and your total time allowed in bed. Ideally, you would get in bed about 1/2 hour before you are likely to fall asleep and wake up at the time you need in the morning. You'll probably need to compromise, adjusting the in-bed and out-of-bed times to get the best fit.

Ideal schedule: Time in bed: _____. Time out of bed: _____. Total time allowed in bed: _____.

Write those times on this sleep log and follow them for Week 2, still recording the time you spent asleep and awake in bed.

Date	Med?	Hours awake in bed (fill in boxes)									Time in and out of bed		Hours asleep (fill in boxes)																							
		4.5	4	3.5	3	2.5	2	1.5	1	0.5	IN	OUT	0.5	1	1.5	2	2.5	3	3.5	4	4.5	5	5.5	6	6.5	7	7.5	8	8.5	9	9.5	10	10.5	11	11.5	12

Sleep Log: Week Three and Beyond

Date	Hours slept	Hours allowed in bed	Sleep efficiency (Hours slept / Hours in bed * 100)	Adjust time allowed for the next night in bed based on sleep efficiency:		
				<80% Subtract 15min	80-85% Keep the same	>85% Add 15min
Ex. 2/7	5	7	5 / 7 * 100 = 71%	7 hr – 15 min = 6.75 hr		
Ex. 2/8	5.5	6.75	5.5 / 6.75 * 100 = 81%		6.75 hours (same)	

8

The Antidepressant Diet

Food and the Brain

Depression can make people passive, and Ralph was about the most passive client in my practice. He came to his visits without goals or complaints, each time with the same grim, bleak expression. He was on long-term disability for depression and seemed resigned to that fate. Then, one day he strolled in with a new glow. His face had a smile and his conversation flowed spontaneously. Perplexed, I asked him what had made the difference. *"I gave up fast food three months ago,"* he said. From motivational interviewing to CBT, I had tried to move the hardened walls of his depression without success, but I had never thought to ask what he was eating.

Ralph's case got me interested in the food-mood connection, but back in the early 2000s when I saw him, there was no proof that food could treat depression. At that time, we only had a rudimentary understanding of the basic science behind nutrition on the brain. In particular, we knew that brain cells looked healthier in the absence of simple sugars, saturated fats, and processed foods. Blood vessels were also less clogged, allowing better delivery of oxygen throughout the brain. What we did not know was that food could treat depression just as medication or therapy can.

Many years later, in 2017, the first clinical study of nutrition and mood came out (Jacka et al., 2017). It was a well-designed study which randomized people with moderate to severe depression to receive either supportive therapy (the placebo) or nutritional counseling for three months. Both groups had the same amount of face-to-face time in counseling, with the only difference being the focus of the sessions. Clients in the nutritional group learned how to change their diet toward a simplified version of the Mediterranean diet (the "ModiMed" diet).

I expected that a healthy diet might have some effect but was surprised by just how big the effect was. In the study, researchers found that shifting from an average Western-style diet to the "ModiMed" diet treated depression much better than supportive therapy, with the kind of large effect that we see with CBT or antidepressants. Given that statistical flukes are common in medicine, it's unwise to jump on the bandwagon of a single study. However, this study was quickly followed by a second randomized-controlled trial that also found significant antidepressant effects with the Mediterranean diet (Parletta et al., 2017).

In the first study, the diet was laid out with specific suggestions regarding how much to eat from each food group. The second study used a more relaxed approach, encouraging clients to eat more of the healthy, Mediterranean-style foods and fewer of the others. Both worked equally well. Neither excluded any particular foods, and neither had calorie restrictions.

Just how significant were the effects across both studies? A good way to estimate this is through effect size, which estimates how big the difference was between the treatment and the placebo (e.g., supportive counseling). Dietary counseling had a large effect size in the first and second study (1.2 and 2.4, respectively). In comparison, the effect sizes for exercise and antidepressants range from 0.3-0.6 (Cipriani et al., 2018; Cooney et al., 2013).

Both of these studies were conducted in Australia, and in this book I've adapted their recommendations for American clients in a form I call the *antidepressant diet*.

Healthy Skepticism

How do we know that it was the food that treated depression in these studies? After all, making dietary changes involves a few steps that could improve mood on its own, such as supportive contact with a dietician, goal setting, and a greater sense of self-efficacy. Healthy habits tend to give rise to more healthy habits, so it's also possible that those who took on this diet started exercising or socializing more.

There are several factors that support a direct role of food in the observed effects. First, reductions in depression were closely correlated with improvements in diet. For every 10% change in diet, there was a 5% drop in depression scores. That suggests it's the food that made the difference, and it offers hope that small changes can still make a difference.

But what about the possibility that their findings were attributable to weight loss or greater self-esteem? The researchers anticipated this quandary and controlled for potential confounds that might have otherwise explained their findings. Although weight loss does improve depression, it did not account for the effects in these trials. Nor did changes in exercise, smoking, or sense of self-efficacy. **In the end, the food itself made a difference all its own.**

Though the benefits of the antidepressant diet are only based on two studies, they do build on other research on food and mood in people without depression. That body of evidence is much larger, and includes 16 controlled trials involving over 45,000 people, which found that shifting to a healthy diet improved mild symptoms of depression in otherwise healthy adults (Firth et al., 2019). As the research continues to build, nutritional therapy is poised to become a new standard of care for depression.

The Science Behind the Diet

To create this diet, the researchers started with a diet *U.S. News & World Report* ranked #1 for medical health: the Mediterranean diet. This diet is particularly good at preventing heart disease and diabetes, which is important because the brain needs healthy blood flow and stable metabolic hormones to stay well.

Next, they sprinkled in some brain superfoods, emphasizing green, leafy vegetables, nuts, berries, and oily fish like salmon. These foods improve brain health by reducing inflammation and oxidation, and increasing brain-growth factors. They also supply the building materials to make brain cells and neurotransmitters, like folate and omega-3 fatty acids. These superfoods carry few risks, so they can be consumed in abundance.

The team then identified foods that do some good and some harm (e.g., poultry, lean red meat, dairy, and eggs) and introduced these in moderation. They provide essential brain nutrients, like choline from eggs or iron, and B-vitamins from red meat. Diets that exclude these foods – whether vegetarian, vegan, or pescatarian – are in fact associated with a higher risk of depression (Matta et al., 2018). On the other hand, these foods carry health risks when overindulged. The solution is to eat them in moderation.

Finally, the team limited foods that appear to do nothing but harm for both the brain and the body. Diets high in saturated fats, simple sugars, and processed, fried, or fast foods raise the odds of depression, as does excessive alcohol use. They clog blood vessels, set off depressogenic cascades of inflammation, and cause metabolic hormones to surge, crashing into the brain much as stress hormones like cortisol do.

Antidepressant Foods

Foods that improve the health of the brain have these qualities in common:

1. They are anti-inflammatory.

Inflammation is how the body fights off intruders, like infections and harmful chemicals. That battle is healthy when it's short lived, but when inflammation goes on too long, it leads to depression and other health problems, like diabetes, cancer, heart disease, and arthritis.

2. They are rich in antioxidants.

Oxidation is how the body converts oxygen into useful energy. The problem is that oxidation creates harmful by-products called *free radicals* that contribute to aging and disease. Antioxidants clean up those by-products, and foods that are rich in antioxidants are good for physical and mental health. These include flavanols from berries, tea, and dark chocolate; coenzyme Q_{10} from fish, nuts, and vegetable oils; and various vitamins from colorful fruits and vegetables.

3. They are neuroprotective.

The brain is constantly repairing its neurons through a process called *neuroprotection*. Antidepressants, exercise, and a healthy diet contribute to neuroprotection by increasing brain-derived neuroprotective factor (BDNF). Unhealthy fats and simple sugars get in the way of brain repair by lowering BDNF. Foods that increase BDNF include:

- Carotenoids: carrots, sweet potatoes, dark leafy greens, tomatoes

- Probiotics: yogurt, pickled vegetables, vinegar

- Omega-3s: fish, nuts, fruits, dark green vegetables

How to Use Diet in Therapy

You don't need to be a dietician to guide clients toward the antidepressant diet. The changes involved are very basic. After all, this diet was designed for people with depression to follow, so simplicity is at its core. Too much knowledge can get in the way by introducing higher-level debates over the merits of organic farming and steel-cut oatmeal. Those ideas do have merit, but they have not yet proven their utility in treating depression.

Most of the recommendations in this diet are self-explanatory, like eating more fruits and vegetables. There are a few that can be confusing, like whole grains and processed foods, and I've included a crash course on these to guide you and your clients. Perfection is not the goal, for the therapist or the client, so don't worry about doing it wrong. Simply shifting toward brain-friendly foods and away from harmful ones will do your clients a world of good. For that reason, take the portion sizes in the plan with a grain of salt; they are only a rough guide.

As clients follow along the diet, make sure they are enjoying the process by preparing meals they like and feeling more confident about their abilities. Too much focus on the numbers can increase stress, and part of the goal of a healthy diet is to stabilize stress hormones. In addition, rigid adherence to the antidepressant diet can backfire by triggering a ruminative spiral of self-reproach. It also misses out on an important ingredient in Mediterranean foods: fun. Part of the reason that people in the Mediterranean regions are happier and healthier is that they enjoy long, relaxing meals with friends and family, often outdoors under the warm Mediterranean sun.

Introducing the Diet

Most clients are curious to hear that a diet can treat depression and want to know more. I start by educating them about the diet and encouraging them to look for ways that they are already following it. People with depression need to give themselves some credit.

I then ask them to think of a few changes they could start with, ideally something easy and appetizing. For example, they might add berries to their breakfast, shift their breads and pastas to 100% whole grains, or adopt a new snack from the **Antidepressant Food Swaps** list on page 187. The important thing is that the change is something they're likely to follow through with. If they succeed with this first step, we can build from there.

The following steps can help you introduce this diet in therapy:

1. **Assess their current diet.**

   I begin by asking clients about their current dietary patterns. Some are already on board with this plan, in which case I'll give them a copy of the **Antidepressant Foods: Serving Guide** handout (page 186) to validate and encourage the steps they are already taking. Many others look to the floor with chagrin and speak of a vicious cycle where they use sweet-salty-fatty foods to feel better, later feel worse, and then repeat.

2. **Address guilt and shame around food.**

   Many clients have a long history of negative associations around food that can get in the way of this plan. What role has food played in their lives? What does it mean to them? What messages did they get from their family? What has been their experience with diets in the past? This work is more involved for clients with eating disorders, for whom it can help to take the word "diet" out altogether.

3. **Briefly describe the "diet."**

   Provide clients with a copy of **The Antidepressant Diet is Not a Diet** handout (page 178) to help give them a broad overview of the diet and its rationale. Explain that this plan is not a diet in the traditional sense because clients can eat as much as they want. Rather, it is a plan that encourages clients to consider the following three categories of food: those to eat more of (brain-healthy foods), those to eat less of (brain-unhealthy foods), and those to eat in moderation. A detailed description of these categories is provided on page 184 (**Antidepressant Foods: The Full List**). There is also an accompanying handout that specifies recommended serving sizes on page 186, but make sure to emphasize to clients that this is just a rough guide.

4. **Find a few brain foods they like.**

   Drawing from the "eat more" section at the top of the **Antidepressant Foods: The Full List**, brainstorm with the client to create a list of antidepressant foods they actually like. What do they enjoy eating? What cravings does it fulfill? Use the **Antidepressant Food Swaps** handout to help them generate alternatives. Clients with depression have difficulty conjuring up pleasurable ideas, so it helps to name specific ingredients and modes of preparation. For example, instead of "vegetables," say "sweet potatoes" or better yet, "roasted sweet potatoes." Instead of "fruit," say "blueberries" or "whole wheat blueberry pancakes."

5. **Make simple changes and raise awareness.**

   Start by increasing brain-friendly foods before reducing foods in other categories. For the first week, have clients eat more of the foods from their new list. Ask them to keep a food journal listing what they ate at each meal and how they felt a few hours later. Emphasize that the main goal is to become more aware of what they eat and how it makes them feel. Although this book includes a weekly food record (page 189), that's optional. It's best reserved for later when the client is closer to the model diet, or for clients who enjoy that level of detail. At the early stages, the journal should focus on the ingredients, rather than the quantity. Measuring portions is tedious and will make this feel too much like a diet. Instead, it should feel like a journey, an exploration of food.

6. **Review progress and adjust goals.**

   Review clients' food journal at the beginning of each session, highlighting their successes and troubleshooting setbacks. "How were you able to make that shift? What was difficult about it?" Ask how the new foods tasted, as well as how clients felt a few hours after eating them. As clients become more aware of the delayed effects of what they eat, they will naturally shift toward healthier options. If a client is making steady progress, ask if they are ready to make further changes. Comparing their food journal with the recommended antidepressant foods on page 184 will clarify the next steps. If they are falling behind in the diet, problem-solve the matter and adjust the goals if needed. Sometimes it's best to put the diet on hold until they are ready to tackle it again.

Working with Special Medical Diets

The antidepressant diet can be easily modified to meet most medical needs. Below is a list of common medical conditions that require special diets. I've put an asterisk by the conditions that would benefit from a consultation between the client and their physician or nutritionist before starting a new approach. The three conditions at the end of the list require avoiding certain foods, like lactose or gluten, which is easy to do on this diet. In addition, nutrition guidelines for individuals with heart conditions (heart failure, high blood pressure, high cholesterol) advocate lowering salt and saturated fats, which is already built in to the antidepressant diet.

Medical Conditions That Require Special Diets

- Diabetes*

- Renal (kidney) insufficiency or failure*

- Renal (kidney) stones*

- Gout*

- Heart failure

- High blood pressure

- High cholesterol

- Celiac Disease (Gluten intolerance)

- Lactose intolerance

- Food allergies

Consult with physician before adopting the antidepressant diet

---

Antidepressant Cookbooks

- Natalie Parletta, Dorota Zarnowiecki, Svetlana Bogomolova, & Amy Wilson. *HELFIMED Recipe Book (2017)*. This cookbook was used in the original research and is available online at moodtreatmentcenter.com/antidepressantcookbook.pdf

- Felice Jacka. *Brain Changer: The Good Mental Health Diet* (2019). Dr. Jacka conducted the original studies on the antidepressant diet. Her book summarizes the science behind the diet and includes recipes.

- Rebecca Katz. *The Healthy Mind Cookbook* (2015).

- Leslie Korn. *The Good Mood Kitchen* (2017).

- America's Test Kitchen. *The Complete Mediterranean Cookbook* (2016).

The Antidepressant Diet is Not a Diet

A new antidepressant was discovered in 2017: food. For those of you who've experienced sugar highs, caffeine rushes, or alcohol buzzes, this news probably doesn't come as a surprise, but this antidepressant food is a different kind of medicine. Its effects build slowly over weeks and months. Instead of a quick chemical effect, it improves the health of the brain. It lowers inflammation and provides nutrients that strengthen and repair brain cells.

The food that does all this is found in the Mediterranean diet. It's high in vegetables, fruits, fish, nuts, whole grains, and healthy oils. Just as important, it's low in the foods that impair brain health: sweets, fried foods, and fast or processed foods. It's rated among the top diets for physical health, and its benefits in depression are impressive as well. In particular, switching from a Western-style diet to a Mediterranean one treats depression with an effect as powerful as that of an antidepressant. It also improves memory and concentration, and it lowers the risk of dementia by 50% (Morris et al., 2015).

The antidepressant diet is not a diet in the traditional sense. Calories are not restricted, and no food is outlawed. It's also simple enough that people with severe depression have been able to follow it, and even doing it halfway still brings noticeable benefits. Here are some features of this diet:

1. It's a minimal effort diet.

The point of this diet is to feel good. Enjoying your meals, and the way you feel after those meals, is part of that plan. Rigid rules and calorie counting are not.

2. You don't have to count calories.

You can eat as much as you want with this diet, as long as you shift toward more brain-healthy foods and less brain-unhealthy foods.

3. It's not a fad diet.

This diet has been around for centuries. It is grounded in the traditional foods of Mediterranean countries in Southern Europe, Northern Africa, and the Middle East. People from those regions live longer, healthier lives, and the food they eat is a part of the secret to their good health.

4. It can lead to weight loss.

Although this isn't a weight loss diet, weight loss can be a side effect. Calorie counting diets can shed pounds, but their effects are generally short-lived. In contrast, Mediterranean foods work like a good weight-loss medicine by improving metabolism, lowering appetite, and reducing belly fat. In one study, the Mediterranean approach caused more weight loss over the long term than calorie counting.

5. You don't have to give up fats.

Healthy fats from nuts, fish, and extra virgin olive oil are not only allowed, they're encouraged.

6. It's not expensive.

By cutting out snack foods, sodas, and desserts, the savings with this diet can be big. Studies find that people spend less on food when they switch from the Western diet to the Mediterranean diet.

7. Perfection is not the goal.

This diet is about feeling good, not nutritional purity. You don't need to buy organic vegetables or grass-fed, hormone-free meats to see results. Frozen and canned foods are allowed. We'll get picky about a few things, like extra virgin olive oil and 100% whole grains, but beyond that you can relax at the grocery store.

10 Ways to Depression-Proof Your Diet

The steps below will help you get started on the antidepressant diet.

1. Focus on how you feel after the meal.

Sugar, salt, and processed foods taste good in the moment. A few hours later, though, they cause uncomfortable cravings for more. They're designed for addiction. The flavors of the antidepressant diet are more complex and will take some time to adjust to. These foods aren't instantly rewarding, but if you focus on how you feel in the hours after a meal, then you might appreciate a difference. Compared to a fast food meal, you're likely to feel more energized, lighter, and mentally clear after an antidepressant meal. These foods stabilize metabolism, which means fewer sugar cravings and hunger pains throughout the day.

2. Enjoy your meals.

In the Mediterranean culture, people savor their food over long, languid meals. Find foods that you like, eat outdoors, share meals with friends, and fill your plates with beautiful colors of fruits and vegetables. It takes about 20 minutes for the brain to register that you've eaten, so slow down the process and appreciate the flavors as you eat.

3. Swap soda for water.

Make water your go-to drink. Or use tea or flavored water without any sweeteners. That includes artificial sweeteners, which cause more depression and health problems than regular sugar. Sugar spikes strain the brain, so swapping out soda for unsweetened drinks will make a big difference in your wellbeing. Always have a glass of water with an alcoholic beverage. If insomnia is an issue, avoid caffeinated beverages after 2:00 p.m.

4. Snack on nuts and berries.

These are packed with brain-protecting nutrients and appetite-stabilizing protein and fiber. Whole-grain snacks like homemade popcorn or whole-grain bread dipped in extra virgin olive oil are also encouraged.

5. Use sweets as a reward.

Limit sugar, but enjoy a small serving of sweets on special occasions or as a reward for the positive changes you've made. Choose desserts with dark chocolate, honey, nuts, or berries.

6. Swap white flour for 100% whole grains.

For bread, cereal, pasta, rice, and crackers, choose products with "100% Whole Grains" on the label (see "Whole Grain Taste Test" handout). Swap white rice for a whole grain variety, like brown rice, wild rice, quinoa, or farro.

7. Find vegetables you like and include them in every meal.

Aim for variety of colors, and try to include green leafy vegetables and tomatoes. Keep fresh leafy greens on hand and sprinkle them wherever you can: on pizzas, in omelets, between bread, or under a piece of grilled meat.

8. Swap butter and oil for extra virgin olive oil.

Olive oil is good for the heart and the brain, and the extra virgin type is packed with anti-inflammatory nutrients.

9. Shift your protein.

Eat more beans and fish. Enjoy chicken, poultry, eggs, and lean red meat in moderation. Dairy is another good source of protein, and this diet encourages reduced-fat milk, cheese, and plain yogurt. Buy the plain yogurt variety and sweeten it to taste with fruit and honey.

10. Slowly cut back on junk food, fast food, fried food, and highly-processed foods.

These are the foods that cause depression, but they are hard to give up. Save this step for last. After you've made the other changes, you won't have much room for these types of foods. You even may not want them at all as you become more aware of the way they make you feel.

What are Highly-Processed Foods?

Processing helps foods stay shelf-stable. It's also used to improve their color, texture, and taste or, as some would argue, make them more addictive. Technically, bread, cheese, and canned beans are processed, but not in a way that is a problem on this diet. It's ultra- or highly-processed foods that you need to avoid. These include frozen or packaged meals, fast food, fried food, hot dogs, cold cuts, bacon, sausage, soda, chips, microwave popcorn, candy, frozen desserts, sugary breakfast cereals, energy bars, bottled drinks, Frappuccinos, pre-mixed baking items, margarine, and premade sauces.

Be careful, as highly-processed foods can still say "organic" or "natural" on the front, but that doesn't mean they are healthy. To shop smart, count how many unfamiliar chemicals are on the ingredient panel. Stick with products that have the least of these.

Sugar and Salt

When shopping, look for foods that are low in sugar and salt, particularly the "added sugars" which are usually listed separately on the nutrition panel. The American Heart Association recommends keeping these added sugars to a maximum of 25 grams a day for women and 36 grams a day for men, and that's sound advice for the brain as well. Spikes in sugar are not good for the brain, and one common "added sugar" — high fructose corn syrup — has been linked to mania and depression.

It's tempting to switch to artificial sweeteners, but think twice before you do. They may have zero calories, but they still cause as much weight gain as regular sugar. Artificial sweeteners kill the good bacteria in the gut and cause the gut's lining to breakdown, a condition called "leaky gut." The result is that toxic materials leak into the blood stream, causing inflammation, metabolic changes, weight gain, and diabetes. Eventually those changes irritate the brain, which is why artificial sweeteners are linked to higher rates of depression than regular sugar.

Whole Grain Taste Test

Whole grains are good for you because they contain the healthy parts of the grain that are rich in fiber and vitamins. In contrast, those nutrients are stripped away in flours. Those nutrients protect you from a sugar rush. It's the same reason that eating the whole fruit is healthier than drinking fruit juice. The extra fiber in the fruit slows down the rush of sugar.

Unless you bake them from scratch, most of your whole grains will be store bought. When shopping for whole grains, look for products that are low in sugar and salt, high in fiber, and free of chemical additives. The following products have been blessed by professional taste testers and contain 100% whole grains.

Whole Wheat Pasta

Bionaturea Organic 100% Whole Wheat

Barilla Whole Grain Penne

Ronzoni Healthy Harvest

Trader Joe's Organic Whole Wheat

DeBoles Organic Whole Wheat

Rao's Homemade Whole Wheat Penne

Whole Wheat Bread

Sliced Breads

Arnold Whole Grain Double Protein

Freihofer's Country Stone Ground 100% Whole Wheat

Nature's Harvest Stone Ground 100% Whole Wheat

Eureka! Seeds the Day Organic

Whole Foods Market Organic 100% Whole Wheat

Nature's Own: Premium Specialty 12 Grain or Double Fiber Wheat

Pepperidge Farm: Farmhouse Soft 100% Whole Wheat and Whole Grain 15 Grain

Vermont Bread Company Yoga Bread

Rise Organic Bakery 100% Whole Wheat

Martin's 100% Whole Wheat Potato Bread

Rubschlarger 100% Whole Grain Pumpernickel Bread

Sprouted Breads

Most sprouted breads are whole grain. Popular brands include Angelic Bakehouse, Alvarado Street Bakery, Ezekiel, Shiloh Farms, and Silver Hills Bakery Sprouted Breads.

English Muffins

Thomas' 100% Whole Wheat

Orowheat 100% Whole Wheat

Pita and Flatbreads

Flatout 100% Whole Wheat Flatbread

Thomas' Sahara 100% Whole Wheat Pita

Buns

Ozery Bakery Onebun

Nature's Own 100% Whole Wheat Buns

Angelic Bake House Sprouted Buns

Arnold Select 100% Whole Wheat Rolls

Pizza

Angelic Bakehouse Sprouted Flatzza Pizza Crust

Trader Joe's Whole Wheat Pizza Dough

Boboli 100% Whole Wheat Thin Pizza Crust

Pancakes

Hodgson Mill Whole Wheat Pancake Mixes

Kodiak Cakes Whole Wheat Pancake Mixes

Cereal

Oatmeal (avoid "instant" oatmeal)

Muesli cereal, fiber and bran cereals, granola, porridge

Good brands with whole grain options include Fiber One, Ezekiel 4:9, Engine 5, Kashi, and Grape Nuts.

Rice

Brown rice, wild rice, and quinoa

Snacks

Crackers made with 100% whole grains, brown rice, or nuts

Home popped popcorn (pop on the stove with olive oil)

Gluten-free Whole Grains

Corn, buckwheat, sorghum, teff, millet, amaranth, arrowroot, and oats labeled "gluten free." Flours made from beans and nuts will also work. Quinoa, brown, and wild rice are gluten-free. Avoid whole wheat, rye, and barley grains if you're gluten-free.

Antidepressant Foods: The Full List

"Eat more of..." These are brain super-foods. The more you eat, the better.

"Eat in moderation..." These foods support brain health in small doses, but too much can cause harm.

"Eat less of..." You could avoid these foods entirely, but that would be no fun. They do some harm, but your body can repair the damage if you space them out in small amounts.

	Eat more. It's all good...
Vegetables	**Best options:** Green leafy vegetables (the darker the better), tomatoes, eggplant, purple corn, sweet potatoes, and orange, yellow, and red vegetables. However, better to aim for variety than to eat only the "best" options. **Tips:** Frozen vegetables often contain more nutrients than fresh ones. Look for bags of loosely frozen veggies instead of the ones frozen in a solid block of ice.
Fruit	**Best options:** Blueberries, strawberries, cranberries, cherries, blood oranges, citrus fruits, and concord grapes. **Tips:** Unlike vegetables, fruits are better in their fresh form. For dried fruit, look for unsweetened products.
Nuts, seeds, olives	**Best options:** Walnuts, hazelnuts, and almonds. Flax, chia, and hemp seeds. **Tips:** Peanut butter and other spreadable nuts count, but look for low-sugar options. Avoid salted nuts. They can raise blood pressure.
100% whole grains	See **Whole Grains Taste Test** for ideas **Real whole grains:** Labeled "100% whole wheat" or "100% whole grains;" or the first ingredient is "whole grains" or a specific whole grain, such as whole wheat, corn, cornmeal, oats, rye, buckwheat, wheat germ, wheat bran, barley, spelt, sorghum, amaranth, millet, bulgur, kañiwa, farro, teff, or triticale. **Fake whole grains:** Wheat bread (it's only whole if it says whole wheat), multigrain bread, and products labeled "made with whole grains". Those made with enriched or refined flours, white rice, gnocchi, white pasta, or corn flakes.
Fish	**Best options:** Oily fish are high in omega-3s, including salmon, tuna (either fresh ahi tuna or canned light tuna), sardines, caviar, and mussels. Low-mercury options (best for children and pregnant women) include: canned light tuna (not white or albacore tuna), shellfish, salmon, catfish, flounder, sole, trout, black sea bass, tilapia, pollock, anchovies, herring, and perch. **Tips:** Fresh, smoked, canned, and frozen all count. Most "fresh" fish at the grocery store is defrosted, so opt for frozen fish and defrost when ready. Minimize contaminants like mercury by removing the skin and fat before cooking. High-mercury fish include marlin, shark, swordfish, tilefish, pike, king mackerel, orange roughly, and bluefin tuna.
Beans	In addition to beans, edamame, humus, tofu, and falafel count.

Eat in moderation. Good in small doses, harmful in excess...	
Extra virgin olive oil	Olive oil is healthy because it is low in saturated fats, but extra virgin olive oil has brain-healthy antioxidants. **Tips:** Extra virgin olive oil burns at temperatures above 325-375°F. For high-temperature cooking, use oil with a higher smoke point, like regular olive oil (465°F) or safflower oil (510°F).
Red meat	**Best options:** Lean meats like roast beef, bison, buffalo, ostrich, 95% lean ground chunk, and beef cuts labeled "loin" or "round." **Cooking tips:** Trim the fat. To reduce glycation toxins, cook at a low temperature and marinate in lemon or vinegar for an hour.
Poultry	Chicken, turkey, duck, quail, pheasant. **Cooking tips:** Removing the skin will lower the saturated fats. If roasting, remove the skin after cooking so the meat doesn't get too dry.
Dairy	**Best options:** Plain, unsweetened yogurt, Greek, Icelandic (Skyr), and probiotic yogurts (Kefir). For cheese, opt for hard cheese, feta, and ricotta. **Tips:** Vegetarians, vegans, and those with lactose intolerance can opt for soy- or nut-based milk (preferably unsweetened).
Eggs	**Best options:** Look for "free range" eggs and those that are high in omega-3s, a healthy fat that is essential for brain function. **Tips:** Limit to 3 egg yolks per week if you have diabetes, high cholesterol, or heart disease.
Eat less. These mostly cause harm ...	
Fried, fast, sweet, and processed foods	Maximum of three 120 calorie servings per week of: Sweets, sodas, chips, fast food, ultra-processed foods, fried foods, bacon, sausage, deli meats. Bread, pasta, rice, or snacks that are not 100% whole grains. Butter, margarine, and packaged condiments (jelly, ketchup, mayonnaise).
Alcohol	Maximum 1.5 standard drinks/day. Red wine is preferred. Drink a glass of water with each alcoholic beverage. 1.5 standard drinks = 6.8 ounces wine, 2 bottles beer (1 bottle if it's high gravity), 2 ounces spirits, or 5 ounces sherry or port.

Extra credit...
• **Vinegar and spices** are good for the brain, particularly balsamic vinegar, basil, turmeric, cinnamon, garlic, ginger, marjoram, mustard, oregano, rosemary, saffron, sage, and thyme. • **Unsweetened Tea.** 3-6 cups of tea a day lowers the risk of depression, particularly black, green, and white teas.

Antidepressant Foods: Serving Guide

The following chart provides recommended servings for each food group, but these are just a rough guide. Start with the easiest changes and build from there. The more you do, the better you'll feel. You should see a little benefit a few hours after a healthy meal, more improvement in two to four weeks, and a bigger change in depression after two to three months.

Eat more. It's all good...		One serving is:
Vegetables	Ideally 6 servings/day. Include green leafy vegetable or tomatoes in at least one of those servings. Mushrooms count, but minimize potatoes to one serving a day unless it's a sweet potato.	Leafy vegetables: ½ cup cooked or 1 cup raw Other vegetables: ½ cup raw or cooked
Fruit	Ideally 3 servings/day. Include berries every day. Limit juice to one serving a day.	Fruit (fresh, frozen, or canned): ½ cup Dried fruit: 1½ tablespoons Juice: ½ cup
Nuts, seeds, olives	Ideally 1 serving/day	Nuts and seeds: 1 ounce (about ¼ cup) Olives: 3 ounces
100% whole grains	Ideally 5-8 servings/day (eat closer to 8 if you're physically active)	Bread: 1 slice. Rice, pasta, oatmeal, or muesli: ¼ cup. Cereal: ⅔ cup.
Fish	Ideally 2 servings/week. At least one of those should be an oily fish like salmon.	3 ounces cooked
Beans	Ideally 4 servings/week	Beans: ½ cup Hummus or tofu: ⅓ cup
Eat in moderation. Good in small doses, harmful in excess...		**One serving is:**
Extra virgin olive oil	Maximum 3 tablespoons/day	
Red meat	Maximum 3-4 servings/week	3-4 ounces cooked.
Poultry	Maximum 2-3 servings/week	3 ounces cooked (= one breast or a leg + thigh)
Dairy	Maximum 3 servings/day of milk, cheese, yogurt	Milk: 1 cup milk (250 mL) Yogurt: 200 grams Hard cheese: 40 grams Soft cheese: 120 grams
Eggs	Maximum 6 eggs/week	People with high cholesterol or heart disease may need to limit eggs further

Antidepressant Food Swaps

Food	Substitutions
Chips	Popcorn made at home with olive oil (hold the butter)
Crackers	100% whole wheat crackers or crisp breads
Snacks	Celery, carrots, apples, or pepper strips with a dip or nut butter; strawberries with goat cheese; fruit; nuts; or edamame
Ranch dip	Salsa, hummus, chili, tzatziki (or other yogurt dip), baba ghanoush (roasted eggplant), pesto, balsamic vinegar with extra virgin olive oil, olive tapenade, or almond butter
Creamy salad dressings	Salad dressings made with extra virgin olive oil, balsamic vinegar, lemon juice, honey, or mustard
Mayonnaise	Mashed avocados, olive oil, or mustard
Butter	Extra virgin olive oil
Extra salt	Extra herbs, peppers, or spices
Salt cravings	Olives, feta cheese, crackers or pretzels made with 100% whole wheat, hummus, pesto, olive-oil popped popcorn, salted nuts, kimchi, dried nori (seaweed) strips. Sprinkle salt in extra virgin olive oil and dip whole wheat bread in it.
Jelly	Chopped berries with a little bit of honey
Yogurt with sugary fruit	Greek or Icelandic (Skyr) yogurt. Start with plain yogurt and add berries, nuts, and – only if needed – honey or maple syrup.
Sauces with cheese, cream, or butter	Tomato sauce or pesto
Potatoes	Sweet potatoes
White rice	Brown rice, wild rice, whole wheat couscous, or quinoa
Pasta	100% whole wheat pasta
Biscuits	100% whole wheat English muffins
Sandwiches on white bread	Sandwiches on 100% whole wheat bread
Deli meats	Chicken or turkey breast (these are less processed than the packaged slices); hummus
Hamburgers	Bean, veggie, turkey, or salmon burgers on 100% whole wheat buns
Ice cream	Pudding made with skim or 1% milk; canned pears sprinkled with cinnamon and cocoa nibs; frozen grapes
Cookies and candy	Nuts and dried berries, dates, and dark chocolate (>70% cocoa)
Coffee creamer	Coffee creamer has no real cream and is full of trans fats and sugars. Instead, substitute real cream or milk, or even better – almond or soy milk.
Milkshake	Fruit smoothie (try banana, honey, and yogurt)
Soft drinks	Iced tea (unsweetened or sweetened with a little honey), plain sparkling water
Fruit and sports drinks	Use coconut water or make your own water by soaking cucumber, mint, citrus, or berries in a pitcher.
Energy drinks	Green or matcha tea
Beer or cocktails	Red wine (5 ounces a day, about ½ metric cup)

Slightly Healthier Junk Food

If you find it hard to let go of junk food, or just want to make those three servings a week as healthy as can be, try some of the healthier junk foods from the following list. What could go wrong? Well, they still have too much sugar and salt, and they aren't free of processing, but they are worlds better than the old-school junk food. They are the lesser of evils.

Food	Examples
Desserts	Look for recipes that are loaded with fruit, vegetables (e.g., sweet potatoes, pumpkin, or carrots), nuts, nut butter, seeds, whole wheat, oats, olive oil, yogurt, or dark chocolate.
Fruit and nut bars	Kind Bars, Raw Revolution, Rx Bars, Abound, Larabar, Balance, Pure Organic Brand
100% whole wheat crackers	Mary's Gone Crackers Ak-Mak Sesame Cracker 100 Whole Wheat Crisp breads (e.g., Wasa or Finn Crisp Original Rye) Carr's Whole Wheat Crackers 365 Everyday Value (Whole Foods) Woven Wheat Baked Crackers Kashi Heart to Heart Whole Grain Crackers Nabisco Triscuit 100% Whole Wheat Crackers Ritz Toasted Chips 100% Whole Grain
100% whole wheat chips and pretzels	SunChips 100% Whole Wheat Chips Way Better Snacks Tortilla Chips Snyder's Whole Grain Tortilla Chips Snyder's Whole Wheat Pretzel Sticks Beigel Beigel 100% Wheat Pretzels Unique Sprouted 100% Whole Grain Pretzel Splits
Chips made from beans and veggies	Flamous Falafel Chips Beanitos Chips Kashi Hummus Crisps The Mediterranean Snack Food Baked Lentil Chips Dry Roasted Edamame

Weekly Food Record

Track your progress with the antidepressant diet by checking a box every time you have a serving in that food group. The number of boxes represents the recommended servings. More servings may be needed if you're very active, and these optional servings are drawn in light gray (for example, there are 5-8 servings/day for whole grains). For a few categories, there are specific foods that are good to include, like green leafy vegetables, berries, or oily fish. These can be marked by shading the entire square.

	Mon	Tue	Wed	Thur	Fri	Sat	Sun
Eat more...	**Minimum Servings**						
Vegetables	☐☐☐ ☐☐☐	☐☐☐ ☐☐☐	☐☐☐ ☐☐☐	☐☐☐ ☐☐☐	☐☐☐ ☐☐☐	☐☐☐ ☐☐☐	☐☐☐ ☐☐☐
	■ = green leafy vegetables or tomatoes (ideally 1/day). Max 1 potato/day						
Fruit	☐☐☐	☐☐☐	☐☐☐	☐☐☐	☐☐☐	☐☐☐	☐☐☐
	■ = berries (ideally 1/day)						
Nuts	☐	☐	☐	☐	☐	☐	☐
100% Whole grains	☐☐☐ ☐☐☐ ☐☐	☐☐☐ ☐☐☐ ☐☐	☐☐☐ ☐☐☐ ☐☐	☐☐☐ ☐☐☐ ☐☐	☐☐☐ ☐☐☐ ☐☐	☐☐☐ ☐☐☐ ☐☐	☐☐☐ ☐☐☐ ☐☐
Fish	☐☐						
	■ = salmon and other oily fish (ideally 1-2/week)						
Beans	☐☐☐☐						
Moderate...	**Maximum Servings**						
Extra virgin olive oil†	☐☐☐	☐☐☐	☐☐☐	☐☐☐	☐☐☐	☐☐☐	☐☐☐
Lean red meat	☐☐☐☐						
Poultry	☐☐☐						
Milk, cheese, yogurt	☐☐☐	☐☐☐	☐☐☐	☐☐☐	☐☐☐	☐☐☐	☐☐☐
Eggs	☐☐☐☐☐☐						
Alcohol	☐	☐	☐	☐	☐	☐	☐
Eat less...	**Maximum Servings**						
For special occasions	Each box represents a 120 cal serving ☐ ☐ ☐						
	Sweets, sugary drinks, and white breads. Fried, fast, and ultra-processed foods.						
Don't forget...							
Drink lots of water							
Exercise daily							

†Each box is one tablespoon

The Top Antidepressant Boosters

Congratulations! You've reached the end of this book and hopefully have 30 new tools under your belt to treat depression and bipolar disorder. Only one problem remains: 30 is too many. Motivation is in short supply during depression, so you'll need to parse it down to the ones that your client is most likely to succeed with. That list will be different for each client, but there are some interventions with broad appeal. I've listed the ones that offer the biggest returns on investment below.

	Activity	What it is	What it helps	Page
Morning	Brisk awakening	Arise out of bed at the same time each day (give or take 15 minutes).	Depression, bipolar, insomnia	81
	Dawn simulator	By creating a virtual sunrise in your bedroom, these devices improve wakefulness and energy.	Energy, depression	85
	Air ionizer	Originally designed as air purifiers, these devices lift mood. Their fresh scent is reminiscent of the air around a waterfall.	Depression, particularly winter depression	95
Daytime	Absorbing activity	Activities that are so engaging that you lose track of time – and get out of your head – while doing them.	Depression, anxiety, ruminative worry	123
	Brisk walking	Faster than a walk but slower than a jog, 30-45 minutes a day or every other day.	Depression, anxiety, concentration	127
	Nature walks	A stroll in the woods – or along rivers, lakes, or oceans – for one or two hours several days each week.	Concentration, ruminative worry	131
Evening	Evening wind-down	Restful activity before bed can deepen sleep. Examples include meditative music, aromatherapy, dim lights, and a warm bath.	Sleep, bipolar	143
	Blue light blockers	Blue light prevents the brain from entering sleep by shutting down melatonin, a problem that's solved with a special pair of glasses.	Sleep, bipolar, depression, weight loss	145
	CBT for Insomnia	This structured sleep guide realigns the two biological forces that drive sleep.	Sleep, depression, bipolar	163
Meals	Antidepressant diet	This Mediterranean-style diet emphasizes fruits, vegetables, nuts, fish, and olive oil. Calories are not restricted, and no foods are outlawed.	Depression, memory, weight loss	173

Appendix

Antidepressant Apps

There is no end to the number of apps that promise happier, healthier lives, but only a few have undergone clinical testing to prove their effects. Their benefits are real. Self-guided therapy with an app has even treated depression when antidepressants did not work (Mantani et al., 2017). I've listed the best of those apps here.

Cognitive Behavioral Therapy (CBT)

These apps guide clients through CBT: *Moodivate* ($), *Catch It, MoodHacker, Ginsberg,* and *Activities.* They are particularly good for adding antidepressant activities to clients' daily lives.

Intellicare is another series of free apps that was funded by the National Institute of Health to treat depression (intellicare.cbits.northwestern.edu). Clients can try *Worry Knot* for rumination or *Slumber Time* for insomnia. A few of the Intellicare apps also help people get active with engaging activity: *MoveMe, Daily Feats, Boost Me,* and *Aspire.*

Rhythmic Breathing

Rhythmic breathing is a form of meditative breathing that has significant effects on depression. One form of rhythmic breathing, Sudarshan Kriya yoga, has been proven to work for anxiety and depression when medications did not (Sharma et al., 2017). Clients can search for "Sudarshan Kriya yoga" on YouTube or try the app *Breath2Relax* to guide them through the practice.

Mindfulness

Daily practice of mindfulness meditation can improve depression, sleep, and anxiety. The best apps for mindfulness are: *Headspace* ($), *Insight Timer, Smiling Mind, iMindfulness* ($), and *Mindfulness Daily.* Audio guides are also available through CDs, music streaming services, or UCLA's free guided meditations website: www.marc.ucla.edu/body.cfm?id=22.

Stress and Anxiety

There are several available apps that can help clients reduce stress and anxiety. *Stress Free* improves general anxiety and stress management. *Agoraphobia Free* helps people out of the paralyzing anxiety that keeps them from leaving the house.

Suicidality

Virtual Hope Box is based on the cognitive-behavioral model of suicide prevention. In a crisis or emergency, it reminds clients of reasons to live, supportive contacts, and distress tolerance skills.

Sleep

CBT-I Coach is a free app that allows clients to track their progress in CBT-Insomnia along with a therapist. It was created by the Veterans Administration but suitable for civilians.

References

Aiken, C. B. (2019). The bipolar spectrum. In G. Parker (Ed.), *Bipolar II disorder: Modelling, measuring and managing* (3rd ed.), pp. 16–32. Cambridge, UK: Cambridge University Press.

Akiskal, H. S., & Akiskal, K. K. (2011). Overview of principles of caring for bipolar patients. In H. S. Akiskal & M. Tohen (Eds.), *Bipolar psychopharmacotherapy: Caring for the patient* (2nd ed., pp. 487–508). West Sussex, UK: Wiley.

American Psychiatric Association. (2013). *Diagnostic and statistical manual of mental disorders* (5th ed.). Arlington, VA: American Psychiatric Publishing.

Anderson, T., & Wideman, L. (2017). Exercise and the cortisol awakening response: A systematic review. *Sports Medicine – Open, 3*(1), 37.

Angst, J., Gamma, A., Bowden, C. L., Azorin, J. M., Perugi, G., Vieta, E., & Young, A. H. (2012). Diagnostic criteria for bipolarity based on an international sample of 5,635 patients with DSM-IV major depressive episodes. *European Archives of Psychiatry and Clinical Neuroscience, 262*(1), 3–11.

Asai, Y., Obayashi, K., Oume, M., Ogura, M., Takeuchi, K., Yamagami, Y., … Saeki, K. (2018). Farming habit, light exposure, physical activity, and depressive symptoms. A cross-sectional study of the HEIJO-KYO cohort. *Journal of Affective Disorders, 241*, 235–240.

Babyak, M., Blumenthal, J. A., Herman, S., Khatri, P., Doraiswamy, M., Moore, K., … Krishnan, K. R. (2000). Exercise treatment for major depression: Maintenance of therapeutic benefit at 10 months. *Psychosomatic Medicine, 62*(5), 633–638.

Barcaccia, B., Balestrini, V., Saliani, A. M., Baiocco, R., Mancini, F., & Schneider, B. H. (2018). Dysfunctional eating behaviors, anxiety, and depression in Italian boys and girls: The role of mass media. *Brazilian Journal of Psychiatry, 40*(1), 72–77.

Bratman, G. N., Hamilton, J. P., Hahn, K. S., Daily, G. C., & Gross, J. J. (2015). Nature experience reduces rumination and subgenual prefrontal cortex activation. *Proceedings of the National Academy of Sciences U.S.A., 112*(28), 8567–8572.

Bromundt, V., Wirz-Justice, A., Kyburz, S., Opwis, K., Dammann, G., & Cajochen, C. (2013). Circadian sleep-wake cycles, well-being, and light therapy in borderline personality disorder. *Journal of Personality Disorders, 27*(5), 680–696.

Carvalho, A. F., Takwoingi, Y., Sales, P. M., Soczynska, J. K,, Köhler, C. A., Freitas, T. H., … Vieta, E. (2015). Screening for bipolar spectrum disorders: A comprehensive meta-analysis of accuracy studies. *Journal of Affective Disorders, 172*, 337–346.

Chan, M. F., Chan, E. A., & Mok, E. (2010). Effects of music on depression and sleep quality in elderly people: A randomised controlled trial. *Complementary Therapies in Medicine, 18*(3-4), 150–159.

Chao, Y. Y., Scherer, Y. K., & Montgomery, C. A. (2015). Effects of using Nintendo Wii™ exergames in older adults: A review of the literature. *Journal of Aging and Health, 27*(3), 379–402.

Chatterton, M. L., Stockings, E., Berk, M., Barendregt, J. J., Carter, R., & Mihalopoulos, C. (2017). Psychosocial therapies for the adjunctive treatment of bipolar disorder in adults: Network meta-analysis. *The British Journal of Psychiatry, 210*(5), 333–341.

Chiba, S., Yagi, T., Ozone, M., Matsumura, M., Sekiguchi, H., Ganeko, M., … Nishino, S. (2018). High rebound mattress toppers facilitate core body temperature drop and enhance deep sleep in the initial phase of nocturnal sleep. *PLoS One, 13*(6), e0197521.

Cipriani, A., Furukawa, T. A., Salanti, G., Chaimani, A., Atkinson, L. Z., Ogawa, Y., … Geddes, J. R. (2013). Comparative efficacy and acceptability of 21 antidepressant drugs for the acute treatment of adults with major depressive disorder: A systematic review and network meta-analysis. *Lancet, 391*, 1357–1366.

Cooney, G. M., Dwan, K., Greig, C. A., Lawlor, D. A., Rimer, J., Waugh, F. R., ... Mead, G. E. (2013). Exercise for depression. *Cochrane Database of Systematic Reviews, 9,* CD004366.

Cunningham, J. E., & Shapiro, C. M. (2018). Cognitive behavioural therapy for insomnia (CBT-I) to treat depression: A systematic review. *Journal of Psychosomatic Research, 106,* 1–12.

Curtin, M. (2017, May 30). Neuroscience says listening to this song reduces anxiety by up to 65 percent, Inc. Retrieved from https://www.inc.com/melanie-curtin-neuroscience-says-listening-to-this-one-song-reduce-anxiety-by-up-to-65-percent.html

Delle Chiaie, R., Trabucchi, G., Girardi, N., Marini, I., Pannese, R., Vergnani, L., ... Biondi, M. (2013). Group psychoeducation normalizes cortisol awakening response in stabilized bipolar patients under pharmacological maintenance treatment. *Psychotherapy and Psychosomatics, 82*(4), 264–266.

Dimidjian, S., Hollon, S. D., Dobson, K. S., Schmaling, K. B., Kohlenberg, R. J., Addis, M. E., ... Jacobson, N. S. (2006). Randomized trial of behavioral activation, cognitive therapy, and antidepressant medication in the acute treatment of adults with major depression. *Journal of Consulting and Clinical Psychology, 74*(4), 658–670.

Dong, X., Yang, C., Cao, S., Gan, Y., Sun, H., Gong, Y., & Lu, Z. (2015). Tea consumption and the risk of depression: A meta-analysis of observational studies. *Australian and New Zealand Journal of Psychiatry, 49*(4), 334–345.

Dorsey, C. M., Teicher, M., Cohen-Zion, M., Stefanovic, L., Harper, D., Satlin, A., ... Lukas, S. E. (1999). Core body temperature and sleep of older female insomniacs before and after passive body heating. *Sleep, 22,* 891–898.

Elias, L. R., Köhler, C. A., Stubbs, B., Maciel, B. R., Cavalcante, L. M., Vale, A. M., ... Carvalho, A. F. (2017). Measuring affective temperaments: A systematic review of validation studies of the Temperament Evaluation in Memphis Pisa and San Diego (TEMPS) instruments. *Journal of Affective Disorders, 212,* 25–37.

Erikson, E. (1993). *Childhood and society.* New York, NY: W.W. Norton.

Erren, T. C., & Lewis, P. (2019). Hypothesis: Folklore perpetuated expression of moon-associated bipolar disorders in anecdotally exaggerated werewolf guise. *Medical Hypotheses, 122,* 129–133.

Fava, G. A., Rafanelli, C., Tomba, E., Guidi, J., & Grandi, S. (2011). The sequential combination of cognitive behavioral treatment and well-being therapy in cyclothymic disorder. *Psychotherapy and Psychosomatics, 80*(3), 136–143.

Feng, F., Zhang, Y., Hou, J., Cai, J., Jiang, Q., Li, X., ... Li, B. A. (2010). Can music improve sleep quality in adults with primary insomnia? A systematic review and network meta-analysis. *International Journal of Nursing Studies, 77,* 189–196.

Firth, J., Marx, W., Dash, S., Carney, R., Teasdale, S. B., Solmi, M., ... Sarris, J. (2019). The effects of dietary improvement on symptoms of depression and anxiety: A meta-analysis of randomized controlled trials. *Psychosomatic Medicine, 81*(3), 265–280.

Francesca, M. M., Efisia, L. M., Alessandra, G. M., Marianna, A., & Giovanni, C. M. (2014). Misdiagnosed hypomanic symptoms in patients with treatment-resistant major depressive disorder in Italy: Results from the improve study. *Clinical Practice and Epidemiology in Mental Health, 10,* 42–47.

Frank, E., Kupfer, D. J., Thase, M. E., Mallinger, A. G., Swartz, H. A., Fagiolini, A. M., ... Monk, T. (2005). Two-year outcomes for interpersonal and social rhythm therapy in individuals with bipolar I disorder. *Archives of General Psychiatry, 62*(9), 996–1004.

Galvez, J. F., Thommi, S., & Ghaemi, S. N. (2011). Positive aspects of mental illness: A review in bipolar disorder. *Journal of Affective Disorders, 128*(3), 185–190.

Gamma, A., Angst, J., Ajdacic-Gross, V., & Rössler, W. (2008). Are hypomanics the happier normals? *Journal of Affective Disorders, 111,* 235–243.

Goodwin, F. K., & Jamison, K. R. (2007). *Manic-depressive illness: Bipolar disorders and recurrent depression* (2nd ed.). Oxford, UK: Oxford University Press.

Grosso, G., Micek, A., Castellano, S., Pajak, A., & Galvano, F. (2016). Coffee, tea, caffeine and risk of depression: A systematic review and dose-response meta-analysis of observational studies. *Molecular Nutrition and Food Research, 60*(1), 223–234.

Guo, T., Xiang, Y. T., Xiao, L., Hu, C. Q., Chiu, H. F. K., Ungvari, G. S., ... Wang, G. (2015). Measurement-based care versus standard care for major depression: A randomized controlled trial with blind raters. *American Journal of Psychiatry, 172*(10), 1004–1013.

Guo, X., Park, Y., Freedman, N.D., Sinha, R., Hollenbeck, A.R., Blair, A., & Chen, H. (2014). Sweetened beverages, coffee, and tea and depression risk among older U.S. adults. *PLoS One, 9*(4), e94715.

Harvey, A. G., Soehner, A. M., Kaplan, K. A., Hein, K., Lee, J., Kanady, J., . . . Buysse, D. J. (2015). Treating insomnia improves mood state, sleep, and functioning in bipolar disorder: A pilot randomized controlled trial. *Journal of Consulting and Clinical Psychology, 83*(3), 564–577.

Harvey, S. B., Øverland, S., Hatch, S. L., Wessely, S., Mykletun, A., & Hotopf, M. (2018). Exercise and the prevention of depression: Results of the HUNT cohort study. *American Journal of Psychiatry, 175*(1), 28–36.

Henriksen, T. E., Skrede, S., Fasmer, O. B., Schoeyen, H., Leskauskaite, I., Bjørke-Bertheussen J., ... Lund, A. (2016). Blue-blocking glasses as additive treatment for mania: A randomized placebo-controlled trial. *Bipolar Disorder, 18*(3), 221–232.

Hill, N. T., Mowszowski, L., Naismith, S. L., Chadwick, V. L., Valenzuela, M., & Lampit, A. (2017). Computerized cognitive training in older adults with mild cognitive impairment or dementia: A systematic review and meta-analysis. *American Journal of Psychiatry, 174*(4), 329–340.

Howland, R. H. (2016). Hey mister tambourine man, play a drug for me: Music as medication. *Journal of Psychosocial Nursing and Mental Health Services, 54*(12), 23–27.

Huedo-Medina, T. B., Kirsch, I., Middlemass, J., Klonizakis, M., & Siriwardena, A. N. (2012). Effectiveness of non-benzodiazepine hypnotics in treatment of adult insomnia: Meta-analysis of data submitted to the Food and Drug Administration. *British Medical Journal, 345*, e8343.

Hwang, E., & Shin S. (2015). The effects of aromatherapy on sleep improvement: A systematic literature review and meta-analysis. *Journal of Alternative and Complementary Medicine, 21*(2), 61–68.

Irwin, M. R., Olmstead, R., Breen, E. C., Witarama, T., Carrillo, C., Sadeghi, N., ... Cole, S. (2015). Cognitive behavioral therapy and tai chi reverse cellular and genomic markers of inflammation in late-life insomnia: A randomized controlled trial. *Biological Psychiatry, 78*(10), 721–729.

Jacka, F. N., O'Neil, A., Opie, R., Itsiopoulos, C., Cotton, S., Mohebbi, M., ... Berk, M. (2017). A randomised controlled trial of dietary improvement for adults with major depression (the 'SMILES' trial). *BMC Medicine, 15*(1), 23.

Jamison, K. R. (1995). *An unquiet mind: A memoir of moods and memories*. New York, NY: Knopf.

Kaplan, K. A., Talavera, D. C., & Harvey, A. G. (2018). Rise and shine: A treatment experiment testing a morning routine to decrease subjective sleep inertia in insomnia and bipolar disorder. *Behaviour Research and Therapy, 111*, 106–112.

Kotin, J., & Goodwin, F. K. (1972). Depression during mania: Clinical observations and theoretical implications. *American Journal of Psychiatry, 129*, 679–686.

Leubner, D., & Hinterberger, T. (2017). Reviewing the effectiveness of music interventions in treating depression. *Frontiers in Psychology, 8*, 1109.

Liao, W. C. (2002). Effects of passive body heating on body temperature and sleep regulation in the elderly: A systematic review. *International Journal of Nursing Studies, 39*(8), 803–810.

Lin, H. T., Lai, C. H., Perng, H. J., Chung, C. H., Wang, C. C., Chen, W. L., & Chien, W. C. (2018). Insomnia as an independent predictor of suicide attempts: A nationwide population-based retrospective cohort study. *BMC Psychiatry, 18*(1), 117.

Linehan, M. (1993). *Cognitive-behavioral treatment of borderline personality disorder*. New York, NY: Guildford Press.

Lunn, R. M., Blask, D. E., Coogan, A. N., Figueiro, M. G., Gorman, M. R., Hall, J. E., ... Boyd, W. A. (2017). Health consequences of electric lighting practices in the modern world: A report on the National Toxicology Program's workshop on shift work at night, artificial light at night, and circadian disruption. *Science of the Total Environment, 607*, 1073–1084.

Lyall, L. M., Wyse, C. A., Graham, N., Ferguson, A., Lyall, D. M., Cullen, B., ... Smith, D. J. (2018). Association of disrupted circadian rhythmicity with mood disorders, subjective wellbeing, and cognitive function: A cross-sectional study of 91,105 participants from the UK Biobank. *The Lancet Psychiatry, 5*(6), 507–514.

Maguire, M. (2017). Epilepsy and music: Practical notes. *Practical Neurology, 17*(2), 86–95.

Mantani, A., Kato, T., Furukawa, T. A., Horikoshi, M., Imai, H., Hiroe, T., ... Kawanishi, N. (2017). Smartphone cognitive behavioral therapy as an adjunct to pharmacotherapy for refractory depression: Randomized controlled trial. *Journal of Medical Internet Research, 19*(11), e373.

Matta, J., Czernichow, S., Kesse-Guyot, E., Hoertel, N., Limosin, F., Goldberg, M., ... Lemogne, C. (2018). Depressive symptoms and vegetarian diets: Results from the Constances cohort. *Nutrients, 10*(11), e1695.

Morris, M. C., Tangney, C. C., Wang, Y., Sacks, F. M., Bennett, D. A., & Aggarwal, N. T. (2015). MIND diet associated with reduced incidence of Alzheimer's disease. *Alzheimer's Disease, 11*(9), 1007–1014.

Naumann, J., Grebe, J., Kaifel, S., Weinert, T., Sadaghiani, C., & Huber, R. (2017). Effects of hyperthermic baths on depression, sleep and heart rate variability in patients with depressive disorder: A randomized clinical pilot trial. *BMC Complementary and Alternative Medicine, 17*(1), 172.

Neria, Y., Olfson, M., Gameroff, M. J., Wickramaratne, P., Pilowsky, D., Verdeli, H., ... Weissman, M. M. (2008). Trauma exposure and posttraumatic stress disorder among primary care patients with bipolar spectrum disorder. *Bipolar Disorder, 10*(4), 503–510.

Obayashi, K., Saeki, K., & Kurumatani, N. (2017). Bedroom light exposure at night and the incidence of depressive symptoms: A longitudinal study of the HEIJO-KYO cohort. *American Journal of Epidemiology, 187*(3), 427–434.

Otto, M. W., Henin, A., Hirshfeld-Becker, D. R., Pollack, M. H., Biederman, J., & Rosenbaum, J. F. (2007). Posttraumatic stress disorder symptoms following media exposure to tragic events: Impact of 9/11 on children at risk for anxiety disorders. *Journal of Anxiety Disorders, 21*(7), 888–902.

Parletta, N., Zarnowiecki, D., Cho, J., Wilson, A., Bogomolova, S., Villani, A., ... O'Dea, K. (2017). A Mediterranean-style dietary intervention supplemented with fish oil improves diet quality and mental health in people with depression: A randomized controlled trial (HELFIMED). *Nutritional Neuroscience, 22* (7), 1–14.

Peres, J., & Nasello, A. G. (2008). Psychotherapy and neuroscience: Towards closer integration. *International Journal of Psychology, 43*(6), 943–957.

Perez, V., Alexander, D. D., & Bailey, W. H. (2013). Air ions and mood outcomes: A review and meta-analysis. *BMC Psychiatry, 13*, 29.

Potts, R., & Sanchez, D. (1994). Television viewing and depression: No news is good news. *Journal of Broadcasting & Electronic Media, 38*(1), 79–90.

Primack, B. A., Swanier, B., Georgiopoulos, A. M., Land, S. R., & Fine, M. J. (2009). Association between media use in adolescence and depression in young adulthood: A longitudinal study. *Archives of General Psychiatry, 66*(2), 181–188.

Quillen, J. (2015). *Inside Alcatraz: My time on the rock.* London, UK: Random House.

Riley, K. E., & Park, C. L. (2015). How does yoga reduce stress? A systematic review of mechanisms of change and guide to future inquiry. *Health Psychology Review, 9*(3), 379–396.

Rosenthal, S. R., Buka, S. L., Marshall, B. D., Carey, K. B., & Clark, M. A. (2016). Negative experiences on facebook and depressive symptoms among young adults. *Journal of Adolescent Health, 59*(5), 510–516.

Rothbart, M. K., Ellis, L. K., & Posner, M. I. (2004). Temperament and self-regulation. In R. F. Baumeister & K. D. Vohs (Eds.), *Handbook of self-regulation: Research, theory, and applications* (pp. 357–370). New York, NY: Guilford Press.

Schmitt, K., Holsboer-Trachsler, E., & Eckert, A. (2016). BDNF in sleep, insomnia, and sleep deprivation. *Annals of Internal Medicine, 48*(1-2), 42–51.

Sharma, A., Barrett, M. S., Cucchiara, A. J., Gooneratne, N. S., & Thase, M. E. (2017). A breathing-based meditation intervention for patients with major depressive disorder following inadequate response to antidepressants: A randomized pilot study. *Journal of Clinical Psychiatry, 78*(1), e59–e63.

Sharpley, C. F. (2010). A review of the neurobiological effects of psychotherapy for depression. *Psychotherapy: Theory, Research, Practice, Training* (Chic), *47*(4), 603–615.

St-Louis, E., Manaugh, K., Lierop, D., & El-Geneidy, A. (2014). The happy commuter: A comparison of commuter satisfaction across modes. *Transportation Research Part F: Traffic Psychology and Behaviour, 26,* 160–170.

Swartz, H. A., Rucci, P., Thase, M. E., Wallace, M., Carretta, E., Celedonia, K. L., & Frank, E. (2018). Psychotherapy alone and combined with medication as treatments for bipolar II depression: A randomized controlled trial. *Journal of Clinical Psychiatry, 79*(2), 16m11027.

Sung, Y. H, Kang, E. Y., & Lee, W. N. (2015, May). *A bad habit for your health? An exploration of psychological factors for binge-watching behavior.* Presentation at the 65th Annual International Communication Association Conference, San Juan, Puerto Rico.

Torrent, C., Bonnin C'del, M., Martínez-Arán, A., Valle, J., Amann, B. L., González-Pinto, A., … Vieta, E. (2013). Efficacy of functional remediation in bipolar disorder: A multicenter randomized controlled study. *American Journal of Psychiatry, 170*(8), 852–859.

Trappe, H. J. (2010). The effects of music on the cardiovascular system and cardiovascular health. *Heart, 96*(23), 1868–1871.

Wang, C. F., Sun, Y. L., & Zang, H. X. (2014). Music therapy improves sleep quality in acute and chronic sleep disorders: A meta-analysis of 10 randomized studies. *International Journal of Nursing Studies, 51*(1), 51–62.

Watkins, E. R. (2016). *Rumination-focused cognitive-behavioral therapy for depression.* New York, NY: Guilford Press.

Wehr, T. A. (2018). Bipolar mood cycles associated with lunar entrainment of a circadian rhythm. *Translational Psychiatry, 8*(1), 151.

Wehr, T. A., Turner, E. H., Shimada, J. M., Lowe, C. H., Barker, C., & Leibenluft, E. (1998). Treatment of the rapidly cycling bipolar patient by using extended bed rest and darkness to stabilize the timing and duration of sleep. *Biological Psychiatry, 43*(11), 822–828.

Yokoyama, S., Okamoto, Y., Takagaki, K., Okada, G., Takamura, M., Mori, A., … Yamawaki, S. (2018). Effects of behavioral activation on default mode network connectivity in subthreshold depression: A preliminary resting-state fMRI study. *Journal of Affective Disorders, 227,* 156–163.

Made in the USA
Columbia, SC
12 June 2022